THE GLASS MOTHER

ROSIE JACKSON lives near Frome, Somerset, where she works with the creative arts in community and health settings. Born in Yorkshire, she has degrees in literature from the Universities of Warwick and York. After lecturing at the University of East Anglia and in London, Bristol and Nottingham, she left academia, spent time in India and the United States, and began writing creatively. Her work is widely published. *Fantasy: The Literature of Subversion* was translated into Italian and Spanish; *Mothers Who Leave* was translated into German. Her poetry collection *The Light Box* was published by Cultured Llama in 2016. *www.rosiejackson.org.uk*.

Also by Rosie Jackson

Jan –
best wishes for your own writing –

The Glass Mother

ROSIE JACKSON

warm wishes

Rosie

* * *

September 2017
Bristol.

So few grains of happiness
measured against all the dark
and still the scales balance.

The world asks of us
only the strength we have and we give it.
Then it asks more, and we give it.

Jane Hirshfield, 'The Weighing'

Published by
UNTHANK BOOKS
2016

First published in Great Britain in 2016
by Unthank Books of Norwich and London
www.unthankbooks.com

Every reasonable effort has been made
to trace copyright holders of material in this book,
but if any have been inadvertently overlooked
the publishers would be glad to hear from them
Unthank Books, PO Box 3506,
Norwich, NR7 7QP

A CIP catalogue record for this book is available
from the British Library

ISBN 978-1-910061-36-7

Cover design & typesetting by Lyn Davies Design
Text design © Lyn Davies

Printed in Devon by Imprint Digital

CONTENTS

PROLOGUE

L ATE IN 2015, after I'd completed the manuscript of *The Glass Mother*, I came across a photograph of a repaired ceramic vessel; a simple round bowl, with two cracks on one side which had been filled with lacquer mixed with powdered gold: an example of the Japanese practice of *Kintsukuroi*, or *golden repair*.

The number of 'Shares' of this photo on Facebook – over 165,000 – suggested that this philosophy of treating breakage and repair as part of the history of an object, and an event to be celebrated rather than disguised, was something people liked and recognized. The bowl, far more beautiful now than it would have been without the cracks, seemed to have come into its own precisely because of the visible damage and careful repair work.

This struck me as a perfect analogy to my own story in *The Glass Mother*. Among its other themes, my memoir offers a personal account of how, in a society unskilled in matters of human relationships, the wounds caused by damaged mothering can be passed on from one generation to the next, and how, though it's no easy task, pouring love and understanding into the wounds can effect a form of golden repair.

It has taken me nearly fifty years, and the writing of this memoir, to start to fill in the cracks in my life. The writing evolved as a kind of detective story, moving from known facts to things hidden in the shadows, eventually making connections that linked my own struggle for healing with wider cultural issues of our time.

From when I began to read at the age of four, words have been my way into experience: they held me, contained me, offered meaning and connection, when nothing else did. Words loved me into being and I loved them in return. I have trunks and suitcases full of the journals I've kept since my teenage years, as if I relied on writing my life to make it real, to give me a human shape, an edge, an identity. At times, poems have literally kept me alive.

It was no surprise, then, that at university I chose to study literature as a source of nourishment, and my memoir begins in the year when I first left 'home', left a 'mother' whom I had always found to be as cold and brittle as glass, and entered the world of words and ideas. Only later, much later, after rejecting some of the negative aspects of institutionalised intellectual life I encountered at the University of East Anglia and else-where, did I begin to recognize more fully what had happened to me. By re-visiting my childhood and early years, and re-examining my own subsequent role as an 'absent' parent, I was eventually able to understand my history and to arrive at compassion for my parents, and for my mother in particular.

The writing of *The Glass Mother* has been my own form of spiritual alchemy. Precisely through this process of naming what has often been difficult to acknowledge, finding 'the words to say it', I have found that the cracks in one's life can be filled with gold after all. The wounds may still be visible, but they can also lead to places of remarkable beauty.

The Turquoise Hat

You must try,
the voice said, to become colder.
I understood at once.
It is like the bodies of gods: cast in bronze,
braced in stone. Only something heartless
could bear the full weight.

Jane Hirshfield, 'The World Loved by Moonlight'

ON A HOT SUMMER'S DAY IN 1969, I stood by the A1 hitching a ride north. I was eighteen, wearing a cotton shift dress my mum had made and flat shoes in orange cord. I carried no luggage, only a brown paper bag that I clutched as if it held the crown jewels. With the sun warming my bare arms and the first car stopping as I raised my thumb, I felt on a lucky streak. I'd left home less than an hour before, my first lift had brought me to this roundabout, and from here the A1 stretched all the way to Newcastle-upon-Tyne. That was where my brother had just finished his degree in physics – he got a first – and where my parents were also heading in Dad's old Morris Minor to attend the graduation ceremony. For some reason, perhaps the unaffordable cost of an overnight stay, I'd not been invited. But now, welcome or not, I was chasing after them. I had to take my mother her hat.

For weeks now, after tea each evening, my mother had cleared the dishes, extended the leaves on the living room table and worked on her outfit for the ceremony: a Crimplene suit in pale turquoise – knee-length skirt, collarless jacket – with a hat to match. She was adept at tailoring; she'd sewn our clothes for years, but this was the first time I'd known her attempt a hat. My dad and I watched in awe as, from various scraps of cardboard, stiffener and fabric, Mum constructed an object that did indeed resemble the kind of hat Jackie Kennedy often wore: the shape of an upturned cake-tin, with round base and solid sides, designed to perch on the back of the head. A layer of net in identical turquoise added to the professional effect. That last night, Mum modelled the whole outfit – how proud she was, this woman who'd been forced to leave school at fourteen for factory work, to have her only son graduating – then she packed the suit carefully, and first thing in the morning I waved her off with my father in the car. But no sooner had I returned to the living room, wondering what I would do for two days in an empty house – A-levels were over, we were waiting for results – than I noticed it on the table: a crumpled brown paper bag holding the carefully wrought hat.

I had no idea how far it was to Newcastle, and only a scrap of paper with the name and address of their B & B scribbled on it, but I didn't hesitate. Whatever unspoken thread still pulled me to try to please my mother, to protect her, had me in thrall. I thought of her weeks of labour over the outfit, the disappointment she would feel when she realised she was hatless, how it would bring home to her she was less well-dressed than the other mothers, would feed her profound sense of social inferiority, make her feel she'd let my brother down. I grabbed the bag, locked the back door, hid the key in the coal house and walked across the field to the main road.

As far as I recall, nothing untoward happened on the upward journey. Two or three lifts in trucks, a high cab ride which afforded wonderful views over the Tyne Bridge, and by early afternoon I was in Jesmond, a suburb just north of Newcastle city centre, at the address on the scrap of paper. I can still see the maroon swirls of the paisley stair-carpet, the polished wooden banisters. I knocked at the door of their room. The couple who answered bore some resemblance to my mum and dad, but they were pale and didn't seem to recognise me.

'Hello,' I said, as if I'd just walked down from our house to the garden gate. 'I've brought your hat. You forgot it.'

Mum took the bag, but neither of them spoke. They looked numb, babes in a wood, lost in a foreign country. There was no question as to how I'd got there, or what I would do now.

'Shall we have a cup of tea?' I asked. 'I could do with one.'

But they looked so out of their depth, away from all that was familiar, I felt my unexpected presence was merely adding to their discomfiture. They clearly couldn't cope with being away from home, the last thing they needed was the added pressure of worrying about a daughter who should have been guarding the house 150 miles away.

'Sorry,' I said. 'I just thought you wouldn't want to be without the hat tomorrow. Not after all the work you've done.'

Again no comment. We were all underwater, struggling with a reality we couldn't quite process. After a few minutes, when I realised they weren't going to invite me to stay, or offer a drink, I shrugged. 'Well, I'll be off then.' And turned back down the stairs for the long hitch-hike home.

I didn't shed a tear on the return journey. The heartache and depression I felt were all too familiar. As a child I would do anything to try to elicit a response from my mother – saving up pocket money to buy her bunches of flowers, doing the cleaning, getting impeccable grades at school – yet nothing had worked. And now, though I hadn't wanted to be the hero of the hour, I had hoped for something more than apologising for my presence when I'd tried so hard to please. This feeling of exclusion, of the hopelessness of effort in earning love, was nothing new, but that day it registered on a deeper level. I felt suddenly harder, colder, more reckless. I barely cared what happened to me on the return journey, barely cared what happened to me in life at all. I had similar luck as on the way up, never waiting more than a few minutes for a lift, but I didn't really give a damn whose cab I climbed into. When a driver unzipped his pants and put his hand down into them, I simply acted nonchalant and looked out of the passenger window.

That day proved a turning point. From then on, I lived my adult life travelling blind, on a wing and a prayer. I did things that were beyond my emotional reach, years beyond my level of maturity, took risks, pretended I was cool, grown up, I could manage. I would even pretend to be a mother myself, though I had no idea what it meant. And all the time I was bereft, heartsick, longing for someone to care where I was, who I was, what happened to me. When my parents returned late the next evening, they made no mention of my visit to Newcastle, didn't ask how I'd managed with lifts, it was obvious I'd got home safely. My brother didn't even know I'd been.

And I sensed then what I'd suspected for years: that I wasn't real to them, that we all lived in a zone of unreality, a planet where daughters appeared and disappeared by magic, where hats were plucked from paper bags and parents were as perplexed as white rabbits.

Things Can Get Lost

*The future enters into us, in order to transform
itself in us, long before it happens.*

Rainer Maria Rilke

MY A-LEVEL RESULTS arrived through the post that summer, 1969, one sunny August morning. When I saw the envelope on the floor in our tiny hall, I felt compelled to take it outside before I opened it, as if I needed protection from the negative forces I sensed at home to ensure the best results. I slipped across the cul-de-sac of council houses, through the garages and climbed down a steep bank into old railway sidings. Here I walked along the cinders to one of my favourite haunts under an ash tree, hidden from view by rosebay willow herbs. I felt sick with nerves. Everything was hanging on this piece of paper. Exeter and Warwick had made me offers involving Bs and Cs; they were the only places I'd been for interviews because Mum said they couldn't afford for me to travel to the other universities on my list.

I took a deep breath and unsealed the envelope: three A's in English, French and History, an A in S-level English. Ascribing this success to superstition and prayer as much as my years of over diligence, I gave thanks for the magic. I'd be going to my first choice: Warwick. When I got back to the house, I left the letter on the table for Mum to read. She never said anything to me about it, but soon some of the neighbours knew. Dad's verdict was simple. 'I wish I was as sure of winning the pools as you were of passing your exams. Then I'd be a happy man.'

I left home on a wet Sunday in October 1969, not sent to Coventry but driven there by my dad in the black Morris Minor. Who knows how different the future might have been, had I won the lodgings lottery and started my undergraduate career in the new halls on campus with hundreds of peers. Instead, I landed digs on one of the city's noisiest ring roads in a brick-built semi, with grey pebbledash between the two storeys. The landlady, Joyce, who took in students to supplement her widow's pension, stood on the doorstep looking apprehensive as I unloaded my boxes of books. Dad saw me into the house, then, never the most confident of drivers, swerved back into the scrum of traffic.

My room was upstairs at the front, its single-glazed windows rattling every few seconds as long-distance lorries thundered past. In no time I unpacked my few clothes and went down to the back living room hoping to meet the other lodger. She appeared in the doorway as Joyce served bland fish with boiled potatoes: a plump girl clutching a magazine, her eyes concealed by a thick blonde fringe. I introduced myself, explained I was reading English.

'History,' she returned. 'I'm Jane. From Twickenham. I shall go back every weekend. We go to the National all the time.' She brandished the magazine of actors. 'Have you seen Olivier?'

I admitted I hadn't. 'But I used to go to Nottingham Playhouse. John Neville,' I said. 'Have you seen *Close the Coalhouse Door*? Alan Plater? That was brilliant.'

Perhaps Jane hadn't heard my accent before. From her glance, I felt I was covered in coal dust. She declined the supper of white food, drew away from the door, and for the next ten weeks we barely exchanged a word.

Joyce's back room had no TV, but I was used to this. We'd never had a TV at home, in case it might distract us from homework and 'ruin our education.' So I sat and tried to read, pushing away my loneliness by thinking of my boyfriend. A school mate of my brother's, David had been invited round to our house for tea the previous year when I was exploring universities. Like my brother, David had gone to Newcastle, but to read English, and when I first met him – twenty years old to my immature seventeen – in his tweed jacket, cord trousers, smoking a pipe, with a Penguin edition of Conrad's *Nostromo* peeping out of his jacket pocket, the first man I'd ever known to share my passion for reading novels, I promptly believed myself in love.

David came from Creswell, one of many small mining towns near ours in Shirebrook, both on the Nottinghamshire-Derbyshire border. We were a mere twenty miles from D.H. Lawrence's Eastwood and, like Lawrence, we were shaped by a landscape scarred by the coal industry and by minds that had been trapped there. We discovered a shared hunger for literature that might transcend where we came from, yet make meaning of it. So as I sat reading, panicking a little at my unwelcoming surroundings, worrying how I would find the bus route to campus next morning, it was David I turned to in my inner world, as if he might be the guide I needed.

The University of Warwick, like its equally new siblings at Sussex, Essex, East Anglia, Lancaster, York and Kent, was summoned into being by the 1963 Robbins Report. Declaring that degree places were to be 'available to all who were qualified for them by ability and attainment,' Robbins opened up access to university education in a way previously unthinkable to someone from my background. The report urged these new universities to promote 'the general powers of the mind so as to produce not mere specialists but rather cultivated men and women' and the transmission of 'a common culture and common standards of citizenship.'

Not that I was a political animal. I had no idea what a relatively rare privilege this still was – just 200,000 full-time students attended UK universities at the time – let alone what an expensive luxury it would become. I'd received first class schooling on the state and now I was on virtually a full grant, with all my student fees paid by Derbyshire County Council.

Despite its name, the University of Warwick was sited on the edge of Coventry, on fields beneath Gibbet Hill. As I headed there on the bus for my first day, culture was not much in evidence. Instead I found a no-man's-land of mud, ditches, drills, machines, cranes, stacks of breeze blocks, the whole racket of a large building site. No ivory towers here, nor the promised 'plate-glass' of the new universities, only a mass of white tiled walls like an inside-out urinal. Thanks to the din of the ring-road I'd had no sleep, but spent the night trying to lose myself in one of my books, burrowing into a familiar thicket of words. Now, bombarded with the sound of machinery as I picked my way through a labyrinth of mud to the English department, I felt sick and homesick. But then, I'd been homesick for as long as I could remember.

Addressing us as the head of English was a man modestly dressed and clean shaven, an unmistakeable Scottish lilt in his voice. This was George Hunter, who had arrived in Warwick as one of the founding professors in 1964, head-hunted by the new Vice-Chancellor, Jack Butterworth. Hunter was a polymath, fluent in five languages, with a D.Phil. from Oxford. Articulate and scholarly, his evident devotion to the exactitude of reading and writing commanded instant respect. But over and above that, there flamed a fire in him: the fervour of a visionary who believed profoundly in the value and power of literature to change lives.

'Studying literature,' Hunter warned, 'is not an impersonal activity. It is about a way of life, a way of being. You cannot expect to go through the next three years unscathed. You must be prepared for a serious engagement with literature to alter you, to throw you, to deliver you to places you have not been before, to prove disquieting. We will not be analysing texts in the abstract; we will be engaged in a rigorous and demanding re-making of life through the world of the literary imagination. And both life and the imagination can take us far beyond what we know or can easily handle.'

Prescient words indeed, but they simply filled me with gratitude and awe. I'd never heard anyone so learned or eloquent, let alone expected such a mirror of my own deepest longings. Hunter went on to explain what was unique about his Department of English and Comparative Literary Studies: how we would read no English authors before Chaucer; how we would trace European culture to its roots through epic works in Greek, Latin and Hebrew.

'This first year you will read the *Epic of Gilgamesh*, Homer's *Iliad* and *Odyssey*, the *Old Testament*, Dante's *Divine Comedy*, Milton's *Paradise Lost*, T. S. Eliot's *Waste Land*.' We also had to be fluent in either French or Italian, and study medieval literature. 'An ambitious first year syllabus,' Hunter conceded, 'but how else will you be prepared for what comes next – the European novel and theatre, Shakespeare and his contemporaries?'

This encyclopaedic scope was exactly what had drawn me to Warwick. But the way Hunter spoke had the effect on me of a kind of awakening. He not only validated my life-long hunger for literature, but transformed it from being a sign of snobbery or difference (to my council estate peers I was a swot, a stuck-up grammar school girl) into a meaningful activity with deep human value. When he reeled off some of the magical names on future reading lists – Tolstoy, Dostoevsky, Sophocles, Strindberg, Ibsen – I was in rapture. In the company of these literary Titans, everything else fell away. The lonely Coventry digs, Joyce's blue perm and tasteless food, the anecdotes of her bowel problems, no longer mattered. Sleepless nights were of no concern. Nor the isolation, the absence of a convincingly real family, the mud on my patent leather shoes, unfashionable home-made clothes; they signified nothing on this brave new planet a million grateful light years away from the drab streets, narrow minds and council estates of the dark heart of the mining Midlands. Now I knew what James Joyce meant by a secular epiphany. I was having my own 'sudden spiritual manifestation'; never had I felt such life and hope.

When the other students drifted away from the lecture room in twos and threes, tramping back across a muddy campus towards bars and cafes in the student union, I hurried to the library. Why would I waste time socialising? I didn't know what the word meant. Posters advertising clubs, sport, films, music, discos, were a foreign language to me. For as long as I could recall, my life had consisted of studying, reading and managing my solitude as best I could; why would I choose a new template now? All I wanted to do was read more, learn more, earn my pass into the universe Hunter had just evoked.

In the library, I found one of the carrels, a small cubicle with a desk for private study, and stacked up a pile of library books. A whole day, a whole week, month, term, year, nay three whole years devoted to reading. Bliss! That first day and the days that followed, I sat cocooned in the library, taking notes and ignoring the noise of the drills outside. Elated by my immersion in this treasured world of literature, I was oblivious to how many hours I was devoting to study compared with my peers. C.S. Lewis said we read to know we're not alone; now, to my relief, though I knew I'd always read to banish my aloneness, it was no longer an activity signifying failure. Thanks to George Hunter, my reading now had legit-imacy and purpose in the adult world.

When the main library building closed in the evening, I slipped with the handful of bookworms, mostly male, into the neighbouring glass-walled annexe which allowed us to work until 10pm. Only then did I saunter to the bus-stop on the edge of campus, shivering as I waited for the almost empty double-decker to take me back to Coventry.

Like a premium football coach, George Hunter had gathered round him a first-division team. Some of his department were already established scholars and critics: Bernard Bergonzi, well-known for his study of mod-ernism and poetry, Claude Rawson, a distinguished 18th-century scholar,

Ken Gransden, a renowned man of letters. But Hunter also wanted new brooms to sweep things clean and, unusually for the time, had appointed some outstanding women. Germaine Greer, with her Cambridge Ph.D. on Shakespeare, already notorious for her involvement with OZ magazine and its trial for indecency, was about to achieve greater celebrity with *The Female Eunuch*. I'd glimpse her in the distance, her six feet of presence wrapped in a thick fur coat, summoning a taxi. But Greer was reserved for teaching Shakespeare, the jewel in the crown in our final year. Beyond the dramatic contrast she made with any woman I knew back home, Greer didn't yet have much impact.

But one of her female colleagues did. As I wandered the corridors that first week, through the open door of one of the meeting rooms I caught sight of a woman sitting at a table, waiting for the other faculty to take their seats. She was dressed all in white – a tailored trouser suit and silk shirt – and light from the window behind her created a halo which added to the radiance. More handsome than pretty, with high cheekbones, strong profile, full lips, long dark hair swept up into a perfect French plait, she was the most beautiful woman I'd ever seen. Next day, as I knocked at the office of my medieval tutor, the same woman opened the door. This, I discovered, was Gay Clifford. Once again, everything about her was utterly impeccable: pinned up shoulder length hair, elegant Italian clothes and jewellery – ornate silver ear-rings, and on the middle finger of her left hand, a huge oval ring of black onyx striated by one white vein. Even her office was meticulous, the view from her window not the Somme of campus but the lush green of adjacent woodland.

Gay was to have the most profound and enduring effect on me, as both mentor and friend. She was then twenty-six, and had been the youngest female academic in Britain when she came fresh from her own postgraduate studies in Oxford. In reality, there were a mere eight years between us, but I assumed she was much older and knew we came from different planets. How gauche, dumb and ungainly I felt, in the checked mini-skirt my mother had sewn, my clunky black patent shoes, cheap beige jumper. And how graceful Gay was, artfully putting me at my ease, talking as if my IQ were as brilliant as hers, quickly surmising what I'd already read, lifting a perfectly groomed eyebrow as I enthused over my dog-eared copy of C.S. Lewis' *Allegory of Love*.

'This world seems so unreal to me sometimes,' I admitted. 'I love the idea of it being the copy of another, invisible one – that all this is just an imitation of something much better.'

'The Hermetic philosophy,' Gay nodded, 'making everything here partial, equivocal. But what if there is no greater model we're copying? What if we've reached a world where all the old symbols are dead, emptied of meaning? Then symbolism seems mere nostalgia, and allegory, which takes nothing for granted, comes into its own.'

I was used to relishing ideas in books, but I'd never before experienced them issuing from the mouth of embodied beauty.

'That's why allegory is my passion,' Gay said softly, as if I was the first person she'd trusted with such confidence. 'Why should truth not be told in a roundabout way? Are not the greatest truths hidden and disguised, so we have to tease them out? Is there not something beguiling about saying one thing in the guise of another? How better to bypass the reductive literalism of this blunt modern age?'

With a few deft brushstrokes, she painted connections between *The Romance of the Rose* and Kafka, sketched the poverty of one-dimensional thinking.

'Perhaps this whole world,' Gay gestured, 'is a giant palimpsest, one thing hidden in another, its meaning endlessly elusive.'

When your own mother has been an icy absence, it's easy to fall in love with women who seem full, vibrant, alive. As I watched Gay's beautiful red lips, I felt I'd stepped into a medieval tapestry, a world of enchanted woods and unfolding mystery, where nothing would ever be the same again. The teachers at my all girls' grammar school had been inspired women, gifted at sharing knowledge, but physically they were dowdy, most of them spinsters following the loss of their young men in World War II. Gay Clifford, unashamed of her brilliance, which she wore lightly, seemed equally unabashed by her beauty. I wasn't sure if I was becoming more of myself or less, growing or shrinking, as I drank her words, amazed to be in a universe where Gay existed, and I had the privilege to be her student.

As I turned to leave, she stood and flashed me a smile, taking between her ringed fingers my red crêpe scarf.

'I've always coveted scarves like this,' she said. 'Scarlet. It suits you.'

At once I wanted to tear it off and give it to her, but somehow knew to hold back. This was the first compliment I remembered receiving, the only thing about my outfit that could possibly have been selected for approval, and I went out flattered on every level. If George Hunter had sown the seeds of an academic hunger for learning, Gay Clifford had suddenly made the quest more sensuous, vital. And my ambition raised itself a few bars higher. 'Enthusiastic admiration,' wrote Blake, 'is the first principle of knowledge and the last.' What wouldn't I do to win this woman's praise? What midnight oil wouldn't I burn?

My days and nights of solitary study intensified, broken only by lectures and seminars. I never considered eating in the cafeterias on campus, let alone joining in with social activities. I needed to make my grant stretch so I could afford the books I wanted; my diet consisted of apples, cheese and packets of biscuits. I never drank or smoked; the idea of wasting money on clothes, proper food or entertainment, was totally alien.

Yet as I watched students who were housed on campus quickly form themselves into cliques and cartels, I felt emotionally unmoored. Had I been in hall, or had Jane from Twickenham responded to my overtures, all might have been different. But, stranded in the digs in Coventry, I turned all the more to David and my link with him. I didn't receive letters from my family, but I wrote and phoned David, sharing my news with him, waiting for his replies.

We'd become lovers that summer, 1969, just before I got my A-level results, when we went to London to see the musical *Hair*. How my parents condoned this excursion, I'm not sure. Dad had made a mild protest to the school when he saw me devouring Joyce's *Ulysses* as part of my S-level English, and the only musical I'd ever seen was when he took me to the film of *The Sound of Music*. But with no TV and little awareness of the outside world, they were probably ignorant of *Hair*'s sexual excess, and trusted the newly graduated David to have reliable moral judgement.

I felt very grown up, as we went to the West End theatre together and watched the gyrations of semi-naked figures. But I was totally lost. Beyond the famous soliloquy from *Hamlet*, '*What a piece of work is man/How noble in reason/How infinite in faculties/In form and moving/How express and admirable...*', the lyrics left me mystified. What on earth did they mean by, '*Sodomy, Fellatio, Cunnilingus, Pederasty... Why do these words sound so nasty?*'

Neither at home nor school had I received an ounce of sex education. Either Mum didn't like to admit we had bodies, or was so ungrounded in her own, it was easy to believe I'd sprung fully-formed like Athena from the head of Zeus. Flesh was invisible, our sexual bits especially denied. And though she'd had two live children and one stillborn – a girl, my perfect double, often invoked as the ideal I would never become – Mum seemed to know nothing about her own body. She cautioned me against using Tampax because 'things can get lost *up there*'. Her solution was re-used winceyette pads which dried in the airing cupboard. When I did defiantly buy Tampax from the chemist, I had to hide them in a brown paper bag.

School was equally uninformative. After passing the eleven-plus, I'd gone to Queen Elizabeth's Girls' Grammar, an excellent old school in beautiful grounds in Mansfield. (The whole place, thanks to Thatcher, is now a hotel). But despite an all-female establishment – five hundred girls, women only teaching staff, just two men who taught science – issues of sex and gender were never addressed. At assembly in the grand school hall, our headmistress, the formidable Miss Batty (her actual name) would bellow from her wide girth that 'Abstention is the best method of prevention'. We were taught to regard boys with suspicion and sex with contempt; any girl who 'got into trouble' was an invisible and unspoken embarrassment.

So when, after the performance of *Hair*, David and I stayed at his friend's flat in Wanstead, and were shown to a tiny single bedroom, I didn't blink at the assumption we were sleeping together, nor did I think once about contraception. Here was a chance to prove I was an adult, and I lost my virginity with fierce disdain for the Puritanism that had so far kept it intact. I had no idea what I was doing, but it felt subversive, my own small contribution to the dawning of the age of Aquarius.

All that summer and through my first year at Warwick, on the few occasions David and I slept together, I gave no conscious thought to protection. David made it clear from the start that he didn't believe in it. For this, I don't blame him, but his intellectual heroes: F.R. Leavis and D. H. Lawrence. Leavis' study of Lawrence sat in pride of place on David's bookshelf, and he'd taken on board their idealised, romantic view of sexuality. When David quoted Lawrence as his reason for rejecting contraception – an offence against 'the mystery of nature' – I didn't protest. This was the first time I'd tasted love and intimacy in my life, and I didn't intend to lose it. I had such low belief in my own attractiveness, the very fact that David seemed to desire me, wanted to sleep with me, was a triumph over humiliation and loneliness, and linked me to him in a debt of gratitude as much as love. I'd had a couple of short-lived boyfriends before – Ken, a coal-miner from Shirebrook pit, and Ron, from Bolsover coal-lite plant – but we'd done nothing more than kiss. I had my pride, after all. Not, as Mum thought, that they were socially 'beneath me'. But how could I possibly sleep with men who'd never heard of Ted Hughes or Sylvia Plath?

I still lived, and would for many years more, in a magical universe, one without consequence, where I never thought through the implications of things. Indeed, for someone so good at school and skilled with words, I had a strange incapacity to think at all. George Hunter observed as much. At the end of one of my essays which he second marked, he noted in his perspicacious red pen, 'This woman writes better than she thinks.' It was an astute observation and, paradoxically enough, remained true throughout my academic career. I was always more in love with the sensual side of language, sounds of words and metaphors, than with abstract or conceptual thought; the external world too was a place to be muddled through rather than thought about consciously.

Looking back, I see now that for most of my adult life I functioned on a strange mixture of intellectual overdrive, which could respond well to essay questions, and a profoundly unconscious, at times child-like, stumbling through experience. The written word was my *modus vivendi*. I amassed quotations and lived inside them. When I travelled to and from grammar school each day, a twenty-minute journey on a green double-decker between Langwith Junction and Mansfield, I would memorise great chunks of literature: Shakespeare, Plath, Joyce's *Portrait of the Artist as a Young Man*, with its apt description of my own alienated state: 'an abyss of fortune or temperament sundered him from them...'

Now, at Warwick, I used bus journeys to campus to learn similar quotes from Pound or Eliot, even revelling in Nietzsche's declaration of unashamed aestheticism: 'Only as an aesthetic phenomenon is the world forever justified.' Literature mattered more than life, after all, and the quotes that made me up were my buttress against what lay outside. The first poem I ever had published, in the students' literary magazine *Yorick*, expressed this state of spectatorship I inhabited – a hived-off place made up only of language.

Strange, that I should look upon my life as if I did not live, but present at it merely to record...

In this looking-on at life, I had no idea how to be inside my experience or my body in a responsible adult way. There was no parent inside me, no internalised father or mother, only an absurdly precocious yet profoundly immature child who didn't feel taken care of and didn't know how to take care of herself.

When I was seventeen, I'd gone hitchhiking to France with Rachel, a girlfriend from school. We'd been on our way to my pen-pal and her mates camping in the Loire valley, when we were picked up near Paris by two middle-aged men, who made a long detour to Chartres, stopping by a hayrick in a cornfield. Happily, our French was near fluent, we'd understood their muttered conversation and were ready for a tough battle. We fought and kicked, saved from disaster by the arrival of an elderly woman on her bike, riding back from a service in the cathedral – it was Easter Sunday. I never see photos of Chartres Cathedral without remembering that woman's kindness: how she took us to her old stone farmhouse, its garden full of daffodils, ran us hot baths, bandaged Rachel's cut hand, fed us fresh coffee and crusty baguettes stuffed with slices of ham.

Yet even this hadn't woken me to greater self-care. I lived as if nothing could happen to me, still hitch-hiked alone, either not feeling any fear or being so accustomed to living with subliminal terror, adrenaline was my constant companion.

There was one weekend, that first term at Warwick, when the loneliness grew so acute, I headed out on the ring-road early one Saturday morning and hitched north once more, up the A1 to Durham, where David was studying for a PGCE. But when I eventually reached his hall of residence, his door was locked. I hadn't warned him I was coming.

'I think he's gone to Newcastle for the weekend,' a neighbour told me. 'To see some friends.'

He found me a key and after I'd walked round Durham and visited the cathedral, I spent a solitary night in David's room, eating his packet soup and reading F.R. Leavis on George Eliot. I felt so stupid. This was such a perfect re-run of the scene with my mother's hat: hurling myself up north through the same roundabouts in the vain hope someone might be there to catch me. Why couldn't I function like other people? Why was I so invisible?

Next morning I headed back to Coventry in the rain, climbing into the cab of yet another articulated lorry, pretending not to mind the driver's cigarette smoke. Thank God for Gay Clifford's medieval course, and the essay I had to write. It was something to live for. Huddling down into the seat, I took out my copy of *Gawain and the Green Knight*. In the soporific fug, the green man's huge presence could have been a description of the thick-set driver at my side: *from the nape to the waist so swart and so thick, and his loins and his limbs so long and so great half giant on earth I think now that he was…*

My mind ran on as I scrawled notes in the margins of the text. Under my seat lay a jack which could serve as an axe. If the driver tried anything on, I could whip it out and behead him. Then he would turn into the green knight, his head under his arm as he calmly sat at the wheel, and we belted on south down the motorway. I scribbled more notes on the theme of regeneration, stumbled back to Joyce's lodgings in Coventry as it grew dark. I may be a toddler in the ways of the world, I thought, but I can write damn good essays. That one, as usual, got a first.

3

Warwick University Ltd.

Sometimes I want to flee with everything
I possess into a few words, seek refuge in them.
But there are still no words to shelter me.
That is the real problem.

Etty Hillesum, *An Interrupted Life*

I HAD ALWAYS BEEN A SWOT. I devoured the correspondence relating to my starting infant school, which meant I could read fluently by the time I was four, presumably taught by my mother. The alphabet was my primary way of interacting with the world, books infinitely more real and satisfying than any human connection, and I'd soon consumed the few volumes we had in the house: Palgrave's *Golden Treasury*, much of the St. James Bible and the tiny print of the claret coloured *Pears' Cyclopaedia*.

Yet there lingered a longing for something I couldn't clearly name. As a child, I would wander the streets of our council estate staring into lit windows, looking on with envy at what I assumed were happy families, and now the same feeling persisted at Warwick, watching my contemporaries as they lounged around laughing and being together, and I once more puzzled over how to enter the tribe.

One of the students I particularly admired was Gail. She was everything I was not: an urban girl from Birmingham and utterly cool. On my diet of cheese, biscuits and no exercise beyond walking to the bus stop, my teenage anorexia had given way to slight plumpness, but Gail was as skinny as Twiggy. She had long, dark, fashionably straight hair, tight clothes and an effortless sex appeal. What Gail derived from befriending me I failed to fathom, but she would chat after our seminars, and towards the end of our first term suggested we share a flat together. She too had been dumped into shabby digs and, although it defied first-year regulations to take independent lodgings, I was too desperate to care. This was more than my get-out card from Joyce and the grinding all-night lorries; it was a chance to smash the bell jar.

We found a ground-floor flat in another dingy part of Coventry, amidst row upon row of redbrick terraces edged by corner shops. We shared the one double bed; the small lounge had a gas fire and beyond that lay a tiny kitchen. I still read and studied obsessively, but now I watched how a normal girl lived, devoting time to washing and combing hair, eating little but well, paying attention to outfits, wearing mini-skirts that showed off skinny legs with knee-length boots. I also gained a new perspective on sex. Gail had a hunky boyfriend, Bob, who played guitar in a Birmingham band and, at weekends, I would be ousted from the double bed to three red sofa cushions on the living room floor.

This was the first time I'd overheard ecstatic sex. In eighteen years at home, I never once saw my parents touch, kiss, caress, hold hands, or display an ounce of emotional or physical tenderness. The walls of our council house semi were thin enough to admit noises of neighbours raking out their fire or turning on the TV, but no sounds of passion ever crept through from my parents' bedroom. The only sound I remembered from recent years at home was poignant sobbing from my father, already ill, as, late at night, he lamented to my mother his shortcomings. 'I'm sorry I'm not good enough for you.'

But now, lying in front of the gas fire in Coventry, feeling the draught from the gap under the kitchen door, and staring at the legs of the folding dining table which I'd piled high with books, I was proud to have progressed this far. I may not have reached the same level as Gail, but I was, however obliquely, part of her sexy adult world. Not that I knew what to say to Bob as our paths briefly crossed on the Saturday morning.

'Are you coming to the gig tonight?' he asked.

I guessed that 'gig' translated as the band performing. 'Thanks, but I've got my essay to write.'

'It's a lovely day, though. Aren't you going out?'

'I don't think so.' And I sat down with my large hardback of Chaucer's complete works. *For hym was levere have at his beddes heed / Twenty books, clad in blak or reed...*

Bob, with his shoulder-length blond hair, looked dumbfounded. He found it as hard to understand why I wanted to stay in all day with books as I found it hard to understand why he wanted to be out all night playing in a band when he could be reading Chaucer, Langland, Dante.

With no TV and just one radio downstairs, I'd been largely secluded from the world at home. On weekdays we had the one o'clock news and *The Archers*, at weekends *Three Way Family Favourites*, *Round the Horne* and *Sing Something Simple*. (Dad tried to be droll by dubbing it *Sing Something Sinful*). The *Daily Express* plopped onto the mat each morning, but I never trusted its reliability. We knew when President Kennedy was shot, because a neighbour in our cul-de-sac, knowing we were TV-less, knocked at the door to tell us, but most political events, including the huge student riots in Paris the year before I left home, passed us by. Queen Elizabeth's Grammar School had a similar cocooning effect. When I told Miss Batty of my ambition to go to Sussex to read philosophy, she was adamantly opposed.

'Sussex is far too radical,' she said. 'Reds. You should read literature somewhere safe.'

But if she'd assumed Warwick would shield me from radical thought, Miss Batty was mistaken. When student unrest spread from the continent in 1969, Warwick was foremost amongst the new universities to spearhead student protest, earning the nickname 'red Warwick'. The University Registry was discovered to hold secret files on students, and as Gail and I ventured into the union building that new term early in 1970 – I was more daring with Gail at my side – we were caught up in a large crowd of students agitating for action. Although I'd never really defined my own politics, I was easily roused by oppression or injustice, and discovered I was instinctively left-wing. We cheered the lunch-time speakers who denounced the university administration, and voted to storm the Registry and stage a sit-in to protest against the secret files.

Gay Clifford, perhaps proud to be thought a socialist, was prominent at these meetings, a striking, dramatic figure in an operatic black cape with scarlet lining. Standing beside her was an equally handsome man in his mid forties, his impassioned oratory as brilliant as his intellect. This was E.P. Thompson, Reader in the History of Labour, whose *Making of the English Working Class* (1963) had confirmed his reputation as one of the country's foremost socialist historians. He and Gay were visibly close friends, and in my mind they became a romantic couple defying the academic establishment, their wild edge bestowing upon them a Bonnie and Clyde glamour.

When Thompson took the floor, he pointed out how profoundly Warwick's integrity as a university was compromised by its defining links with commerce, notably the nearby motor industry. That February, his arguments appeared in the *New Statesman*, where he accused the university of raising private funding through close relations with industry, aiming to become a 'Massachusetts Institute of Technology for the Midlands.' Research in science at Warwick, he pointed out, was heavily subsidised by the car industry: metal fatigue (Massey Ferguson), vehicle instrumentation (Rootes and Ford Motors), fatigue in tyres (Dunlop). Didn't this make a mockery of intellectual independence? Wasn't the Vice-Chancellor less an 'academic organiser' than 'the managing director of a business enterprise' with a 'commanding influence over an input of some millions of money'? Didn't this bend the meaning of education, making the administration 'so intimately enmeshed with the upper reaches of consumer capitalist society that they are actively twisting the purposes and procedures of the university... and threatening its integrity as a self-governing academic institution'?

As a Marxist historian, Thompson was particularly sensitive to the alienating nature of the new campus universities and their isolation from human community. He lamented the way the Warwick campus was pitched in cold fields three miles from any urban facilities, with most of the staff and students weekday visitors. Students' facilities were marked by a 'lack of privacy, noise and dehumanised utilitarianism'; there was nowhere for staff and students to meet together; the architects were denounced for their over-generous use of divider and ruler.

Inspired by Thompson's personal address to the union, urging us to resist any erosion of intellectual and human values, many students took direct action and stormed the Bastille of the Registry to recover their personal files. Gail and I arrived there too late, and I knew my history was far too tame to have anything on file against me, but the whole episode confirmed my alignment with the left and E.P. Thompson always remained one of my heroes. The following year, 1971, his principles led him to resign from his lucrative readership and he published *Warwick University Ltd.*, extending his arguments into book form.

In many ways, Thompson's voice proved prophetic. He denounced what was in effect the development of universities into institutions 'in symbiotic relationship with the aims and ethos of industrial capitalism, but built within a shell of public money and public legitimation.' This was the business model which would encroach more and more into higher education over the next few decades, introducing managerial methods and top-down decisions. Students became numbers rather than people; teaching and publications were measured by efficiency and quantity more than quality; academics became administrators. What Thompson's idealism also bequeathed me, though I would be unconscious of it for several years more, was a role model for turning away from a bureaucratic and cold-hearted system of education. He legitimised and made honourable saying no to a dehumanised way of learning. But for now, I was still wanting to drown in a literary universe and continued to incarcerate myself in the white-tiled library, reading more books in a sitting than the human brain can properly compute.

The brightest man in our year was Clive, a working-class hero and Heathcliff-like outsider, who knew how to brazen his romantic way into the hearts and beds of many of the women in my year. One day he peered over the side of the carrel where I was taking notes from a tall stack of books.

'Why do you work so hard?' Clive asked. 'Are you after a first or something?'

I said nothing. He was a good looking man, with wild curly hair, a cross between Dylan Thomas and Norman Mailer.

'You'll just end up a lecturer in some redbrick provincial university,' Clive went on. 'Is that what you want? Is that your idea of a life?'

It clearly wasn't his, and I let myself be invited for a coffee. Lured by the promise of books he could lend me, I also agreed to visit him at his home later that week. He lived in a semi-detached house a couple of miles' walk from campus, the downstairs room filled with more books than I'd ever seen outside a library. Overflowing from shelves and stacked on the floor were literally thousands of volumes, including every left-wing publication from the last twenty years.

'Good God!' I said. 'How do you afford all these?'

Clive gave me a look with which I'd become familiar, as fellow students betrayed surprise at my naiveté. 'You don't think I *bought* them, do you?'

'No?'

'Of course not. Why buy something you can steal?' Clive pointed to the state of the art TV in the corner, the stereo system, the sexy brown leather jacket.

'You *took* it all?'

'How else?'

If I was shocked, I was also impressed. Nothing was further from my parents' law-abiding existence. My father was ill for months after a minor car accident, terrified he'd somehow broken the law.

Clive sat on the sofa and gestured for me to join him. 'You should get out of these home-made clothes,' he said. 'You don't make the most of yourself.'

Realising I'd mistaken the code, I was relieved to hear a key in the front door. Clive leapt to his feet – 'Shit!' – and a pretty woman with long wavy hair came into the room. A few months pregnant, she looked serene, confident, smiling as if nothing could trouble her.

'Hello,' she said. 'Would you two like a cuppa?'

I stayed for an awkward cup of tea with chocolate biscuits, then got up to leave.

'You didn't tell me you were married,' I said, as Clive saw me to the gate.

'I'm not.'

'But she's -'

'We have an open relationship. She wasn't supposed to be back till tonight.'

From then on I merely watched from afar as Clive chatted up the best-looking women on campus, and I stuck ever more firmly to my assiduous note-taking from paid-for books.

My favourite times were tutorials with two or three other students at Gay Clifford's small cottage in Kenilworth. Gay had a knack of putting students at ease, of making everyone feel singled out and special. What better antidote to the dehumanising campus than her beautiful lounge-cum-study crammed with books, art, colourful textiles and furnishings, her tiny kitchen with its Italian majolica pottery and cans of olive oil, bottles of wine, her garden prolific with herbs and cats? As long as the debate stuck to set texts, I could join in, but I was out of my depth discussing ideology or politics. At home, we'd see relatives occasionally, but we had little contact with neighbours ('not our sort') and no friends casually dropping by. I had no social confidence.

My other favourite place was Coventry cathedral. Following its heavy shelling in World War II, the city was still a hotch-potch of post-war construction, with 1960s high rises and – again, thanks to affluence spawned by the car industry – burgeoning shopping centres. The rebuilt cathedral, rising from the ruins of the bombed 14th century church of St Michael's, was completed in 1962 and smelt still of novelty. Graham Sutherland's larger than life tapestry of Christ hung over the high altar – my first real encounter with 20th century art – and I was overwhelmed. The stained glass baptistery window by John Piper and Patrick Reyntiens; my first Elizabeth Frink sculpture – her bronze eagle lectern; a metal crown of thorns screen by Basil Spence; ceramics by Hans Coper; all drew me back to the cathedral again and again. And Beyer's 'Tablets of the Word', eight beautiful sandstone panels set into walls flanking the nave, incised with familiar Biblical texts. This was the first time I'd seen letter carving on such a scale: words as sculpture, and I couldn't pull myself away from their beauty.

I always felt at peace in the Cathedral and wondered about coming back for a service, but knew already that faith was an embarrassment in the secular world of the university; Nietzsche's definitive statement that *God is dead* went uncontested. Anyway, the church was too linked to the family I was trying to leave behind; we'd gone twice every Sunday throughout my childhood.

When I walked back outside, there hung the huge bronze relief of Jacob Epstein's St. Michael, his wings pinned against the brick wall, arms stretching out in victory over a cowering human devil. And lines from Baudelaire would come to me: *En tout home, à toute heure, il y a deux postulations simultanées, l'une vers Dieu, l'autre vers Satan.* (In everyone, at every moment, there are two simultaneous pulls, one towards God, the other towards darkness.) These words had imprinted themselves on my memory because they captured one of my recurrent childhood nightmares – a nightmare that always felt as if it was happening when I was still awake – when I would be lifted out of my bed to the ceiling and opposing forces would fight for my body: God pulling from one corner, and devils from the other. Epstein's sculpture gave me at least temporary assurance that God could win.

So I worked away through the spring and summer terms, barely noticing the seasons. At the end of year, we sat our exams, almost late for our Epic exam because, as we were leaving for the bus, Gail discovered a button on her white blouse had come off and insisted – to my astonished impatience – that we go back in to sew it on. I wrote a passionate paper for the exam on Milton's *Paradise Lost*, arguing on behalf of the idea of the *felix culpa*, the 'happy fall': how it is the very lapse from perfection, the fall from grace, which is necessary to make us fully human. Little did I know then how unhappy such a happy fall could be.

As soon as the exams were done, I was lost, not knowing how to spend my days without books to read or essays to write. I would have leapt into the second year syllabus straightaway, had Gail not taken me with her to parties and social events. I was amazed how she knew so many people, how she had so many good and good-looking male friends as well as boyfriend Bob.

One of these friends, James, arrived at the flat on his motorbike one sunny afternoon just before the end of term. Gail welcomed him in a knowing way, and I wondered if this might be another night for sleeping on the cushions. After a few whispered words whose meaning I didn't catch, James took from his pocket a small package in silver foil. He unwrapped it and Gail let him put its contents – white and square – into her waiting mouth. It seemed to be a ritual, for they smiled knowingly, and again I felt on the edge of a grown-up universe whose language I simply didn't speak.

'What's that?' I asked.

'Acid.'

I must have looked blank.

'LSD,' James explained. 'Do you want some?'

I had no idea what this new acronym stood for, any more than I'd understood the three letter word 'gay' a few weeks before. But so frustrated was I by my ignorance, so hungry for everything from which I felt excluded, that, like the evening I'd seen *Hair*, I sprinted over the threshold.

'Yes please,' I said.

Then James repeated the ritual, popping a second cube of sugar into my mouth. Rather like Holy Communion, I thought, with the host delivered onto the tongue; when James smiled, like our vicar with a blessing, I had to stop myself making the sign of the cross.

Minutes later, I was staring at an orange in a basket on the folding leaf table as if I'd just created the universe and here it was: the whole globe in miniature. I wondered at its luminosity, its infinite depth and, as James peeled it for me, stared at the segments as if I'd never seen a citrus fruit before. His hands too became worlds, the fingers working so slowly, miraculously, as they removed the peel. *What a piece of work is man... How express and admirable... how like an angel...*

Then I was lying next to Gail on the double bed, staring at the polystyrene squares on the ceiling, probably fifty or so tiles which now divided and multiplied into five times fifty, fifty times fifty, then infinite squares moving back and forth across my field of vision. From somewhere across a chasm, I heard James agree with Gail, 'Yes, it's strong stuff. Very pure. Very potent.' Then I was lost again, fallen into a looking glass world which was the original one seen backwards, distorted, magnified, turned inside out, the hidden suddenly made manifest, the familiar infinitely strange and new.

We went out into the back garden. No longer a shabby suburban patch of weeds and grass, it was now a miraculous jungle. The dandelions were as tall as palm trees, the daisies as wondrous as lilies. And, greatest miracle of all, I had ceased to exist. I was no longer me! I had *become* the dandelion and the daisy and the crack in the concrete path leading to the metal post that held the washing line. I *was* the cerulean sky, the white wisps of cumulus. I was Gail's long hair blowing in the breeze, her suddenly over-bright teeth, her sharp nose – now perceived as remarkably angular. I was the stray magpie feather on the uncut lawn, that spent firework of cat poo.

James, our Virgil guiding us through this visionary landscape, suggested we go to the university campus. Perhaps he was bored of watching two young women on an acid trip while he remained sober and wanted to return to his room so he could safely swallow his own fix of sugar; I suspected he'd given me his. Maybe he'd wanted to trip with Gail and see where it led them. But now he urged a change of scenery, insisted we would not believe how the trees would look. Gail nodded, laughed, urged me to ride there first, on the back of James's motorbike. And, as usual, I agreed. Of course I'd go on the bike if that was what Gail wanted.

By now I was feeling disassociated, dragging my body some miles behind me. I'd not been on a motorbike before. Ron, the boyfriend I'd had in the sixth form, had a sports car and motorbike but no spare helmet, so I'd never been allowed on. Still, despite my co-ordination being severely retarded, I had an idea where to put my backside, on this leather seat, where to put my legs, somewhere down the side here, and how to wrap my arms around James's leather clad body. It was all hallucinatory, a slow motion blur as we set off, shapes and fragments moving and multiplying around me. I wasn't sure what was real and what wasn't, but somehow I clung on, registering in a distant region of my mind a sense of triumph at crossing the threshold at last, naive brain-box that I was, pressed against gorgeous James as we wove through Coventry's rush hour traffic. No, you couldn't say I wasn't living now.

With the congestion and traffic lights, the journey took about twenty minutes to the road that led from the by-pass to campus. Here, at the edge of a path, near the woods he'd promised, James stopped the bike and waited for me to lift myself off. We both waited. But my limbs were no longer obeying my brain. James stood and tried to help me off, when I saw that my brain was not the problem. My right leg was, simply, in the wrong place. Instead of bending at an angle in parallel with James's leg, it was further back where, for the last twenty minutes, it had been pressed down against the hot exhaust. I was wearing a mini skirt, my legs bare from the knee, and my inner calf from mid leg to ankle was stuck to the exhaust pipe as stubbornly as raw meat cooked on hot metal with no oil.

LSD, lysergic acid diethylamide, is a synthetic drug, its main constituent ergotamine tartrate, named after ergot, a fungus found on rye. It achieves its hallucinogenic effects by disrupting the interaction of nerve cells and serotonin, distorting the visual perception of reality and disturbing sensory perception. In my case, the acid completely blocked all sensation of physical pain: not only did I feel nothing during the twenty-minute ride to campus, but even when I lifted myself off the bike and tore my leg away from the hot metal exhaust, leaving behind a considerable chunk of flesh, I was totally numb.

Far from lamenting my injury, I bent over in fascination, examining the wound with the same awe and wonder I was devoting to everything in my close field of vision. I stared in amazement at the purple mass of burnt tissue, broken blood vessels, flayed skin crinkled at the edges. The colours were rich and radiant – crimson, mauve, claret, plum – and I knew they must belong to some anatomy outside myself, for despite the enormity of the wound, I was completely pain-free. Perhaps I suggested visiting the health centre to take care of this stranger's leg, for I heard James arguing against the folly of such an idea, given that he was the one who'd administered an illegal drug. So, blithely and blissfully transcending any attention to my limping, bleeding leg, I wandered into the woods that edged the campus, while James motored back to the flat to ferry Gail.

With acid by this time illegal in the US as well as the UK, what we took was probably home-made in England rather than smuggled in. Its famous advocates in the 1960s had included Timothy Leary, the Beatles and Ken Kesey, author of *One Flew over the Cuckoo's Nest*, their main defence being that the drug promoted mystical experiences and led to consciousness of a transcendental reality. Kesey, interviewed for the *Sunday Times* in 1999, claimed he knew no-one who had not come back from an acid trip 'more humane, more thoughtful, more understanding.' Psychoanalyst Sidney Cohen, an early proponent of LSD, described his experience of the drug as conferring a 'majestic, sunlit, heavenly, inner quietude.' They all drew heavily on Aldous Huxley's *The Doors of Perception*, his title lifted from Blake's *Marriage of Heaven and Hell*: 'If man would cleanse the doors of perception, he would see everything as it is, infinite.'

That afternoon on Gibbet Hill, I certainly shared this illusion of having some toehold into the infinite. Every barrier between me and the world seemed to have disappeared. I stepped beneath trees astonishingly verdant, able now to observe the sap pulsing through the complex system of veins in each leaf. The same life force was running in every plant, nettle and blade of grass, and I knew it was inside me too. I had stepped into the mystery.

But gradually this unnatural stretching of awareness tipped beyond endurance. The doors of perception were not only open, but jammed too wide, and I longed for the extremity to stop, for the vision to return to normal and for the translucency of things, their excessive vibrancy, their over-presence, to disappear.

By the time the sun set, I was with Gail in a room on campus, probably James's, feeling deeply weary. If only everything would revert to an ordinary, even banal level, finite and discrete, and this hyper-vision, which allowed no simple rest inside the self, would cease. But the trip showed no sign of abating. The infinite kept pushing through with its exaggerated claims and attendant loss of natural human sensitivity and ordinary pain. Dead too were our appetites for food and drink, or any ability to sleep. Not until the following afternoon, almost twenty-four hours after we had swallowed our innocent-looking sugar cubes, did the effect start to diminish and the pain in my right leg begin.

The glimpse I had that day of heaven and hell was not one I was ever tempted to repeat, yet in some ways it has never left me. LSD stores in the brain and can be suddenly reactivated months or years later, an involuntary phenomenon known as 'flashback'. It would be two years before this particular nightmare struck me, but I don't believe I've ever fully returned to the state of visual innocence I had prior to the LSD experience. The world has since then been impossibly glorious, invasively present, at times almost too colourful, too beautiful. And yet, at the same time, even its most solid forms have been visibly illusory and translucent.

LSD exacerbated the sense I already had of a feeling of unreality, of occupying a dream world which is perceived in the most intricate, precise, impacting detail, miraculous and sensuous, yet at the same time is apprehended as insubstantial, as transient as Prospero's cloud-capped towers; a world both too much and too little all at once. Negotiating this overfull yet vacuous reality has, at times, felt akin to insanity. Many spiritual traditions, including the one I eventually came to follow, insist on the ephemeral and illusory status of this gross world, saying it is itself nothing but a grand illusion, a dream. But my own experience of seeing 'through' reality, a legacy from that summer's day in 1970, left me with a profound longing for its opposite: for finding the material and mundane world solid and anchoring, something to make me feel secure and substantial, as if this world, not some other, is indeed my home.

I was still feeling fragile and vulnerable from this experience when the end of term finally arrived and I sat in the ground floor flat in Coventry for the last time. Gail had already left and I was waiting for my parents to collect me in the old Morris Minor. They were late, my books all packed, and I wandered into the unkempt back garden. Despite the heat, I was wearing trousers to cover the bandage on my right leg, determined to keep it concealed. It had been treated by doctors who swallowed some lie about a domestic burn, but I spent most of that summer wearing trousers or dark tights; it would be nearly ten years before the scar completely disappeared.

I stared at the long grass, trying not to recall the way this concrete path had opened so completely into the underworld that afternoon of the LSD trip. By some miracle, I'd survived my first year at university, and my over-application had won me the first-year English examination award – a welcome lump sum for buying books – but I had little sense of triumph. Indeed, as scenes from the past few months replayed themselves, I felt more defeated than ever.

I remembered the noisy bedroom at Joyce's, night after sleepless night, how I would stare into the mirror, unable to identify with the woman who stood there. I'd thrown a party with Gail that I had no idea how to run; tried to copy the way Gail applied her make-up, but not known where to start; responded to friendly overtures from other students with frozen fear. Small wonder I'd compensated with intellectual overkill, indulged myself in the one arena where I had some competence. But what had my thousands of hours of study brought me? I was no wiser, no more intelligent than when I'd started my first year, as far from myself as ever, even further from others. I still felt locked inside a glass dome, cut off from reality, longing for ordinary human love and joy.

When Mum and Dad eventually arrived, having lost their way round Coventry, we had no real contact. We stuffed my boxes and case into the car and I crawled into the back seat for the almost silent journey home. They seemed terrified of my unknown new life and equally terrified of me. I knew I couldn't bear to spend the summer with them and, as we arrived back in Langwith Junction, re-entering the familiar spools of circular roads and cul-de-sacs of red brick houses, I felt, with my over-wrought imagination, that we were driving into the circles of Dante's Inferno, where nothing ever changed.

Better then to take up David's suggestion of working in London for the summer and saving up for a holiday together in Ireland. That at least would be different. I quoted Rimbaud to myself. '*Au fond de l'inconnu, pour trouver du nouveau.*' To the depths of the unknown, to find the new.

4

My Thin Little English Wedding

We are not hurt only by tragedy:
the grotesque too carries weapons,
undignified, ridiculous weapons.

Graham Greene, *The End of the Affair*

THROUGH THE SAME friends of David who'd hosted us a year earlier, we borrowed a room in East London and started hunting for summer jobs. David was taken on by an industrial bakery and returned each night with loaves of white sliced bread under his arm. I found work in Hackney, at a huge five-floor factory where Lesneys manufactured their famous Matchbox toys, the world's biggest selling brand of die-cast model cars.

On the factory floor where the miniature vehicles were made, and which reeked of molten plastic, I was taken to a large machine whose mysterious furnace converted plastic chips into the neat roofs of tiny VW camper vans. It should have been a relatively simple, if hot and smelly job, to top up the plastic chippings and check the roofs emerged faultless. But as my trays emerged, what should have been pristine cream roofs were shot through with crimson-purple streaks like burst varicose veins.

'What's happened here?' asked the floor manager.

'I don't understand it,' I said. 'I did exactly what you told me.'

'They'll have to be binned.'

I tried again, but something went wrong with the second batch, then the third and by the end of the day I was fired for my incompetence. I suspected sabotage from the permanent workforce, girls who dangled their cigarettes out of loo windows and resented the summer's invasion of students. But just as likely my mother was right, and I was too impractical for anything but having my nose in a book.

For a few days I sat in the flat reading Dostoevsky for my European novel course, then, despite my lack of an equity card, one of David's friends arranged some work for me as a dresser at Drury Lane Theatre. *The Great Waltz*, a schmaltzy musical based on the lives of Johann Strauss senior and junior had just opened. The original play had been the inspiration for Hitchcock's 1934 *Waltzes from Vienna*, a film he called 'the lowest ebb of my career'.

The Great Waltz opened at Drury Lane on July 9, 1970 and was to run for more than six hundred performances. I worked on three dozen of the earliest shows, taking the tube from Walthamstow to the Strand early each evening, with matinees on Wednesday and Saturday. I was not ideal dresser material, all fingers and thumbs and knowing nothing about clothes. I was meant to look after the frilly costumes of five of the chorus, check for tears or stains, hook-and-eye the women into tight bodices, fluff out their skirts and smile compliments as they raced down dozens of stone stairs to the stage. I soon knew by heart the sentimental numbers crackling through the tannoi: *The Kaiser Waltz, The Artist's Life, The Emperor's Waltz, The Blue Danube*; indeed, whenever I hear a few bars of Strauss, I smell again the jars of Ponds' cream and cheap perfume. This was a far cry from my previous experience of theatre at Nottingham Playhouse, then under John Neville's brilliant directorship. I would take two buses at weekends to see Brecht's *Mother Courage*, or Bond's *The Narrow Road to the Deep North*. The Strauss musical, by contrast, was utterly saccharine, and I relied on *Crime and Punishment* squashed in my bag to get me through.

Late that August, David and I had the two week holiday we'd saved for in Galway, in an isolated white-washed cottage. Our cash was immediately stolen by a neighbour's teenage son, but we weren't about to go on a spree anyway. Photos show us sitting at a cast iron garden table avidly reading, my wavy hair parted down the side as it had been since childhood, my feet still wearing those patent black shoes. David devoured the fat newly-published translation of Hitler's *Mein Kampf*. I graduated to Dostoevsky's *The Idiot*.

Somehow, over the previous year, our meetings had been rare enough to protect us from the consequences of feckless sex. But as soon as we got back to England, our fate caught up with us. We were in Nottingham, visiting one of my teachers from Queen Elizabeth's Grammar, Pam Ashley, a bright, curly haired blonde, and her then husband, an English lecturer. The huge rooms of their ramshackle first-floor flat in Mapperley had more books than furniture and the walls were covered with Athena reproductions of Pre-Raphaelite paintings. We slept on a bare wood floor beneath a print of Waterhouse's luscious *Lady of Shalott* and there Adam was conceived.

For someone so in her head and out of touch with her body, it may sound strange to say I knew the very moment I conceived, but I did. I was pregnant. I knew it. Of course, I prayed and hoped I was wrong and that something might happen to reverse it. After all, magical thinking had so far kept our sexual life in a realm of its own with no repercussions in the real world, and I knew that making the news public would have dire consequences in both our families, especially in my overtly Christian one.

In those brief weeks before I risked having my intuition confirmed by our old-fashioned G.P., I went for long walks around my well-trodden haunts on the Nottinghamshire-Derbyshire border. For hours I tramped along farm tracks, wandered through woods ripe with colour, heavy with autumn fruit, and memorised chunks from Baudelaire's *Les Fleurs du Mal*. Like bunches of garlic, words were meant to save me from a vampiric reality, poetry was to cushion me from the barbaric family attacks I knew would follow. *Mon enfant, ma soeur,/ Songe à la douceur/ D'aller là-bas vivre ensemble!/...Là, tout n'est qu'ordre et beauté,/ Luxe, calme et volupté.* (My child, my sister, dream of the gentleness of going to live there together. There, everything is order and beauty, luxury, calm, bliss.)

As I expected, our G.P. Dr Kelly, was visibly shocked. Wasn't I that bright grammar school girl, the one who'd done so well and got a full grant to go to university? Weren't my family practising Christians, didn't I go to church with my father twice every Sunday? Oh dear, how disappointed your parents will be to learn this.

Films like *The Magdelene Sisters* and *Philomena* have captured the extreme moral opprobrium facing unwed mothers in Ireland in the 1950s and 60s, and small town Puritan England in 1970 was not far behind. To both our families, pregnancy outside marriage was a deeply shameful thing. Indeed, in our household, the very terms 'pregnant' or 'pregnancy' were taboo at the best of times, and I'd noticed my mother quickly avert her eyes from a woman's swollen belly. The sacrament of marriage might earn forgiveness for the unholy act of sex, but without it women were sinners. And now I was one.

David and I were both terrified of our parents' reactions, and tried at the thirteenth hour to reverse the damage. One afternoon in Creswell, when his parents were out, David administered quinine as I sat in a scalding hot bath. When that old wives' tale failed to work, he tried fierce punches in the abdomen. We did consider the more rational option of abortion and visited the Pregnancy Advisory Clinic in Birmingham, but by this time my body had taken over and all my instincts were staunchly on the side of my unborn child. While we waited in the clinic's reception area, and I battled with morning sickness, we looked at each other.

'This doesn't feel right,' I said. 'I can't go ahead with it.'

'I know,' David said. 'We'll have the baby.'

When the counsellor appeared, we told her we didn't need her help, and had decided to get married.

'Good,' she beamed back. 'That's brave of you. All the best.'

Outside, we made our way to a greasy spoon café, where David ordered a full English breakfast and started reading their copy of *The Daily Mail*. After I'd retched in the toilets a few times, I sat reciting more lines from Baudelaire – *Sois sage, ô ma Douleur, et tiens-toi plus tranquille...* (Be wise, oh my Grief, behave more calmly...) – and hoped against hope that, once he'd finished his bacon and eggs, David might propose in a more romantic fashion.

While the counsellor at the advisory clinic realised this was indeed a brave and honourable decision on both our parts, there was no such acknowledgement from our families. David came with me to tell mine, but even the magic word 'marriage' didn't lessen their horrified response.

Dad sat on the little chintz covered armchair by the coal fire in our living room and sobbed all night. Unable to talk to me or look me in the eye, he seemed to take on my moral failure as a way of confirming his own. He was a sweet, kind but melancholic man, never robust in body or spirit. He'd suffered T.B. of the spine when I was an infant and spent two years flat on his back in Wakefield hospital, since when he'd been subject to repeated illness and self-doubt. My pregnancy was the straw that once more broke his back. With his secret pride in his baby daughter gone, from then on he went ever more deeply inwards, succumbing to quiet despair and a number of strokes that would fell him completely three years later, when he was fifty-six.

Mum was tight-lipped, silent until David left, when her withering look turned me into the Whore of Babylon. I was used to her lack of compassion, but this hostility was raw and blunt.

'Look what you've done to your father,' she said, as his weeping continued.

Next day, while I was out, she ransacked my bedroom, trying to trace back the extent of my crime. I returned to find her holding out an old five-year diary, once a Christmas present, its zipped red leather shiny but scratched. Mum looked at me in disdain.

'*This* has been going on for some time, hasn't it?'

I squinted towards the entry she pointed to, from the summer I'd hitched to the Loire with my school-friend Rachel. We'd camped with my French pen-pal and her mates, and I'd proudly slept (fully clothed) next to (not with) Jean-Luc, a very good-looking French boy. The entry declared this feat with various asterisks and exclamation marks to signify my triumph at achieving normality, but of course my mother read it in a different way.

'You broke into my diary,' I said. 'That's unforgiveable.'

'If I'd known *this* was going to happen,' Mum continued, 'I'd never have let you go to university. Filling your mind with all those strange ideas. What's the point of all that education now? You might as well have gone to the Metal Box factory.'

'Nothing's changed,' I said. ' My brain's still working. I'm still going to finish my degree.'

'That's what you think.' Now there was a streak of sadism in my mother's voice. 'You wait. It won't be as easy as you think.'

'If you'd taught me something about contraception,' I pointed out, 'then maybe it wouldn't have happened.'

But Mum was too lost in her martyred clichés to listen. 'I'd never have thought this would happen to a daughter of mine. Not after all we've done for you. Your brother would never let me down like this. I always said boys were better.'

Back at Warwick, fellow students were dumbfounded when I told them I was getting married.

'In the middle of term?' Gail looked at me in bewilderment. 'That's a strange time for a wedding.' Then the penny dropped. 'You're not *pregnant*, are you?'

I winced.

'You can have an abortion, you know,' Gail went on, as if I was even greener than she'd realised. 'It's easy. Lots of women do.'

Our thin little English wedding took place on an overcast morning, 14 November 1970, at Chesterfield Registry Office. The ceremony was short and sour, with three of the four parents crying and the fourth, my mother, grim faced in her silence. The bride wore a long-sleeved floor-length button-down-the-front dress in cheap maroon crepe, a wedding ring she'd bought from Woolworths and the ubiquitous patent leather shoes. I don't remember any flowers. The groom wore a grey suit and made the concession to his dad of having a haircut. The reception, whose only guests besides parents were my brother and a best man, was held at the nearby station hotel, with its stained paisley carpet, stale smell and cold buffet. I have no idea who paid for it. The bride disappeared to the bathroom every few minutes to throw up and quote poems to her reflection in the mottled mirrors, only by now Baudelaire had been replaced by Larkin. *Man hands on misery to man. It deepens like a coastal shelf. Get out as early as you can, And don't have any kids yourself.*

It was too late to obey this injunction. David's father had presented him with a packet of contraceptive pessaries a couple of days after he'd heard the news. 'Fat lot of good that is now,' David said, when he told me. But none of our four parents seemed to think this wedding had anything to do with their own dereliction of duty in failing to teach us the most basic facts of life. The pill had been available in the UK for all women, married or not, since 1967, but no one had discussed it with me, not even Gail. Nor did any of our parents air the pros or cons of abortion, let alone congratulate us on taking the courageous step of embracing and welcoming a new human life.

The best man, Malcolm, a pal of David's from university, did his utmost to inject some humour, grace and dignity into the happy day, but he could barely be heard as my dad sniffled into his pressed white handkerchief and the dramatic sobs from my now mother-in-law grew ever louder.

'You'd think life was going out of the world rather than coming into it,' Malcolm whispered. I nodded. The message from both sides of the family was clear: we were doomed, our baby was doomed, and this was the worst day in our parents' lives.

We were all relieved when the travesty was over and we could head back to the car park. On the horizon rose the dark silhouette of Chesterfield's most famous landmark: the notorious Crooked Spire of the parish church. I've never forgotten the sight of it that day, as a slight drizzle began: a huge failed erection, sex twisted and gone horribly wrong.

At that very moment, women across the country were avidly reading *The Female Eunuch*, which had been published the previous month. I'd seen copies in the university bookshop: white dust-jackets with title letters in a lurid pink. But brushing against Germaine Greer in the corridors had come too late for me. It seemed I was already one of the eunuchs, and any hope that I could step into my female power and slough off the limits of my narrow background had been fatally compromised by ignorance and a teenage pregnancy.

Now I felt a failure in both worlds. To the still Victorian mores of my parents, I was a fallen woman. To my liberated street-wise peers, I was an old-fashioned wife with a shotgun wedding. No wonder, when I had my first seminar with Germaine Greer and she read out the student list accusingly, 'It says here *Mrs* Jackson,' that I stammered 'Guilty!' The group burst out laughing. Germaine joined in. But I wasn't trying to be funny. Guilt was exactly what I felt.

5

This Love That Makes My Heart's Blood Stop

What is this flesh I purchased with my pains
This fallen star my milk sustains,
This love that makes my heart's blood stop
Or strikes a sudden chill into my bones
And makes my hair stand up?

W.B. Yeats, 'The Mother of God'

THERE WAS NO HONEYMOON. We returned to my room in the halls of residence beneath Gibbett Hill, where David slept on the floor by night and went flat-hunting by day. In retrospect, I realise we were surprisingly mature about the decision we'd made, David especially. We never reproached one another for the pregnancy, then or since, and dealt as amicably as we could with its consequences, negotiating our way towards our new future with what seems now like remarkable courage and equanimity. I was lost in a world of unexpected and unfamiliar bodily changes, and took David's support for granted, not really acknowledging how flexible and ungrudging he was, stepping into the responsibilities suddenly thrust upon his twenty-two-year old self.

Everyone recommended Leamington Spa as the best place to live, a white-housed Regency town eight miles from campus. When I had no classes, David and I trudged the handsome streets together, searching somewhere to rent. With its elegant squares, curved crescent, splendid balconied houses, pump rooms and gardens, Leamington was a miniature Bath, aspiring to gentility, too far from campus to be a real university town and pushing its more deprived areas out of sight to the south of the river. As we stood on doorsteps, more than one door was closed firmly in our faces when we admitted a baby was on the way. 'Sorry. Two rules. No coloureds. No children.'

In the end, we had to compromise with the nearby city of Warwick: a flat on one of its narrow main streets, down which traffic squeezed between the terraced black-and-white Tudor houses. We had the first and second floors of one of these old buildings, above a ladies' hairdresser. A small door in the street opened onto a yard by the hairdresser's toilet, then a rickety metal fire escape climbed to our tiny galley kitchen. Beyond that, a lounge with its corners shaved off, half the room taken up by a protruding drinks bar covered with dimpled brass, while at the back hung a mirror and light fittings with red velvet shades; it had the ambience of a brothel. Upstairs were two interconnecting bedrooms with sloping roofs which made it impossible to stand. The fitted carpets were all deep red, the walls stark white, the fake inner timbers black. From the bedroom window we could almost reach across to touch the leaning walls above the supermarket opposite. We inhaled a permanent smell of shampoo and bleach, while from eight a.m. to six p.m. the salon ceiling piped its sound of muzak into our floor, so to hear only traffic in the evenings was a relief.

When I was in the sixth form, I'd had a Saturday job at a women's hairdresser in Mansfield, trying to save up for my trip with Rachel to France. Also from eight to six, not even classified as a 'junior', I'd washed hair, massaged scalps, handed plastic rollers, swept up cuttings, made instant coffee, run errands for the 'seniors' and earned £1 a day. This doubtless added to my innate mistrust of our new landlord, a young spiv with oily hair and mercantile manner, who owned the hair salon. When he came to collect the rent, he was visibly bewildered by the hundreds of books that were our only possessions and gestured to the overflowing shelves.

'What do you need all these for?' he asked. 'Once you've read them, I mean. They must weigh a fair bit. I tell you, you'll be liable if anything happens to this floor.'

To help pay the extortionate rent, we let out the top bedrooms to two students in my year. Elaine, a bouncing, effervescent girl, was wonderfully indifferent to all the rules I'd been told women should observe. Irreverent, funny, casual in both dress and manner with her floppy dungarees and wildness, Elaine seemed permanently high from the joke of life itself. Meg, by contrast, tiny and androgynous, was more earnest, elfin with her short-cut black hair. With no adequate public transport to campus, all three of us hitched the eight miles to and from lectures, sometimes in a trio, sometimes alone. David found work teaching English in one of

Leamington Spa's secondary schools, and we spent our spare time reading.

I never considered abandoning my degree, nor did anyone at Warwick suggest it. With my new antennae I registered a couple of women on campus carrying babies around, and gratefully breathed in Germaine Greer's liberated air that deemed anything possible. Gay Clifford was especially adamant.

'You mustn't for a moment lower your sights. This changes nothing for you. You're one of our best students.'

The English department went out of its way to be helpful. I would split my second year, taking the assessed modules as usual, but deferring the end of year exam. From early summer 1971 to summer 1972 I would be with the baby full-time, return for the delayed second year exams, then do the final year – with a free place in the University crèche – before graduating in 1973.

'But isn't it kind of cheating?' I asked one of the tutors. 'I mean, it gives me an unfair advantage. A whole extra year to do background reading.'

The tutor gave me that now familiar you-know-nothing-of-the-world look. 'You will have a baby as well.'

I don't recall going to pre-natal classes, nor consciously making any special preparations for this new life in my life, other than knitting one white matinee jacket. The pregnancy was relatively straightforward. I walked around Warwick, with its leafy lanes, river and castle, ate as healthily as our budget allowed, and behaved with the blithe ignorance of the young. Once the morning nausea abated, my only worrying symptom was low blood pressure, which meant I frequently passed out. One afternoon, standing in a long check-out queue at the supermarket, I fainted, coming round to find the elderly woman behind me had collapsed in sympathy and all the staff were huddled over her, as I contemplated my broken front tooth on the floor.

Not knowing that kleptomania often affects pregnant women, I assumed it was just my own recklessness that drove me to slip into the second-hand book-store a few doors away, find a coveted title hidden in a cranny and carry it out under a folded *Guardian*; or hover in the old-fashioned chemist and lift one of the luxury tissue-wrapped lemon-shaped soaps in the basket by the door. We bought no soap for a year. Once, perhaps inspired by Clive's example, I stole a two-volume hardback edition of Flaubert's complete works, in French, on the most exquisitely thin paper. But I was so shocked this went without mishap – long before the days of CCTV – I knew better than to risk my luck again.

What I wanted to steal but never quite dared was a decent outfit. We had no money for clothes, and for the last four months of pregnancy, literally every day I wore the same loose tunic dress that fastened down the front, a paisley patterned soft Viyella, the colour of Victoria plums.

On 28 May, sitting alone in one of the upstairs rooms as far away as possible from the hairdressers' muzak, I wrote a poem about being ready to give birth. And next morning, Saturday, 29 May 1971, our baby was born. But I could hardly have been less ready or equipped to deal with a new child. I'd just turned twenty, was emotionally immature and lived still in a disembodied universe made up more of words than matter.

Even during pregnancy, I didn't really inhabit my body. I floated through the world in an unconscious way, unmoored. I'd often wished invisibility on myself. Throughout adolescence I'd been prone to anorexia, trying to erase myself from sight when I looked in the mirror. At some stage, something had to break into this rarefied zone, to smash through the bell jar and try to wake me up. If the clumsy pregnant body of which my family was so ashamed could not bring me down to earth, anchor me with some rope of humanity, then perhaps my own body giving birth to another would persuade me I was actually inside one. Thus childbirth did its best to wake me up, in the most violent way possible, to the fact that I was a real woman.

The claim that the body does not remember pain, that the experience of childbirth is quickly covered over by a welcome amnesia, was, for me, completely untrue. I remember it clearly more than forty years on. That hour when my body pushed out a large healthy boy – 8lbs 8ozs wrested from narrow hips – was only one clock hour, 8.30 to 9:30 a.m., but it was the longest of my life, and shocked me into an awareness of suffering I'd not known before. Every second felt a drawn-out eternity, and at each return to the world from my ineffective mask of gas and air, the hand on the clock seemed stuck in the same implacable position. I kept reciting to myself like a mantra, 'It will end, it will end.' But the only thought I understood was that the word *unendurable* now made sense. In the midst of it, I swore to David, who was present throughout, I would never have another child. Of course, had I been more prepared, more mature, more inside my body, I might have been better equipped to deal with it. As it was, I felt traumatized, and the experience triggered nightmares of childbirth for years to come. Needless to say, I made sure I never got pregnant again.

Theories of the importance of close mother and child bonding from the moment of birth onwards had not reached Warneford Hospital in 1971. Perhaps they felt they'd made enough concessions by letting the father be present at the birth. But no sooner had we caught a glimpse of our new baby, his slippery body purple, his face strangely old and wise, his head elongated from the swift passage through a narrow birth canal, than he was snatched away into hospital procedure and bureaucracy. Too bewildered to protest, I lay waiting to be stitched up by a nervous male doctor, then was wheeled through a labyrinth of corridors to a ward where several women were happily suckling their babies. David had been sent home, and I felt distressed. I wanted my baby. Where was he? I called out to the other women to ask for help, then to the first nurse who appeared.

'What have you done with my baby?' I shouted. 'I need to see him. Where is he?'

Unfortunately, this was the same Nurse Ratchett who'd been callous during the labour, telling me to stop making such a noise.

'Don't make a fuss,' she said. 'You'll be glad enough of time on your own in a few days, I can tell you.'

I looked at her in disbelief. Did she have any children? I'd just gone through the most traumatic physical experience a woman can endure, and now I couldn't even hold my own baby.

'Where is he?' I persisted. 'Where have you taken him?'

'It's hospital policy,' she explained. 'The babies all get taken away for the first twenty-four hours. Just until they've passed a motion. You'll see him tomorrow morning.'

I lay back and tried to accept this edict, but the sound of the other new mothers cooing, oohing and aahing was too much. I had to find my baby. I threw off the covers and walked unsteadily towards the door. During the birth I'd had a huge shot of pethidine – I recalled a syringe aiming for my thigh – which probably accounted for the slight feeling of hallucination as I wandered the hospital corridors, in search of anything that resembled a nursery.

I was not attired like the other mothers. On the rare occasions I slept in night-wear, it was a man's shirt. I hated the current nylon lingerie. But I'd found in one of Warwick's second-hand shops a beautiful floor-length Victorian nightgown, white cotton with smocking down the front, which I thought would do for the hospital stay. This added to the Gothic melo-drama, as I drifted barefoot through the old hospital trying to find my abducted baby. I seemed to be wandering forever, unable to interpret doors and signs, everything surreal, looking for someone I didn't yet know but whom I did know was a lost part of me.

Eventually a nurse, racing after me and recognising from my voice that I would not be pacified by any substitute, led me to the nursery. And there, confronted by row upon row of almost identical babies stuck in plastic cribs like battery hens, I felt more foolish than ever. Which of these look-alike infants was mine? Another nurse took pity on me, double-checked the label on the most gorgeous baby of them all and scooped him up.

'This one's yours,' she said, and allowed me to hold him for a few brief moments in all his wondrous newness. I took a deep breath to absorb the smell of him.

'Can I take him with me to the ward?' I pleaded. 'Just for a little while?'

'Sorry. It's for baby's good. We have to observe the rules.'

And I was escorted back to the maternity ward, left waiting another impossibly drawn out sixteen hours, restless and sleepless, until I could have him with me again.

When we all three returned to the Warwick flat a couple of days later, with the baby swaddled in a white babygro and the matinee jacket I'd knitted, I was in bliss. I felt I'd been returned to the beginning of life: that every-thing I'd ever done or read till now needed to be redone, reread, in the light of this epiphany. Poetry I wanted more than prose and I picked up Yeats' *Collected Poems*, a hardback I'd left on the drinks bar in the lounge, and opened it at random – *What is this love that makes my heart's blood stop...?* – thinking I'd be able to read every poem anew, relish each line, each word in the world, in a new way now life was so utterly transformed.

David had filled the flat with flowers, and Elaine and Meg left us to be alone for a few days with our astonishment at our good fortune. We were both deliriously happy. We seemed to have an increased respect for each other, a mutual acknowledgement that we'd done this, we'd come through and created a perfect new human being, and we did what we could to be mutually supportive. We may have been ignorant about much of the world, inexperienced in love, but we were kind and thoughtful with each other, grateful to the other for being the second parent of this wonderful baby, channelling whatever love we might fail to give each other into our love for our child.

And now a healthy grandson had arrived, our parents changed tack. David's parents sent us money and congratulations and wanted to visit. Still in the pop charts was 'Grandad', Clive Dunn from *Dad's Army* singing with a children's choir, which had reached Number One in January that year. This became David's mother's favourite song for his father. *Grandad, granddad, you're lovely. That's what we all think of you. Grandad, grandad you're lovely. That's what we all think of you. Grandad. Grandad.* Suddenly what had been the most shameful of events turned into a cause for proud celebration, all the embarrassment that had been projected onto my pregnant body miraculously erased now the baby was out.

My own mother came to stay for a few days in the flat to help with cooking and washing. This was the era before disposable nappies and we had no washing machine. But I soon sensed that our delight in the baby was not something Mum fully shared. One afternoon, when David was out teaching, I had just put the baby down to sleep when I was hit by intense pain in the lower abdomen. It felt like labour contractions all over again.

'Oh my God,' I said. 'What shall I do?'

I lay down on the red carpet, breathing deeply to try to control the agony. I thought I was dying. Like me, Mum didn't know the medical explanation, that this was the uterus contracting further, but instead of moving over to help, she looked down at me writhing on the floor as if I were an earthworm she would like to squash with all the weight of bitterness of her own failed life.

'Now you know,' she said, her voice cold. 'It's not all a bed of roses.'

And once again, as with the turquoise hat episode, something in my heart closed further. I'd done my best to stay open to her, to not mind the little digs she'd made at me over the years: the preferential treatment of my brother, odd nasty comments, occasional pinches, sadistic jibes. But now I was more wary. I couldn't cut her out completely, that would be too cruel, and anyway some part of me never did relinquish a hope she might magically transform into the warm nurturing mother she had never been, the mother I'd always craved. But I was determined she would not contaminate my new life. Wedded to resentment she might be, unable to mother, but I would not let this pollute my relationship with my own child, and I ceased to pretend to confide in her.

David's parents visited a few days later. David was their only child, they adored him and now they adored his child too. They were good people, kind and generous and David's early polio had made them especially protective and conscientious. But with his mother, Jean, I always felt lacking. She tolerated rather than liked me and, by taking over when they came to stay, made it clear I was not the wife she would have chosen for the apple of her eye. She always brought with her a box of fresh cleaning materials and would set to in the bathroom and kitchen.

Whilst I was bathing the baby, I overheard her talking to Dave's father, Ernie.

'Do you think she's a good mother?' The implication being that Jean clearly thought not.

Ernie came to my defence. 'I think she's doing a grand job. They're young, don't forget. She'll settle in to it.'

But I never felt I was good enough in Jean's eyes; perhaps no woman could have been. Our first major run-in was over a name. David and I both wanted something with a literary association. We spent hours animatedly discussing names from Dickens, Hardy and other 19th-century novelists. The top runners were Barnaby, Martin, Jude, Dmitri, Pascal and, from David's beloved George Eliot, Felix (after *Felix Holt*). This was the era before eccentric names became fashionable and when David's parents heard the options, they pointed out how selfish we were being, putting our preferences first.

'Have you thought how it will be for him at school?' Jean said. 'How they'll laugh at him with a name like Dmitri? Felix? That's the name of a cat!'

'No,' I fought back. 'It means joy. Happiness.'

But they wouldn't give up until we accepted a compromise, and chose two names they approved. We didn't reveal they were both from George Eliot: Adam (from *Adam Bede*) and Daniel (*Daniel Deronda*).

When the parent visits were over and David was out teaching, I took time to relish and absorb my new identity. I lay in the bedroom, with Adam curled asleep on top of me. For hours I cuddled and stroked his warm body, kissed his head, remembered my book of medieval poems. *Lullay, myn lykyng, my dere sone, myn sweyting, Lullay, my dere herte, myn owyn dere derlyng.*

'Nothing will ever come between us,' I whispered. 'You are the most precious baby in the world. No one will ever come between us. I promise. You are loved, loved, loved. No one will tear us apart.'

6

Two Funerals and a Graduation

O the mind, mind has mountains; cliffs of fall
Frightful, sheer, no-man-fathomed. Hold them cheap
May who ne'er hung there.

Gerard Manley Hopkins, 'No, worst there is none'

WE FINALLY MOVED to Leamington Spa that autumn, thanks to colleagues at David's school who told us of a flat to rent above theirs. The house was a large Georgian terrace divided into five flats, with a benevolent ageing landlord who bought the paint for us to decorate. I chose tomato soup red for the kitchen, where we hung a busy Breughel scene. David chose lichen green for the lounge, and Adam's little nursery was duck-egg blue. We were on the second floor, with an attic above, which meant a lot of tramping up and downstairs, the carry cot wheels then baby buggy left in the collective hall at the bottom. But the climb gave us far-reaching views from the front windows onto an untamed patch of green and trees, with the river and Regency streets in the distance.

When the room at the back proved too damp to use as a bedroom we placed our double mattress on the floor in the lounge, its only furniture other than one armchair. This gave Adam plenty of scope to sit, play, crawl and eventually speed around the floor in the mobile baby walker provided by David's parents.

Despite the lack of heating, we settled into a mutually affable rhythm through that winter and spring. I taught myself to ride a bike (I'd never had one as a child), wore long cotton skirts with little tank tops – at last I was slim again – and hunted down colourful picture books. There was no need to buy baby clothes as parents competed to provide. We had no car; David was close enough to school to walk. I looked after Adam and while he slept, I read and studied in the primitive garret overhead. When we both wanted to study one weekend, David's parents came to take the few-months old Adam to them to stay. But neither of us could bear his absence and we caught the first train to go and fetch him back.

After the claustrophobia and noise of Warwick, Leamington Spa was heaven. The river Leam divided the town into 'upper' and 'lower', and we were in the 'upper' middle class area favoured by students and academics. I would push Adam in his baby buggy on daily walks through the fourteen acres of Jephson gardens, where we fed the ducks, then past the Royal Pump Rooms and Baths to large squares of old white houses with wisteria-draped wrought iron balconies; down the wide Parade, along the curve of Lansdowne Crescent, through the little road to the back of our house on Leam Terrace. I might catch sight of E.P. Thompson, his handsome face lined with thought, or Germaine Greer, the tallest and most dynamic woman in town, striding across one of the squares in her thigh-high canary yellow boots.

But it was a lonely time, being a new mother at home. Gay Clifford occasionally dropped by to offer a few words of encouragement, reminding me of her beauty and brilliance, but no one from my student year at Warwick came to visit. We had neither TV nor telephone. Neighbours downstairs let us use their phone for emergencies. I don't remember a radio, but I suppose there must have been one.

David was more gregarious, with a generous ease in socialising that I lacked. He went for drinks with colleagues, particularly his head of department, Mike, whose politics on education were similar and who proved an ally. When we visited Mike and his wife Lyn in their perfect little white town house a few streets away, Lyn, blonde and gorgeous in her mid-pregnancy, was confidently constructing bookshelves. The pair of them were highly articulate and I found them totally intimidating, as I did the married couple in the flat immediately beneath us. Jane, like David, had a degree in English from Newcastle; Phil was doing a doctorate in biochemistry at Warwick. Jane was a willowy blonde, with the slenderest fingers and finest features I'd ever seen. Phil was more of a gipsy, with a mass of dark curls and the Jewish good looks I'd always admired.

When I got up to find Adam stirring, I would hear the door below us shut as Jane and Phil left for their early morning shift handing out *Socialist Worker* at factories on the edge of town. Their flat was filled with radical book titles and framed prints of Leonardo da Vinci drawings. Awed by their cosmopolitan taste when David and I went to dinner, I felt like a child in the adult house of life. I was mortified when I offered to put the red wine we'd brought into the fridge, and Jane replied with a laugh, 'You don't cool red wine.'

I was even more humiliated when the dinner table conversation turned to circumcision. Having only ever slept with one man, how was I to know which was which? I turned to David for clarification.

'Are *you* circumcised?'

David looked embarrassed, while Jane and Phil covered their astonishment in laughter. 'You mean you don't *know?*'

My addiction to voracious reading and prolific note-taking was far too deeply ingrained to be broken by having a baby. I lodged an old drawing board on the lounge armchair and worked while Adam was napping a few feet away. Although I was officially having a year 'out', my second year spread forwards and my third year ran backwards into it, so I was simultaneously revising for novel and poetry exams and preparing for the following year's courses on Shakespeare and European theatre. My head was a mass of quotes and ideas. Gay Clifford's course on allegory had introduced me to authors outside the mainstream, and I soon became obsessed by the Gothic visions of Mary Shelley, Edgar Allen Poe, Bram Stoker, Robert Louis Stevenson. I'd always been drawn towards the unconscious, and in my first year had adored E.R. Dodds' *The Greeks and the Irrational*, studying mysticism and psychic life in Greek culture up to the time of Plato.

Now I became ever more preoccupied with what lay outside and beyond rational experience. I consumed R.D. Laing's *The Divided Self*, relieved to find in his category of the 'ontologically insecure' a perfect description of how I experienced myself: a see-through person who 'cannot take the realness, aliveness, autonomy and identity of himself and others for granted' and often feels 'more dead than alive'. Reassured too, to find that in *Self and Others* and *Sanity, Madness and the Family*, Laing linked depression and mental illness to a family nexus, showing how so-called 'normal' families could mask huge dysfunction, with the most vulnerable member, often the youngest child (as I was), carrying the family's hidden 'madness'.

Suddenly my own history started to make sense and I extended my reading of Laing into literary outsiders and 'madmen' who mirrored what I felt was my own condition. On the Shakespeare course, I would focus my essays around the madness of *King Lear*, the role of the fool, the breakdowns of Hamlet and Ophelia. I was particularly drawn to the motif of the double – Mary Shelley's *Frankenstein*, Hogg's *Private Memoirs and Confessions of a Justified Sinner*, Dostoevsky's *The Double*, Conrad's *The Secret Sharer* – and this would thread through my final year dissertation for Gay Clifford. Later, it became the basis for my post-graduate work. Little did I know it was also the subject of Sylvia Plath's dissertation at Smith's.

But the price for this intellectual over-reaching – being a full-time mother during the day and a passionate student through the night – was physical and mental exhaustion. David had severe eczema, his skin often as rough as sandpaper, bleeding raw, and we rarely got much sleep. I sat the second year exams as planned, relieved to shed some of the heavy 19th century novels I'd been carrying in my head, but it wasn't long before the backlog of sleep deprivation and blithe neglect of my own health took their toll.

A few days after the exams, on the usual routine of taking Adam out in his buggy, its blue-and-white striped canvas like a mini deckchair, we took a route back through the Jephson gardens by the side of the lake. I had to duck to avoid the overhanging branches of a particularly fine copper beech tree and, as I did so, noticed how the leaves, caught by the dappled sunlight, were a particularly intense translucent pink.

I started to admire them more closely, pulling them down to show Adam the colour. Then something suddenly tore in the side of the world and I was tipped into the hyper-real world of an LSD trip. It was exactly two years since that first and only one, and was definitely not the place to be with a year-old toddler. Once again, everything invaded too closely. The surface of each leaf was polished into extra vibrancy, the roughness of the bark magnified. I felt like Alice tumbling into a distorted universe where I had no wish to be. I started to panic. I needed to wake myself. I closed my eyes, counted to ten. But when I opened them again, the world had not reverted to normal. Instead, the hallucination intensified. Objects grew and shrank as if I'd stepped into a hall of distorting mirrors. I didn't dare look too closely at Adam, for even he was losing his beauty and becoming grotesque.

I raced back to the flat, head down, the baby buggy bouncing before me, trying not to look at anything that would feed the nightmare. I carried Adam up the two flights of stairs, settled him on the double mattress in the lounge with his favourite toys and prayed with what was left of my disintegrating mind that our familiar surroundings would return me to normality. Sensing something was wrong, Adam crawled towards me for a reassuring cuddle, but I couldn't bear for him to touch me. No longer my adorable child, he was now part insect, his fingers rasping, his soft torso hardening, as if we'd stepped into Kafka's *Metamorphosis* and the human body itself was under threat. I paced around until David returned from school to take over caring for Adam, then fled to the attic, hoping rest might dispel the unwanted vision. But it stayed with me all night, allowed no sleep, and persisted through the following day.

Somehow I traced Gail and phoned for advice.

'It's only a flashback,' she said. 'Take lots of Vitamin C.'

I swallowed several bottles of Vitamin C, drank gallons of water, but the trip remained as intense as ever. I felt I'd been sentenced to the worst conceivable experience: conscious, but out of control of my mind, more than half of me in the land of the insane, yet trying to behave with Adam as if nothing was wrong. When David returned that second afternoon, I walked into the countryside to try to anchor myself. But nature made it worse. If the previous trip had given me an illusion of heaven, this one took me over the threshold into hell. Fields of golden corn shimmered too fiercely, mockingly. Cracks in the parched soil were too large, opening onto black vaults in the underworld. Beetles were the size of mules. And that night too I paced the flat, terrified I would never get back, that my over-wrought mind had at last given way.

It took almost a week for the flashback to fade. All that time, I was unable to sleep, unable to step back into the normal world where my child was waiting for me. David, as ignorant around drugs as I was, brought back terrible stories from talks with Mike at school, tales of people driven to psychosis when their re-triggered LSD trips never abated, locked permanently in psychiatric institutions. I was in absolute terror this would be my fate.

Happily, I have never experienced a flashback in such extreme form again, but at times of stress and fatigue, I've sensed the same chemical residue waiting in the wings, ready to ambush me and tip an already fragile reality into complete breakdown. From then on I became strongly averse to all forms of drugs and avoided excess alcohol, not from Puritanism, but because I knew now how vulnerable the human mind can be.

Letters arrived that summer from Gay Clifford in Italy. Delighted she was treating me as a friend, I was nevertheless surprised she chose me for her confidences. Closely typed in red ink on A4 sheets of airmail paper, the letters were filled with lyrical descriptions of the area around *Pianelli*, a beautiful old farmhouse she was renting, 'set high up at the end of a valley running down to the plain between Cortona and Lake Trasimene; chestnut and oak trees giving way lower down to the more usual cypresses and olives of Tuscany; terraces below and above with fruit trees and vines... So quiet, so perfectly remote and lucid a place I've never known before: it has become part of me, an image of the kind of living I most desire...'

The poetry of her words made a great impact on me, and I felt honoured she should share her idyll in such detail. My only experience of going abroad had been two trips to my pen-pal in France, and the near disastrous escapade at Chartres with Rachel. Gay's letters were like dispatches from a romantic landscape I felt destined to visit only in my imagination. *Pianelli*, she wrote, was 'a retreat, a place for reflection and quiet and the unhurried observation of small wild things, the lizards and snakes and butterflies and owls that move around the place as if it were a part of their world rather than a habitation of men.' She also confided her 'passionate' envy when Germaine Greer, a friend she dearly loved, was able, on the back of the success of *The Female Eunuch*, to buy *Pianelli* outright. 'I've never before wanted any *thing* so much ... The leaving it was like being expelled from Paradise.'

What surprised me more was the negative tone she used about her work at Warwick University. 'I approach the next term and the return to England with something approaching terror, feeling that Warwick is less and less doing what it should or might do, that the very idea of an institution is inimical to learning with joy. And thinking that, I can't really delude myself that another institution, a job elsewhere, would be more than a frivolous and temporary escape... it's the sense that most of us teaching are teaching without passion, without love, that dispirits me... the sense that it's probably impossible to teach subjects like literature with confidence, in a society that's largely oblivious or hostile to the values that literature has commonly asserted.'

Little did I know then how uncannily prescient these words would prove, both in Gay's life and my own. But I preserved them carefully. Over forty years, through countless house moves and disruptions which

saw the loss of many possessions and most of my personal correspondence, Gay's tissue-thin letters survived. Their almost sepia envelopes lie
on my desk now: reminders of a world long since vanished, like the visionary works she so loved, 'the last way into a kind of world that is not ours,
but perhaps has much to show us.'

Meantime I washed nappies that had soaked overnight in buckets of
Napisan, watched Adam grow, clapped when he took his first steps in the
tomato red kitchen. With the arrival of the autumn term, we started
travelling to the university crèche each morning, a small nursery with
excellent staff where Adam settled in quite happily. I'd been dreading
hitching to campus with a baby and buggy, but one of our neighbours
who travelled to the university each day offered us lifts in his little white
van. This would have been a perfect arrangement, had I not been so scared
of jeopardising the lifts that I was willing to pay any price for them. How
angry I am now thinking back, not knowing I was allowed to say no to
the quick bouts of sex that seemed expected in return.

Sexual permissiveness, of course, was part of the legacy of the 60s,
especially in university circles and this kind of behaviour was not at all
bizarre. But I never felt comfortable with the general assumption that
sexual freedom was a necessary thing for women to prove themselves; it
made it harder to decline, and for girls like me, brought up to believe men
came first and had superior claims, it was all too easy to lose power and feel
pressured to say yes when we wanted to say no. I was left feeling cheap and
compromised, yet fonder of David, grateful for his loyalty and kindness,
hoping he wouldn't discover the shadow of this unwanted secret 'affair'.

It was all part of the craziness of my final year at Warwick. From being
constantly on the run, I was slim at least, dashing from washing nappies
and making porridge with golden syrup, to Germaine Greer's office for
seminars – often she was on the phone discussing publicity – or taking
notes in her brilliant lectures as she argued against the myth that women
of intellectual substance were merely 'flying pigs'. Pop into the campus
supermarket for supplies, collect Adam from the crèche, make supper, do
bath-time, settle him in bed, climb to the attic to write essays on divided
selves and the disintegration of the mind.

Gay Clifford gave me a spare key to her office so I could study in quiet
privacy on campus. Her room was always immaculately tidy, even the
pencils in her drawer newly sharpened in a neat row. I sat at her desk,

hoping her intelligence and beauty might be contagious, determined to justify her faith in me.

One warm Saturday morning, in the garret with its tiny broken window, I sat writing an essay on Shakespeare and madness for a deadline two days away. As usual at weekends David was out with Adam, walking and shopping while I did my assignments. I was on the wild heath with Lear and the fool, in the kind of deep trance writing often delivered me to, when I heard a doorbell ringing persistently. I tried to ignore it, then, worried David might have forgotten his keys, tramped down three flights of stairs to the front door. Jean and Ernie, David's parents, stood on the doorstep cradling a carton of groceries. Ernie was a dapper man, short and clean-shaven, a stores inspector for the Colliery Board. Always neatly dressed, he wore a herring-bone suit, white shirt and dark tie. Jean's hair was freshly permed and her clothes too were meticulously ironed. Through the fog of Lear's descent away from social niceties, I stared at their bright eyes and expectant smiles.

'Should I have known you were coming?' I wondered. 'David and Adam are out at the moment.'

'We thought we'd surprise you,' Jean said. 'Let's get these groceries upstairs.'

I followed her up to the kitchen, its red walls far too visceral for Jean and Ernie's pastels. I'd been leaving the morning's dishes for later, likewise the stinking bucket of Napisan. Jean rolled up her sleeves and started unpacking the box of groceries. Everything came from the Co-Op in Creswell where she worked: instant coffee, milk chocolate digestives, tinned meat and salmon, cans of fruit.

'We'll soon have this sorted,' she said. 'You put the kettle on. We've had a hot drive.'

Eyeing the clock to calculate when David might be back, I did as I was told. We had coffee and biscuits, then Jean washed the pots and cleaned the kitchen. Many awkward silences later, sounds from the hall told us David and Adam had returned. Ernie and Jean hurried downstairs to greet them, commenting on the buggy tipping over with carrier bags of food on the handles and looking at me askance as they carried child and groceries upstairs.

'Did you invite them?' I whispered to David. He shook his head. 'They're not expecting to stay over, are they?' He shrugged. 'You know

I've got my essay to do.'

A laborious lunch preparation began: salad, cheese, tinned corned beef, spring onions, boiled eggs, buttered rolls, all master-minded by Jean, while Ernie dandled his grandson on his shoulder. I wasn't hungry and soon, feeling totally superfluous, slipped back up to the garret.

Quickly back in my trance, tramping over the heath with the poor King, I heard his words with renewed vehemence. *Blow, winds, and crack your cheeks! Rage! Blow! You cataracts and hurricanoes, spout Till you have drench'd our steeples, drown'd the cocks!* I'd written another page on how the mind breaks into madness at times of stress, how close insanity can be, when Lear's footsteps sounded more loudly than ever. *Singe my white head! And thou, all-shaking thunder, Strike flat the thick rotundity o' the world!* Only they weren't his, they were my father-in-law's, as he stormed over the bare floorboards that led from the storage room to the garret.

'We've never been so insulted in our lives,' he raged. 'We make all this effort, drive down through the heat, bring you a week's free groceries, and you can't even say thank you. Can't deign to have lunch with us.' *Crack nature's moulds, all germens spill at once, That make ingrateful man!*

'You don't deserve this marriage, you know that? You don't deserve a family at all. You don't spend time with your own husband and child. You dump your baby in a nursery all week and at weekends let our son do all the work.' He gestured to the shelves of books under the sloping roof. 'You think these matter more, don't you? Well, they don't. Nothing good will come of it. You won't have a life this way. You won't ever be happy. You won't have any friends. You're too selfish. You don't deserve to be a mother. You don't deserve a child at all. Don't expect us to ever visit you again.' With that parting shot, he stamped back downstairs and within minutes I heard the front door of the house slam.

Sadly, he was right. They never did visit again. A couple of weeks later, police knocked at the door. Ernie had died from a heart attack. Once the police had left, David and I stood in the bay window contemplating distant trees and rooftops.

'It was like a curse,' I said. 'What he said last time he came. That's the last thing he ever said to me. That I didn't deserve to be a mother. I'm stuck with that now.'

'It was in the heat of the moment,' David said gently. 'I'm sure that's not what he would want you to remember.'

But Jean was less forgiving. She was devastated by her husband's death and someone had to be held responsible.

'He was so upset that day we visited,' she said, when we went to Creswell. 'His blood pressure shot right up. That's what brought on the heart attack.'

Thus, compounding my sins as an inadequate wife and bad mother, I was now, in Jean's eyes at least, a murderer. Perhaps this accounted for her behaviour towards me in years to come; perhaps, consciously or not, she needed some kind of revenge.

At the end of the academic year, I hitched alone to campus to examine the notice-board where the degree results were posted. Out of sixty students in my year, under BA Honours in English and European Literature Class One, only one name was listed. How relieved I was. Not just for ego grati-fication, but as proof that some inner yearning had been met, my deepest priorities and love of literature recognised. I felt the world had finally acknowledged who I really was, granted me my own place in it, conferred a kind of homecoming. I hurried back to Leamington to find David sitting in the armchair in the lounge with Adam standing between his legs.

'We've done it,' I beamed as I entered the room. 'Got a first.'

David didn't move. 'Don't say we,' he said, his face dark. 'This has nothing to do with me.'

I recoiled as if I'd been slapped. 'But I couldn't have done this without your help. Aren't you pleased? It means I'll get a grant to do post-grad work.'

No, it seemed he wasn't pleased, and the joy I'd felt in my result rapidly drained away. Why was he so angry? Had I hurt his male pride by getting a first class degree when his own, in the same subject, was second class, a 2ii? Surely not. I walked forward to take Adam from him, saying I'd look after him for the rest of the day, but David's legs simply tightened around our two-year old son. His body language seemed to say it all. I might have gained the better degree, but he would be the better parent, have the stronger link with Adam, and if anyone was the outsider in our little family unit, it was me.

Of course, I may have imagined some of this. A lack of praise for my achievements was so familiar from my history, I had a heightened sensitivity to it. My passing the 11-Plus, my ten O-levels, three Grade A A-levels, Grade A S-level, my first-year examination award at Warwick, all had been met with a notable silence in my family. I was once awarded a silver pencil for a run of successful Children's Hour competitions on the radio, which won for the whole family a day's outing to a BBC studio, but that was the only time my parents showed much interest in my achievements. I couldn't recall any words of congratulation, not one celebratory meal. No matter how I excelled, nothing seemed good enough. When I wrote some short stories and read them out, Dad suggested sending them to the BBC, but Mum snorted. 'They won't want *those*.'

Now, whether real or imagined, sensing David's disinterest rather than pride or delight in my first class degree, I immediately plummeted from euphoria into despair. What were all those years of studying for? Why was I reviled for doing something I loved? Was this Ernie's curse, the final words he'd ever uttered to me, coming true? Now he was dead, had his spirit entered David so he could take up the baton of reproaching me?

By the time Adam was in bed that night of my results, the old black hole had opened to swallow me again and I sat in the red kitchen, emptying a bottle of paracetamol. I wasn't trying to commit suicide; I just craved oblivion. David saw what I was doing, made a cutting remark about my stupidity, and walked away. I slept in the attic, where the previous year I'd crept up with Adam for his night feeds so as not to waken David. My well-thumbed books lay in untidy stacks on the floor. *Paradise Lost, Melmoth the Wanderer, The Idiot, The Tragic Life and Deserved Death of Dr Faustus*.

That year I'd totally fallen in love with Christopher Marlowe's *Doctor Faustus* and become obsessed with the myth. Here was my copy of the first chapbook of 1592, with its frontispiece sketch by Rembrandt of the doomed scholar. And here was Thomas Mann's masterpiece novel *Doctor Faustus*. This was my myth, too, I was sure of that, especially now. Hadn't I done what Faust did and put ambition before love? Hadn't I too wanted too much knowledge? I was a bad person, selfish, stupid. The demons had won. I'd killed David's dad. He was right. I didn't deserve happiness. And Marlowe's words, which I knew by heart, repeated themselves as I slipped into my paracetamol-induced sleep. *Ah Faustus/ Now hast thou but one bare hower to live,/ And then thou must be damnd perpetually./ Stand stil you euer moouing spheres of heauen,/ That time may cease, and midnight never come...*

Gay Clifford marked the end of that academic year with a thirtieth birth-day party in her cottage in Kenilworth. David and Adam had already left to stay with his mother and I was to follow them after Gay's party. After days wandering shops in Leamington and Warwick, I found for Gay the most expensive present I'd ever bought for a friend: a beautiful art deco ink blotter with inset porcelain (she always preferred writing with a fountain pen in red or sepia brown ink). Gay gave me the spare room that adjoined hers on the front of the cottage so I could stay late after the party, and here I spent what was left of the small hours listening to her prolonged rapture in the next room as she took to bed her current lover, one of the married men in the English department. It sent me back to my nights in the flat in Coventry, overhearing Gail and Bob, once more a spy in the house of love. But I had a strange feeling that Gay wanted me there, somehow wanted me to know of her amorous adventures, to be a kind of witness. Next morning, as we all emerged insomniac for fresh coffee, the lover lamented the coming day and the social function he had to attend with his wife. 'Still,' he said, in his laconic Scottish drawl, 'night, thank God, will eventually come.'

That summer, too, my own father died. I hadn't known he was critically ill; only too late did I discover he'd had a series of mini-strokes before the swift cerebral haemorrhage that felled him in August.

'Why didn't you tell me?' I asked my mother.

'You weren't interested,' she said, in a martyred voice. 'You never visited.'

At the funeral, she made it clear that Dad's illness could in large part be laid at my door. He was 'such a good man'; he'd 'never recovered from the blow' of my pregnancy. So now I had two dead fathers on my conscience. No wonder I didn't feel much like celebrating the results of my ambition.

On my final hitched ride to Gibbet Hill, I travelled in with an English professor I'd never met. He said, 'So you're the girl who got the first. With a baby too. Congratulations. That's quite an achievement.'

But when the graduation ceremony took place, in my beloved Coventry Cathedral, I wasn't there. It would have cost money we didn't have, and anyway, who would have come with me?

7

How Could You?

When I speak about it now
I see November mist.
That damp afternoon of my life …

Opening my freedom

like a letter bomb,
seeing everything
explode…

How do you tell of
amputations this invisible?

Maggie Mountford, 'When I Speak'

I HAD SPENT THE FIRST eight years of my life in Leeds, where I was born, and memory had glamorised the city as a solid, earthy no-nonsense home, close to the wildness of the Ilkley and Otley moors, filled with Henry Moore beauty and grit. As David and I moved north that summer, after my degree, perhaps we were both driven by nostalgia. David had wanted to return to Newcastle, where he'd done his degree, but though I was offered a post-graduate place there, no suitable school-teaching job materialised nearby. We resorted to David teaching in Leeds while I enrolled for a D.Phil at York. I'd been awarded a full grant for three years.

On the map, Leeds and York looked quite close. My fantasy, despite having no car, was to travel effortlessly to York each week to see my supervisor and attend some of her post-graduate seminars, then study at home the rest of the time. But the tangled network of roads made hitching impossible, no buses ran from our side of town and the train journey involved several changes and long waits. No crèche space was available at York for part-time attendance and I could find no nursery near us in Leeds.

Our budget didn't stretch to property near like-minds on the Headingley side of town. Instead, in what was to prove a massive error of judgement, we took out a mortgage on a four double-bedroom three-storey stone terrace in Leeds 15, a working class district off the Selby Road. Exhausted following my final sprint at Warwick and depressed from Dad's death, not wanting to drag Adam around properties with nowhere to stay, I left the house-hunting to David while Adam and I spent a few weeks with Pam and Bob Ashley in Nottingham, who now had two boys close to Adam's age.

Again, my error, but I don't believe I even saw the house on Morritt Drive before we bought it. If I did, I was still appalled by our decision as soon as we moved in. We were far from David's school and on the opposite side of the city from the university or any cultural life. Morritt Drive was on the edge of one of the ugliest areas of Leeds, as down-at-heel as the worst parts of Shirebrook had been, and I felt I'd slid back into the same hostile environment my mother had resented for so long, one which she'd wanted to ensure her children would escape.

The family selling us the house had not yet found a new place and as we waited for completion of the sale, we rented a room off them for the first few weeks. The owners, another Dave and his wife Pat, had no time for education, despised school teachers and to prove their point mostly kept their kids at home all day. I hid with Adam in our bedroom at the top of the house, reading out loud his favourite illustrated books: *The Hungry Caterpillar, Where the Wild Things Are, The Tiger Who Came to Tea*. We tried to ignore the bawling of the bored kids downstairs as their parents rowed, and Dave number two asserted his male authority. He was uncomfortable with our presence and threatened by the fact David and I shared cooking and childcare.

One evening, as though to remind us who was the boss in this household, Dave number two accused Pat of having an affair with their previous lodger. It was obvious to me, from seeing the lodger and Pat together, that this was complete paranoia, but Dave rejected all Pat's denials. He was a small man, a Jack Sprat who ate no fat, while Pat looked as if she ate no lean. But still, before we could stop him, as he kept yelling his accusations, Dave number two suddenly picked up Pat and hurled her through the back door, shattering its sheet of frosted glass.

She returned from hospital a few days later, one leg and arm in plaster. Now, I was sure, Pat would pack her bags, take the children and move out. But she didn't. She had nowhere to go. She accepted Dave's apology, explained to us that this was a result of the stress they were under, and stayed in the marriage.

When I had to go through to York for my first supervision, Pat, still in plaster, along with the next-door neighbour, offered to take care of Adam. He got on well with the neighbour's youngest boy, so I agreed. But I was in panic all afternoon, too worried about Adam to concentrate on the M. Phil. group's discussion of the philosophical niceties of post-modern aesthetics, and raced back to retrieve him. He seemed fine, but I was determined never to use that option again. Eventually I discovered Judy, an intelligent vivacious blonde a few doors away, the only vaguely like-mind on the terrace. We exchanged child-minding – her son Jason was Adam's age – and subsequently, on the few occasions I did go through to York, I left Adam with them with less anxiety.

Happily, I wasn't required to take any set course. My supervisor, Nicole Ward-Jouve, invited me to attend the Masters seminars for stimulus and contact, but my D. Phil. was by research only and I could dispense with the weekly visits if I preferred. Nicole, bilingual, from Marseilles and Provence, was a latter day Simone de Beauvoir, a true French intellectual. Quietly impressive, serious and slender, she was an attractive Angela Carter figure with long wavy brunette hair, glasses and a distinctive brown fedora. Married to Tony Ward, another lecturer in York's English department, with three young children, Nicole was, I thought, the perfect role model for successfully juggling motherhood and academic life.

My initial plan was to do a doctorate on Surrealism and literature. Nicole seemed the ideal supervisor, as many of the texts I was reading, including André Breton's manifestos and fiction, were in French. But I quickly became disenchanted with the deliberateness of Surrealist art as being too forced and mechanical. When Nicole urged me to find some niche I could make my own – 'You need something that is unexplored. Something original.' – I turned instead to the antecedents of Surrealism in Gothic fiction, which delved into unconscious material for no doctrinaire reason and had fascinated me for some time.

At that time, Gothic fiction was still relatively uncharted territory in academic circles. I'd already read the classics by Mary Shelley, Charles Maturin, Bram Stoker, but now I consumed *Caleb Williams* by Mary Shelley's father William Godwin, Ann Radcliffe's *The Mysteries of Udolpho*, Horace Walpole's *The Castle of Otranto*. One of the other post-grads at

York was Elizabeth Wallace (married to trumpeter John Wallace who went on from his musical studies at York to great success). Liz was writing her B. Phil. on 'The Gothic Ethos' and we swapped reading lists and ideas.

What Gothic fiction allowed was an exploration and dramatisation of disorder in the world and psyche alike, all those psycho-sexual obsessions driven underground by the Age of Reason. As I read more widely, I became fascinated by the ways Gothic motifs and themes survived in 19th century novels, especially in the Brontës, Mrs Gaskell and Dickens, where Gothic strands undermined their veneer of social order. This became the main subject of my research: firstly, identifying and defining the Gothic tradition and, secondly, following its progress through Victorian fiction. Nicole's method of supervision was largely homeopathic, giving me a minimal dose of ideas then leaving them to ferment and expand in my own time and space. Pleased I'd found my niche so quickly, she recommended fiction by the Marquis de Sade, theoretical texts by Gaston Bachelard, and I read these alongside the complete works of Dickens, Gaskell, the Brontës and their Gothic forbears.

'All fiction,' Balzac once claimed, 'is symbolic autobiography.' I suspect the same is true of academic theses, especially in the arts. The personal root of my own choice certainly seems pretty obvious to me now. Dickens was a favourite in our family: the dark blue hardbacks of his complete works, in tiny print on tissue-thin sepia paper, were one of the few sets of books on our shelves at home. By tracing the irrational, Gothic features running through his fiction, I also, I now realise, was tracing the subterranean 'madness' that had somehow burrowed its way into our family in hidden, largely repressed ways.

Once again my life took on a strangely fissured nature, though this time without Warwick's daily visits to campus or the network of support and inspiration offered by Gay Clifford. I found a small playgroup for Adam near the esplanade of cheap shops at the top of the road, and took him there for a couple of hours some mornings, but I feared he wasn't happy and felt guilty leaving him. The rest of the day I shopped, cooked, washed clothes and tried to find ways of entertaining a bright two-year old on a working-class terrace where the tiny back gardens of washing lines and tricycles gave onto a wasteland of old tyres and wrecked cars. Play equipment in the local park had been vandalised. By night I once more turned into the madwoman in the attic, climbing to my new study in the top of the house and writing my notes on Gothic topography, irrational motifs and psycho-sexual darkness.

With both our fathers deceased, we only saw our mothers if they trekked up to Leeds on public transport. Mum could drive, but as soon as Dad died, worried about money, she sold their Fiat, and never again got behind a wheel. She rarely visited. Jean, by contrast, missing Ernie dreadfully, wanted more of a role in our lives. She adored David and, now she was alone, he and Adam were her primary concern.

Jean wasn't an unkind woman. I remembered how touched I'd been when I first visited their home in Creswell and she'd run me a bath with bubbles, which we never had at home, and handed me a bag of fresh peaches. Now she was quick to praise the little housework I did – look at my washing in the back garden, how much whiter it was than the neighbour's. But she never understood my passion for my work. Like my mother, she belonged to a generation of women whom the first wave of feminism had never reached, let alone the second, and a woman's place was strictly in the well-kept home, with a little part-time work on the side.

My own mother's attitude to women's education, though less visibly hostile, was shot through with ambivalence. On the one hand, she was too resentful of her own lack of opportunity and education to stop mine, and through my success she must have gained some vicarious pride. But on the other hand, her underlying envy made me feel my success should be tempered, as if I shouldn't have a life too divergent from hers and leave her behind. Her dream, she once confided, was to have me be a school teacher and live round the corner. She lived in terror of social opprobrium, and dreaded her children going out on a limb. My pregnancy had caused her and my father to move house from their quiet cul-de-sac to a busy main road a few miles away, where they could start again without shameful rumour.

In fact, my mother's credo, explicit as well as unspoken, was that men were superior to women and my brother came first. She was vehement in this belief to the end of her life. Many years later, at my brother's fiftieth birthday celebrations, as I stood drinking champagne, my mother – now in her early eighties and drinking more than she was used to – stood next to me. We were surrounded by my brother's colleagues from the Civil Service where he'd worked in the MOD for nearly thirty years, rising to the role of diplomat and personnel manager, with the promotion or demotion of high ranking military staff partly in his hands. Mum, always more garrulous with strangers than she was with me, and never reflecting before she spoke, was chatting to an urbane admiral. He shared he had three daughters.

'No sons?' my mother asked, in blatant sympathy.

The admiral, noticing the tone, seemed surprised. 'No,' he said cautiously. 'I'm very happy with my girls.'

Heady on her champagne, Mum's voice became embarrassingly loud. 'Oh, how terrible!' she announced to the room. 'All daughters. No, no. Sons are so much better. So much better than girls.'

To his credit, the admiral repeated how much he loved his three girls. But he and the nearest guests shot me a puzzled look, as much as to say, I thought you were this woman's daughter? Can she really be so insensitive as to say all this within earshot? Tip of the iceberg, I thought. The day of my father's funeral, when my brother's car left the driveway to return to London, Mum shut the door and sank on the sofa with a huge sigh of relief.

'Thank goodness for that. Now I can stop doing meals. Stop looking after anyone.'

Hello, I wanted to say. I'm still here. Girls eat too, you know. Not that this was entirely true. I had long since ceased to eat much in Mum's presence, another reason for rarely visiting. My appetite died when I was with her, and for years I'd not been able to put anything she'd cooked into my mouth.

My anorexia had begun at sixteen when I went to France for the first time, to stay with my French pen-pal and her family. After tasting the pleasures of real French cuisine, I found I could no longer stomach the pies, pastries, meat and soggy veg at home. Soon I was eating nothing expect a tiny plateful of salad for lunch in the school dining hall and a cooking-apple in the evenings at home – eating-apples were too calorific. When I was starving in the middle of the night, sometimes I would sneak downstairs and raid the pantry for two or three glacé cherries. Of course I lost weight rapidly, and was chucked out of the school hockey team, because I could no longer whack the ball down the pitch with my former gusto.

A few months after the trip to France, the phone went at home, a solid black telephone which squatted on top of the hardboard cupboard housing the meters in the downstairs hall. No matter where you were in the small house, it was impossible not to overhear phone conversations.

'Oh, Miss Batty,' came my mother's voice, ingratiating as she realised it was my headmistress on the other end. Then silence as she listened, followed by defensiveness, 'No, she's perfectly all right,' and finally outright denial. 'She eats very well. I do a good cooked meal every night.'

I stared at the cooking apple on my kidney-shaped dressing table. I'd not realised my mother could lie so blatantly, though I did know she put deference to authority before her children's health. My brother had agonising stomach pains one Christmas Eve, persisting through Christmas Day, but Mum wouldn't call out a doctor until Boxing Day because you 'mustn't trouble them at this time of year'. The fact that my brother's ruptured appendix led to peritonitis and he came close to losing his life failed to impact on this behaviour. In this anorexic phase, one girl teased that my vertebrae stuck out 'like Maltesers', and I had to sit on top of the radiators at school to stop shivering. But my mother's fear of criticism was so strong, she cared only about being thought a 'good mother'. Not until I left home and felt free to eat what I liked did I start to fatten back to normal, then add a bit extra.

Oblivious to this family history, David's mother Jean could not have known that the best way to antagonise me was to tell me the men in the family should come first. Especially now I'd finished my degree, she felt I was going a step too far with post-graduate work and her message when she visited was always the same: it was time to stop.

'Can't you see how tired David is? How he's suffering with his eczema? You can't expect him to work all day then come home and look after Adam.'

'I need time to do my work,' I protested. 'Studying is work too, you know. It brings money in. I get a grant.'

But Jean wouldn't give up. What on earth was the use of a Ph.D. anyway? Hadn't I proved what I could do? Didn't I have a good husband who was working full-time and needed support? Didn't I have a little son who needed constant love and care? Wasn't anything else ambition, pride, stubbornness? She always knew Adam was my Achilles' heel. 'He's only young once, you know. You won't get this chance back to look after him properly.'

Sometimes, in moments of sheer exhaustion, I would think she was right. Yes, it would be easier to give in and stop striving, like the other women on Morritt Drive, their horizons limited to corrugated garage roofs and plastic washing lines. Perhaps that was the Nirvana I needed, to bat away the depression that was always waiting in the wings. But then Jean would go too far, criticise the way I didn't do the ironing or had failed to darn David's socks, and my resistance reared up again.

Despite having Germaine Greer and Gay Clifford as dynamic female role models at Warwick, I hadn't engaged consciously with feminist thought, and was yet to read any of my life in terms of sexual politics. I did though have an instinctive pull towards strong women. For my birthday in 1974, David gave me Claire Tomalin's magnificent new biography of Mary Wollstonecraft, which I devoured for what it told me about Wollstonecraft as Mary Shelley's mother, and her proto-feminism.

That year, too, Jean provided us with our first television, black and white, and I avidly watched BBC's mini-series *Shoulder to Shoulder*, which dramatized Britain's suffragette movement. Siân Philips played Emmeline Pankhurst, with Patricia Quinn and Angela Down as her daughters Christabel and Sylvia. I sat alone in our dark lounge with its imitation stone chimney breast, chocolate brown Habitat chairs on castors, rush matting, my hand clamped over my mouth as I watched women prisoners being force-fed during their hunger strike protests at the Cat and Mouse policies which tried to keep militant suffragettes out of action. I waved my clenched fist in salute at the rousing signature tune by Ethel Smyth, from her 1911 'The March of the Women': *Shout, shout, up with your song!/Cry with the wind for the dawn is breaking;/March, march, swing you along/ Wide blows our banner, and hope is waking...*

Inspired by this rally cry for female comradeship, I sought out a women's group to try to combat my isolation. One Saturday I was leafing through a radical bookstore near the university in Leeds, buying more of the de Sade Nicole had recommended and dipping into Engels for the first time, when a title jumped out at me from a poster. *Wedlocked Women*: a new book by local author Lee Comer, who was inviting women to join her weekly support group in Headingley. At last, I thought. The march of the women. *Shoulder to shoulder and friend to friend.*

The next week, as David baby-sat one evening, I caught the two buses to Headingley. Lee Comer's front room was filled with a dozen well-dressed, middle-class women. I noticed the clever way bandannas wound round their hair to look both revolutionary and sensual – where did they learn to dress with such sexy nonchalance? Then, in a kind of dumb fascination, I listened as they debated theories of the family as a site of oppression, and Marxist versus feminist forms of resistance to capitalism. Knowing no one, longing for someone to ask who I was and why I was there, I kept fantasising they would turn to me next, discuss my situation, find a solution to shoe-horn me out of my depressed loneliness on the other side of town.

But the talk never shifted from theory to practice and, after my first ever herb tea, I left feeling more alone than before. It did wake me up to the fact that Leeds 6 would be a more congenial home for us than Leeds 15 – Headingley, after all, with its solid black stone houses and hidden gardens was where I'd lived as child – and I started viewing smaller properties there we might afford. One was absolutely perfect, with fitted bookshelves already in place and a small allotment. But David said it was too soon to move, we'd barely unpacked our bags. And so we stayed in misery at Morritt Drive.

Though it had never been graced with an official name, severe depression had plagued me since childhood. For as long as I could remember, life had been a trial to be endured rather than enjoyed. I had no idea this was not a normal state. I simply assumed everyone felt much the same, surviving the intolerable from day to day. When I asked my mother how she kept going, she would reply with a Scarlett O' Hara answer – *Gone with the Wind* was her favourite film – that you never knew what tomorrow might bring.

When I first read Hans Andersen's *The Snow Queen*, I was convinced it had been modelled on our family – hearts frozen, broken glass landed in our eyes and blood – people who were jagged and could not be warmed through. There might be a brief outburst of sentimentality on birthdays or anniversaries, but this was no substitute for real feeling or empathy. I felt un-connected, disconnected, a socket that was meant to be running a human appliance but was not plugged in to the mains.

My purpose in revisiting this past is not to indulge in a catalogue of misery, but to name as precisely as possible the conditions that can militate against love and self-belief, creating a tragic lack of inner security that is passed on from one generation to the next; only naming and understanding it clearly can lead to the kind of forgiveness and compassion that lets such history be overcome.

I was fourteen when I first tried to commit suicide, in an unconvincing way one Saturday afternoon when I'd returned home from a school hockey match. We'd played away, near Beeston, Nottingham, and as usual had a good win, in which I'd played my energetic part. But the cheery celebrations of the other girls on the coach returning to school left me acutely aware of my loneliness. Most of them lived near each other in Mansfield, and as they shared their plans for the rest of the weekend – time with families, friends, each other, dogs, cats, horses – I felt cold, etiolated, lacking the essential emotional chlorophyll other people took for granted.

When I walked into our council house after a further lonely bus journey, it was, as so often, eerily empty. The house was small; I never did discover where the rest of the family disappeared to. Still in my coat, standing in the kitchen, feeling in a total vacuum, I opened the blue cutlery drawer and took out the ivory-handled carving knife which Dad honed on a long metal sharpener each week before the Sunday roast. Resting my wrist against the edge of the sink, I was just starting my first incision when footsteps sounded in the passageway. With farcical haste, I hid the knife and disappeared upstairs, bracing myself for more hours of solitary study.

That same hopelessness had dogged me ever since. At Warwick, my love of literature and addiction to doing well, along with tangible encouragement from Gay Clifford, had kept me going, helped by the fantasy of romance with David, then the new-found joy of having Adam, which brought me a little more into the human race and imposed the day-to-day imperatives of looking after a new baby. But now, in Leeds, the old darkness resurfaced.

It wasn't a question of post-natal depression. Being a mother in itself neither triggered nor intensified my despair, but nor could it lift my spirits in a permanent way; it simply could not transform the basic make-up of my psyche. Though I loved Adam instinctively, this didn't generate the love for life itself that was lacking; an underlying feeling of wanting to erase myself was too strong. Amorphous but ubiquitous, this deep depression had always been there, sometimes more prominent than others, as if it came from another planet and had a life of its own. And now we were stranded in Leeds, with no distractions or like-minds, despair rose again like ancient quicksand to pull me down. It wasn't so much that I'd lost a desire to live as that I'd never had one.

Being essentially non-verbal, profound depression is impossible to properly describe, and not susceptible to persuasion or reason. In his autobiographical account *Darkness Visible*, William Styron refers to it as a state where 'faith in deliverance, in ultimate restoration, is absent. The pain is unrelenting, and what makes the condition intolerable is the foreknowledge that no remedy will come...' Any relief is only temporary; hopelessness sets in and the future disappears.

In Leamington Spa, our flat had looked out onto trees, sky, spacious streets; merely walking outside gave a buoyant feeling of hope and possibility. In Leeds 15, the front of our terrace looked onto the triangular steeple of an ugly little church beyond which lay busy roads, the back onto untended gardens and rusting metal. We had no car and no spare money for going anywhere. Gay and I exchanged occasional letters, and I kept in touch with Bernard Bergonzi, one of my professors from Warwick, but this was not the same as face-to-face contact. I had no adults to talk to. The visits to York had become too sparse to be meaningful. Day after groundhog day, I felt trapped and hopeless. Everything was heavy yet hollow, drained of colour and scoured of meaning. I cried a lot and was unable to sleep.

Of course, I did what any sane person would, and frequently begged the nearest G.P. for help. I shared how suicidal I felt, that I had a toddler to look after. His answer was always the same: 'Valium'. I swallowed them, time after time, but they made me so flat and lifeless, I may as well have been dead anyway, and finally threw them down the loo.

David did his best, but we were never real soul-mates. Our initial attraction and affection had blossomed into deeper appreciation and mutual respect when Adam was born; we'd both tried hard to adapt and help each other survive a challenging situation. But since that day of my degree results, when, rightly or wrongly, I'd read David's body language as exclusion and his words as contempt, I'd felt rejected and alienated. After that, we had less and less emotional connection and almost no physical contact. David showed no interest in my research; I probably showed little in his teaching. More and more, apart from arranging things for Adam, or discussing menus, we barely spoke; when we did, it led to arguments. I felt we'd turned at best into our parents, on automatic domestic pilot, at worst into Pat and Dave number two, as if along with the house we'd inherited the haunting template of their disastrous marriage. I couldn't be honest about the extent of my depression for fear of David's negative judgements, as if I should indeed be able to 'will' myself out of it. And as I had insufficient understanding of the psyche to account for my mood in any terms other than personal failure, I felt more and more inadequate, filled with self-loathing.

Dates and events between Christmas 1973, a few months after we moved to Morritt Drive and Christmas 1974, when David and I separated, are mostly blurred as I look back, lost in the thick fog and labyrinth of a depression more severe and sustained than any I'd yet known. I was too ill to keep a journal. Somewhere in the midst of this black cloud, I apparently had a brief fling with a teaching colleague of David's, which was later quoted as his reason for wanting a divorce. I don't remember it, but it was perhaps a wild bid to put some intimacy into my life, a reckless attempt to relieve a sense of intolerable loneliness. I do plead guilty to a psyche out of control, to living in a way with no thought of consequence, oblivious to the impact on others, and I must have been an impossible partner. Whatever the brief 'affair' might have been, it left in its wake no joy, only shame at betraying David, and anger at being wrong-footed as he claimed the moral high ground – a position he was then able to occupy in all our subsequent disputes down the years.

Styron suggests that the reason mental illness so often meets with incomprehension is less to do with 'a failure of sympathy' than with 'the basic inability of healthy people to imagine a form of torment so alien to everyday experience.' I've often met such incomprehension, if not condemnation, from people unversed in mental suffering. David was an only child, the apple of his parents' eyes, loved and nurtured with especial care following polio in his early years. Not only were the inner anguish and loneliness I felt on a pretty much permanent basis alien to him, but, compared with his physical health issues – recurrent asthma as well as the chronic eczema that still plagued him, let alone the lasting impact of polio – something as invisible as mental anguish must have seemed self-indulgent and self-induced. But his apparent indifference merely exacerbated my loneliness and increased the distance between us.

On one of my visits to York, when I shared with Nicole Ward-Jouve how desperate things had become, she invited me to bring Adam to stay with her. She and Tony lived with their three children in a beautiful old stone farmhouse in Butterwick, twenty miles to the north-east of York, where farmland gradually cedes to the wild beauty of the North Yorkshire moors. For a moment, I felt relief. A perfect solution: I could leave Morritt Drive and take Adam to a real family context in a large home full of company, talk, books. As a full-time student, I'd be able to use the crèche at York. I didn't have to choose between Adam and my sanity.

But as I tried to translate this plan into reality, two obstacles arose. Firstly, Nicole's husband, Tony Ward, who had originally approved the idea, changed his mind. I'd met Tony on campus, a big, warm-hearted bear of a man in his late thirties. Elaine Feinstein later described him in an obituary in *The Guardian* as 'rumbustious, physically powerful and generous-spirited', someone who 'relished everything he did: directing Shakespeare at York University, hunting big game in the Canadian wilds, or planting trees around his lovely house in Butterwick in North Yorkshire.' But, like many academics, Tony was also a heavy drinker. This would eventually reach a crescendo, leading to divorce from Nicole and premature death from alcoholism aged fifty-seven. And now, whatever his motives – whether to cover his growing addiction, or simply keep his habits to himself – Tony pulled the plug on the idea of Adam and me moving to Butterwick. With my hopes dashed, I felt more depressed than ever, stranded and filled with panic.

David too was violently opposed to the plan. By this time our hostilities were impossible to disguise, and we both knew we had no choice but to move towards separation. But we couldn't agree over the best arrangement for Adam. When the dream of Butterwick fell through, I fantasised I could take Adam with me to York and he and I could share a rented room. But David quickly disabused me of the illusion that I would cope or survive financially. Anyway, he wanted Adam for himself.

'What every child needs,' David declared, 'is the total security of being able to identify with one parent. So if you take him away on your own, you must do it on your own. That means I won't be there to bail you out. I won't be looking after him at weekends or holidays, or if you're ill. You will be totally on your own with everything. And I won't give you any financial help. No support. No money.'

These were the days before the Child Support Agency. Perhaps welfare benefits would have been available, but if they were, I knew nothing of them. I was already panicking how I would manage with Adam on my own, and without any back-up from anyone, I had to admit the truth that I simply couldn't. I was long since out of my depth, and this was beyond me. My primary motive for leaving was to try to combat the rising tide of depression, a tide that was covering all practical thought and reason with such dark sludge, actions that might have been easy for some seemed to me totally impossible. Ernie's final curse seemed to echo in David's words, conveying the same self-fulfilling prophecy: 'You won't manage.' 'You don't deserve to be a mother.'

Desperate, I called my own mother. If only she could be the parent I needed at last. Right till the end of her life, I never fully relinquished the fantasy that she might step in and be the 'good' mother, or at least 'good enough'. I needed her to say: 'Wait. Don't do anything irreversible. Don't move out of the house. It will make it seem legally like desertion. You'll lose your rights. You'll never get Adam back. Stay, whatever the cost. I'll come and help you. I'll look after Adam for you while you sort things out. Don't worry. We can work this through.' But when she heard me sobbing down the phone, she just said, 'Oh dear. I've been saying my prayers. Did I tell you about the trip I'm going on with the W.I.?'

It was naïve of me to expect anything else. Mum had never been able to cope with me in a state of disarray, nor ever displayed any emotional response. As a child, if I returned from school upset or crying, she would walk out of the room the moment I entered, abandoning her ironing or cooking as she disappeared upstairs. She was never able to comfort or empathise; never intervened in anything. She 'didn't want trouble', hated a fight. We didn't have arguments at home, there were no passionate exchanges, just a blank silence that I read at best as indifference, at worst as hostility. I suspected that her lack of responsiveness to the crisis now was also linked to her friendship with David's mother Jean, whom she was scared to alienate. Anyway, Mum liked David and, he being the man, she would oppose him as little as she would oppose my brother, even when something as huge as Adam's future and my mothering of him were at stake. So I hung up the phone feeling sick and frightened, knowing no help of any kind was to hand.

One of the worst effects of severe depression is the way it renders impossible realistic or long-term thinking. The only priority is getting through the intolerable moment, trying to escape the anguish *now*. Longer term consequences are simply not entertained. When David suggested he have Adam, in the week times at least, and I have him at weekends and holidays when I had somewhere suitable to stay, it sounded vaguely logical, a good temporary solution, a relative and reversible idea. David's love for me might have run its course, but not his love for Adam, so surely I could trust him when he said he was looking after Adam's best interests? Wasn't it better that I left, than stay behind and turn into another Sylvia Plath with her head in the gas oven? In years to come, I often repeated that analogy to myself. It *was* better, surely, for Adam to have an absent mother who was alive, than an irretrievably dead one?

We approached a lawyer in Leeds for help with drawing up a separation agreement.

'We want this to be an amicable arrangement,' David said.

The lawyer laughed. 'Think again. There's no such thing as an amicable divorce.' And he proceeded to pit us against each other, with ripple effects that would last for years.

'We want joint custody of Adam,' I said.

'What about care and control?' he asked.

I didn't really know the difference. 'What do you mean?'

'That's mine,' David replied. 'The primary responsibility will be mine.'

The lawyer raised his eyebrows and considered us as if we were Martians. 'What about when you're teaching?'

'There's a nursery nearby that takes children from single parents,' David said confidently. 'I've researched it. They've agreed to take Adam.'

'What?' The anger I'd been sitting on for months started to flare up. 'You didn't tell me that. If they've got a place, why can't we use it now? Then we might not need to split up.'

'It doesn't take children with two parents.'

'That's bloody stupid,' I snapped. 'Like offering someone help with depression only when they've proved how serious it is by actually committing suicide. Why can't this bloody country try to help people stay together?'

'That's not how it works,' David snapped back.

The lawyer crossed his hands with a look of satisfaction. This was more like it. This was how divorcing couples were supposed to bicker.

We separated on Leeds station just after Christmas, 1974. Adam was three and a half. I was twenty-three and a half. I was going to North Wales for a few days before I moved into a rented room in York.

David held Adam, his arms wrapped tightly around him, and I had the same feeling of exclusion I'd had that day of the degree results. David wore a duffle coat, Adam a padded jacket and knitted bobble hat, blue and white with black fair-isle markings. As David looked at me, I noticed a single tear on his cheek, the only sign of sadness I'd seen him betray, and my heart leapt at the sight. If you're upset, I thought, maybe you don't really want me to go. Maybe you'll ask me to stay. You only have to ask me once, just once, say you need me and want me to stay, and I'll ignore all our differences and stay forever. I'll burn my books, we'll live in our terraced house in Leeds, it was where I started life after all, it can be where I'll live it out. Heart in my mouth, I waited. But whether through pride, rage, indifference or defeat, David said only one word. 'Goodbye.'

I leant forwards and cuddled Adam. His cheeks were red with cold and he was staring at us both, bewildered as to what was happening. Then, in complete ignorance that this was an act which would cloud his life and mine for much of our future in a way I could not foresee, I kissed him, said I'd see him again soon and climbed into the train.

I felt weird straight away. It was like a scene from a Victorian novel. I wasn't leaving for another man and had no other relationship, yet still I had a sense of moral awkwardness, of blame and opprobrium. I knew somewhere that this was not a normal thing to do, yet at the same time it felt inevitable. Other women, other mothers, have often reacted in shock and horror when they imagine the scene. 'How *could* you?' 'I could never do that.' But the tragedy is, given my history, how could I *not* do it? What did I know about being a mother? What did I know about receiving and therefore being able to give a mother's love?

All this sounds tragic, almost absurd, to me now, but the truth is I never seriously thought about the effects of my leaving on Adam. The plan, as I understood it, was to see him every weekend, so this separation was not an absolute thing. And as I recollect that moment on Leeds station, the most painful thing for me is the shocking realisation that I *had no idea my three-year old son needed me.* What does it say about my upbringing, about the education system I'd been through, about its ability to foster emotional intelligence, that a woman who had a first-class honours degree, the best in her year, and was half-way through a doctorate, had *no idea* her own three-year old needed her? What does it say about that woman's lack of self-esteem, her lack of awareness of her impact on others, that she did not know her own motherly loveliness?

Years later, when Jean twisted the knife in my heart further by telling me of days and nights when Adam cried inconsolably for me, I was shocked. At the time, I had no idea he would miss me or cry for me. I even wished she hadn't told me. I couldn't bear to think about his loss. It was so much easier not to know. Easier to stay in the unreal universe of my parents, where my Dad cried all night and no one took any notice, where I cried non-stop and no one took any notice, where grief slid down the walls with the condensation and Mum mopped up the puddles with a tea-towel.

I felt bereft immediately. I knew something irrevocable and tragic had happened and, like many tragedies, it was all the more painful for seeming to be of my own making. The train sped towards the white peaks of Snowdonia, and I sensed my character start to shift in a metamorphosis that would last forever.

I felt myself grow simultaneously harder and softer.

Harder, because I now had to steel myself against the anguish of separation from the most innocent and loved being in my life; and against the misunderstandings, judgements, projections and prejudice that would come from others, from myself and, in time, from him.

Softer, because I now carried that separation as a permanent wound, one which wedged my heart open and would, ironically, drive me to atone for my failure as a mother by being more loving, kinder and compassionate to others.

I knew it was a wound for which I could not openly claim sympathy, because a child had been hurt more than me and, anyway, this decision had been my own choice, hadn't it? But it was a wound nonetheless and, like the injury sustained by Chiron, the mythical wounded healer, it was a wound which could never be closed.

In trying to escape my depression, I was losing the most beloved person in my life. I was literally throwing away the baby with the bath-water. Anyone who knew anything would have been able to tell me that such an attempt to leave despair behind could lead to nothing but greater anguish.

Later, decades later, came this poem, 'Belonging to No One':

It's the moving away from that moment
she remembers, more than the getting there.
Welsh mountains appearing in the train window,
white fields belonging to no-one. Trying too hard
to please people from then on, as if she has a duty
to pour love in all the wrong places; drawn to others
who are inside out, showing their seams.
Not knowing if the father's single tear
was the sting of cold, or grief. Not knowing
if the child understood anything.

The kind of separation that makes it
impossible to stick maps together again;
the world, for all three of them now,
unhomely, incomplete.

Always that one day on a station platform,
the no-man's land between Christmas and New Year,
when time departs down one track and she down another,
looking in railway carriages for suitcases, lost children,
that knitted bobble cap with its festive stripes,
his then smile.

8

A Sound High in the Air

What is that sound high in the air
Murmur of maternal lamentation ...

T.S. Eliot, 'The Waste Land'

I RETURNED FROM WALES to my new lodgings in York: one room in a three-storey student house on one of the arterial roads of the city. In a replay of my first term at Coventry, I once more lay awake through the night listening to the windows rattle and the building judder as long-distance lorries braked to a halt at the traffic lights outside, then revved into gear again.

I didn't really know what I was doing there. I numbed myself from grief by ceasing to feel much at all and muddled through from one lack-lustre day to the next. The student house was joined to its neighbour on the terrace by internal doors and fire escapes, with a total of fifteen to twenty students, mostly young post-graduates: sociologists, scientists, historians and, in the flat below mine, a trumpeter studying music. One couple had a young boy, Sam, blond-haired and blue-eyed, the same age as Adam and a grinding reminder of his absence.

When the small kitchen struggled to cope with the numbers, one of the mature students organised a rota for cooking and cleaning, with a kitty for food. To my surprise, this worked well. People were generous and imaginative, and several nights a week a dozen or more of us squashed round the table to share a cooked meal, with vegetarian menus of lasagne, rice, lentils, pasta, baked potatoes, salad. The collective tubs of honey and peanut butter, though, proved lethal. I quickly turned into Pooh bear, gorging myself at all hours of the day and night on thick slabs of brown bread ladled with butter and honey. They were never enough. I still craved more sweetness. This was the first time I'd put on extra weight since

Adam was born, but I didn't care what I looked like. Indeed, like the masochistic heroine of Mrs Henry Wood's *East Lynne*, the Victorian sensation novel about a woman who leaves her children and meets every possible punishment and physical deformity, I almost welcomed ugliness as something I now deserved. David told me I 'looked pregnant'; perhaps I was trying to pretend I was.

From a distance, of course, I can see this period through a different lens. David too was hurt by our break-up, struggling to look after a three-year-old on his own as well as holding down a full-time teaching job in less than perfect health. He must have found my behaviour as unloving and unfathomable as I found his. We were both young and ignorant, ready to lay responsibility for the mess of our lives at anyone's feet except our own. In retrospect, too, I have to acknowledge that David did make efforts to ensure I had continued contact with Adam over the years, but they were sporadic and never felt enough. Indeed, as the contact diminished more and more, I was convinced it was punitive. It seemed David had all the power and I had none. Agreements I thought we'd made were quickly broken, and I came to resent him for shifting my mothering into an ever more partial role. I felt more and more at a tangent, increasingly dispensable, living in rage and fear that he was pushing me out of Adam's life altogether.

Soon after our separation, the car we'd never been able to afford miraculously appeared, and David brought Adam over to visit me. I'd complained I couldn't sleep for the sound of braking lorries and would love some classical music. To my surprise, David presented me with an exquisite boxed set of Julian Bream, and I remembered other gifts he'd bought me: a leather bound set of George Eliot some weeks after I got the first class degree he couldn't celebrate; the collected poems of Wallace Stevens, 'that it might strengthen you when you need to be strong,'; and a final book just before we parted, in which he'd inscribed a play on my maiden name: '*What – Price liberation?*'

The price of my 'liberation' certainly was too high. I can still feel the agony of Adam's visits and partings. He would sleep with me in the traffic-noisy second-storey room with its on-the-floor mattress; play games; race with Sam round the house. He never cried when we parted, perhaps David's distractions guaranteed that. A few times I visited them back in Leeds, but I wasn't welcome to stay over so my trips were necessarily brief. And with only a few hours with Adam before the wrench of the next inevitable parting, it was hard to anticipate the meetings with much joy.

It soon became clear that we weren't sharing child care at all, that the plans we'd made for my having Adam each weekend were a sham. Bit by bit, especially once the legal agreements were finalised, the visits were whittled down. I was unable at that time to see it from David's point of view; I simply felt excluded, denied the right to see my own child. I would stand in the nearest public phone box, ten minutes' walk from the student house, jamming in coin after coin as I yelled at David in protest at what was happening, but it only made things worse. By the time I got back to the house, shaking in impotent tears, all I could do was stuff down more bread and honey. At least when the huge tubs were empty they could be turned into helmets for Adam and Sam, or buckets for their pretend sandpit in the garden.

In the daytimes, I wandered round York much like any neurotic post-graduate, stifling my honey-eating grief. I discovered the quiet reading room in the university's centre for medieval studies, housed in a beautiful old building a stone's throw from York Minster. When the centre closed at 5 p.m., I dragged myself back with a heavy heart to my bedroom. With no TV in the student house and no radio, I turned once more to my usual panacea of books. As a child, I'd learned how to read the opening pages of a novel so quickly I could trip myself into its alternative world, and I now devoured women's fiction from the nearest second hand bookshop: Iris Murdoch, Margaret Drabble, Muriel Spark, Erica Jong, Margaret Atwood. I was nothing but a welter of chaos, sadness and rage, and I slid into words as a way of giving myself shape, of trying to retrieve some identity.

Under these circumstances, anywhere would have felt alienating, and both city and campus at York felt brittle and unwelcoming. With the splendour of the Minster with its glorious rose window, the ruins of medieval walls skirting the old quarters, the golden banks of daffodils nodding in spring, the cobbled streets full of olde worlde shops and low-ceilinged tea rooms, York seemed to me a twee resort for tourists who wanted a picture perfect past. The campus too, a few miles outside the city, was not much of a community. Like Warwick, it was still in unscarred childhood, barely ten years old, and from the library's new corduroy chairs to the shiny coloured plastics of the cafés and bars, the furniture and fittings were unhomely. The settings of the different colleges were pedantic, with clipped lawns, a plastic-bottomed lake, walk-on ducks and waterfowl straight out of Walt Disney. Amidst the two and a half thousand students, I spotted very few black faces or signs of ethnic difference, and after the rich racial mix of Leeds, where my toddler still lived on a working class terrace, York felt sterile, white, unflinchingly middle class.

If I'd not been carrying such awkward feelings of shame and pain around being a mother who wasn't one, I might have found comfort with the feminists on campus, buoyantly reading Germaine Greer's *The Female Eunuch*, Betty Friedan's *The Feminine Mystique* and Kate Millet's *Sexual Politics*, with its scathing attack on Lawrence's representations of women. But I wanted to be genderless, sexless, to wipe out the painful remembrance of my female identity. If I had no life other than the life of the mind, perhaps I could transcend the pain I was feeling, even transform into an honorary man. I became ever more indifferent to my body, caring little what I put in it or on it, taking no exercise. And, fittingly enough, my closest intellectual affinity came from male post-graduates studying the history of madness.

York was famed for pioneering the first humane lunatic asylum. Founded by a Quaker, William Tuke, in 1796, The Retreat had promoted a more liberal treatment of mental health, moving away from judgements of the mentally ill as wild beasts or moral deficients. Amongst the sociology students who came to examine the hospital's records was Mike Hay, who also used the medieval reading room in town most days. Mike's supervisor was York's current Professor of Sociology, Laurie Taylor (later linked in the press with Howard Kirk, the libidinous lecturer in Malcolm Bradbury's novel *The History Man*). Mike took me for drinks with Taylor, and when I managed to veer the conversation away from George Eliot (would I never get away from her?), they introduced me to the shifting definitions, status and treatments of mental illness.

Mike lent me Michel Foucault's *Madness and Civilization: A History of Insanity in the Age of Reason*, and I read with shock about the barbaric treatments administered to the so called 'mad' over the centuries: long-term immobilization by manacles, sudden immersion in cold baths, imprisonment, painful blistering, debilitating purges, physical punishment, straitjackets, the removal of all shreds of human decency and respect. I started to weave Foucault and other theorists into my own study of irrationality in 18th and 19th century Gothic, and discovered that Dickens too was preoccupied with what defined and separated the 'mad' from the 'sane'. His library was filled with medical and philosophical accounts of insanity, including a personally inscribed copy of John Connolly's 1849 *Lectures on Some of the Forms of Insanity*. Connolly's work in the Middlesex Lunatic Asylum had led him to stress that the demarcation line between 'normal' and 'abnormal' mental health was largely invented. 'They have sought for, and imagined, a strong and definable boundary between sanity and insanity, which has been imaginary, and arbitrarily placed... being supposed to separate all who were of unsound mind from the rest of men.'

Dickens knew Connolly and shared his sentiments. On his lengthy walks round London following his daily stints of writing, Dickens often wandered to Bethlem's psychiatric hospital, known as Bedlam. He would stand outside the walls and muse how only the slenderest of divisions separated him from the incarcerated 'mad'.

'And the fancy was this: Are not the sane and insane equal at night as the sane lie a dreaming? Are not all of us outside this hospital, who dream, more or less in the condition of those inside it?' (*Night Walks*)

One of the inmates at Bedlam, while Dickens was standing outside contemplating the fragility of this divide, was Richard Dadd. A brilliant artist who had trained at the Royal Academy of the Arts, Dadd travelled as a draftsman on an expedition to Greece, Turkey, Syria and Egypt. On the Nile, convinced he was under the influence of the Egyptian god Osiris, he became delusional and violent, and back in Kent, in 1843, murdered his father, convinced he was the devil in disguise. Dadd was committed to Bedlam, where he painted astonishing works, including *The Fairy Feller's Master-Stroke*.

I was introduced to Dadd's troubled genius by Geoffrey Summerfield, another lecturer in York's English department. From a background in the Black Country followed by years of school-teaching, Geoffrey was an intellectual and social rebel, who liked to exist at an oblique angle to the academic establishment. With his heavy rimmed glasses and slightly wild beard, he looked like an English version of beat poet Allen Ginsberg. A passionate believer in the transforming power of the imagination, he was an early champion of Ted Hughes and Seamus Heaney, David Hockney and outsider art. He edited Penguin's *Voices* anthologies of poetry for schools and prepared editions and defences of the much neglected John

Clare. Soon I was visiting Geoffrey's country cottage a few miles outside York, and had dinner cooked by his beautiful partner Catherine. Their library stood in the garden: the whole of a converted ancient dovecote filled with rare and first editions, signs of a love of books that tipped into bibliomania.

Geoffrey was the department's nonconformist, defiant of intellectual snobbery and indifferent to institutional etiquette. Warm, personable, encouraging, he understood my difficult situation and arranged for me to teach on the undergraduate course, which would stand me in good stead when I applied for academic posts. Geoffrey also introduced me to one of his students who'd been paralysed in a car accident when she was sixteen. Her boyfriend, driving drunk, had smashed up the car and she'd been squashed between the front seats, her legs jammed into her spine. We spent hours talking together, as I pushed her wheelchair round the lakes and tried to emulate her lack of self-pity.

I didn't have much contact with the rest of the department, though I was persuaded to present a paper for a staff/post-graduate seminar. Wanting a change from my thesis, I opted to talk about 'Lessing's visionary work'. This met with incomprehension from the male faculty.

'I thought Lessing was a German Enlightenment poet. Who the hell is this *Doris*?'

As I sorted my papers, another commented, 'I thought brains and beauty weren't supposed to go together?' and I gave him a scathing look. I wasn't partial to flattery, and with the weight I was carrying, knew only a rhino would find me attractive.

I did wander into a lecture hall one lonely day to hear York's visiting Professor F.R. Leavis. Here he was, the great man himself, David's intellectual hero, whose ideals and hero-worshipping of Lawrence had, in some fashion, helped create the mess of my life, and whose definitions of the literary canon had shaped the syllabus and teaching of literature in English universities and schools over the previous two decades. Leavis it was who pronounced the greatness of poets T.S. Eliot, Ezra Pound, Gerard Manley Hopkins; who elevated Jane Austen, George Eliot, Henry James, Joseph Conrad and D.H. Lawrence into the first rank of novelists in *The Great Tradition*, and who had no room (at first) for Dickens or Hardy, let alone female outsiders such as Gaskell and the Brontës, to whom I was devoted. But I shared his belief that the life of the mind and one's personal life are deeply connected; it was the same conviction George Hunter had instilled in me, that literature was concerned with a search for meaning. I remembered reading an essay by Leavis on the train en route to my university interview at Exeter six years before – what an eternity away it seemed, that blinkered schoolgirl world – when I'd underlined his words, that a passion for literature was a lifelong commitment. 'Literary criticism,' he wrote, 'provides the test for life and concreteness; where it degenerates, the instruments of thought degenerate too, and thinking, released from the testing and energizing contact with the full living consciousness, is debilitated, and betrayed to the academic, the abstract and the verbal.' (F.R. Leavis, *The Calendar*, 1933).

But if I was expecting some of that brilliance as I entered the darkened lecture hall, I was disappointed. I could count on one hand the other students who had come to witness the legend in action and I sat at the front to add to the illusion of an audience. Leavis had retired from Cambridge in 1962, and it was hard not to doubt the wisdom of his taking on this visiting professorship. Newly octogenarian, he was visibly in his last days. With an open-necked whiter than white shirt, a scrawny, ascetic body, his hair thin and slightly wild, he looked like an ageing Rod Stewart. Even at the front, I could hardly hear his rambling Beckettian monologue, let alone follow it, and one by one the tiny audience sneaked away till I was the only person left. Leavis didn't notice. He was the ghost of himself, talking to a hall of shadows. Three years later, 1978, his obituary in *The Times* would talk of the 'mixture of asceticism and vitality' that marked him, the 'flame-like nimbleness of his speech and glance', the 'almost Socratic powers' which 'compelled attention'. But I discerned little sign of these in the man I saw at York, only evidence of what *The Times* also called 'a rare talent grown painfully awry'.

The situation with Adam, meantime, grew ever more painful. Our too-brief reunions and too-quick partings were heart-breaking. He seemed, on the surface at least, to cope well with the dislocation, fascinated when he stayed with me by the variety of people passing through the student house. But I found his visits excruciating, and when he left again, felt part of myself was missing. Time never dulled this constant pain of his not being there, of my not being part of his life, not sharing and witnessing his growing up.

I was still trying to reconcile myself to the less than ideal arrangement of contact every second or third weekend, when David told me he was selling Morritt Drive and moving down to Creswell to live with his mother. He'd found a teaching job nearby. At that moment, I knew I was capable of murder. I had no car, no money, couldn't drive, and Creswell was far from a railway station. How would I see Adam now? Did the fact of our joint custody give me no rights? I was meant to have a say in all major decisions affecting his life: health, education, where he lived. Surely David couldn't just move Adam round the country without consulting me?

When David wouldn't listen to my protests, I called the solicitor in Leeds who'd sorted the divorce. I rammed into the phone box several pounds worth of coins, begging for help. Yes, the solicitor agreed, I had a legal right to see Adam and police could be called to enforce that right, but he cautioned against it. 'In my experience, it only makes things worse.' His voice was slimy, and I remembered the pass he'd made at me as he gave me a lift to the station after the court hearing. A woman who surrenders care of her child was clearly, in his view, a loose woman, not to be given respect.

I called David and fumed some more. 'I expect this was your mum's idea, was it? Have her son and grandson to herself? Get her revenge on me for Ernie.'

But my anger and grief were not read as signs of my love for Adam, only further proof of instability. All my subsequent displays of emotion, all my dark despair, merely played into David's winning hand. Was he not the stable, rational, adult who had stepped into his responsibilities? And was I not the madwoman, the woman who'd had an affair and forfeited her rights by leaving the family home? I had no case. I'd absconded. I was the absent, and therefore bad, mother. He was simply being practical, and in the absence of a wife to look after his child, he would turn to his mother.

Again, in retrospect, I can see that David was perhaps doing no more than he needed to survive, but I felt punished and persecuted. He knew that his mother and I had an awkward, if not hostile, relationship, and now I would be beholden to her too for seeing Adam. I'd never felt such a sense of impotent rage. Jean had won after all then, and I had lost. Lost care and control of Adam, lost custody in all but name.

A few weeks later, I received a cheque from the lawyers in Leeds: my share of the profits from the house sale: seventy pence, barely worth the spit on the stamp. I stood on the bridge near York station, tore the cheque into scraps and watched them drift down onto the railway tracks. I thought of Anna Karenina and wished I could drift down as easily.

From then on, from the time they moved from Leeds, contact with Adam shrank to occasional weekends and fragments of school holidays. Once, when several weeks had gone by without my seeing him, I did threaten police intervention.

'You can do what you like,' David said on the phone. 'We'll go away in the car. We'll zig-zag across the country if need be. You won't be able to find us.'

I never did actually involve the police, which I came to partially regret. Adam would have seen I meant business, that I felt he was worth fighting for, that my love wouldn't take no for an answer. But I was too much of a pacifist. I'd been brought up on the Bible, after all. I knew by heart the story of King Solomon. When faced with two mothers fighting over a child, Solomon takes his sword and threatens to slice the child in two to give them half each, and the real mother stops him, proves her love by being prepared to lose her son rather than have him harmed in any way.

'Then spake the woman whose living child was unto the king, for her bowels yearned upon her son, and she said, O my Lord give her the living child, and in no way slay it.'

I may have been pathetically weak and unassertive, but I truly didn't want Adam scarred by legal battles, or witnessing the melodrama of visibly warring parents. Instead I raged inwardly, tempered my verbal protests so I could still see Adam when David allowed, and sank into bitter relinquishment.

In the summer of 1975, knowing I needed paid work, Gay Clifford pulled strings with friends of hers to get me a job in London's Anthony d'Offay gallery. On Duke Street in the heart of Mayfair, the gallery specialised in rare art books and *catalogues raisonnés*, which I packed and weighed and took in stacks to the nearest post office. The owner's friends and clients dropped in on their way to Sotheby's, Harrods, Fortnum and Mason, the opera, and I felt as alienated at this end of the social scale as I had been on the other in Lesney's matchbox factory. Where did I belong? I borrowed Gay's flat, which was the basement of Germaine Greer's London home in Ladbroke Grove, careful to keep the rooms in their meticulous state in case Gay suddenly returned.

One hot August day, David brought Adam to the gallery to visit me. This must have been a stretch on his part, taking time out of his summer holiday to make sure Adam and I saw each other. But if it was wonderful to see Adam, it was also utterly heart-breaking. He was four now, a gorgeous chunky boy, beautiful and bright. And I felt a sense of utter wrongness, all three of us being in the wrong place at the wrong time. What were any of us doing there in that airless gallery basement, trying to make sure we got no finger marks on the expensive art catalogues? I looked at David, wondering if he felt the same. Here was the boy we'd made together, no longer a toddler but a child, almost school age. We should be running him along the beach, swinging him in the air, racing into the sea, diving and laughing as we surfaced through the waves. We should be buying Cornish ice-creams, making mud pies, sand castles, hunting for crabs. Instead we walked to the nearest café in Mayfair and consumed over-priced coffee and Cornettos.

When they left and I went back to the esoteric art books, I wanted to disappear. Nauseous with frustration and despair, I was feeling ever more superfluous, the unwanted third in the family triangle, with an ever briefer walk-on part in Adam's life. I knew if I said too much, David might put into action his threat that I wouldn't see Adam at all. So I bit my tongue and remained polite and ingratiating, careful to show the required gratitude for being allowed to see my own son.

But my underlying rage was huge and amorphous. I realise now it should have been directed towards the whole web of circumstances – social, familial, economic – which had delivered us to this sad travesty of family life; instead the anger went towards myself for making such mistaken yet seemingly necessary choices, towards David for not having found a more generous solution, towards Jean for engineering what she wanted and stepping into the surrogate mother role, and of course towards my own mother for failing to do anything at all. How come David's family had been so active and mine so passive? Why couldn't my mother have intervened the way David's mother had?

Mum visited me just twice during my time in York. On both occasions, she brought with her the one gift she always pulled from her carrier bag with a proud flourish on her visits: a jar of home-made chutney. No matter what my distress over Adam, no matter my suicidal despair, I was always given this bottled chutney, topped with a little piece of cloth and rubber band, as the panacea to my troubles. It was clear Mum had no notion at all of what I was experiencing, over Adam or anything else. She had never discussed anything personal with me; not once in her life did she ask me the simple question, 'How are you, what's happening for you?' It seemed she had no capacity at all for emotional curiosity. So now, as always, it was a huge relief when she left again and the charade of pretending she was a flesh-and-blood mother could end. I donated the jar of chutney to the collective kitchen and opened the sash Georgian windows to get rid of her smell of talc.

I'd been fortunate to inherit from Mike Hay the tenancy of a lovely rented room in St. Paul's Square, a quiet enclosure of Georgian houses surrounding a large railed area of grass and giant horse chestnut trees. My first-floor room, painted soft grey, had two floor-to-ceiling windows looking onto the square, so close to the chestnut trees I could almost touch them. The noise came now not from passing traffic, but from the music students in the house and square: a rich array of flutes, trumpets, piano, guitars, played with impressive proficiency.

Twenty years later, one of my short stories, 'Spice Island', published in *Writing Women*, 1997, was set in this grey rented room.

'Do you remember it, that room with the dull ashen paint, every inch the same shade of unpolished pewter? The height of the elaborate coved ceiling only made more space for the greyness. It stretched from window to door, darkening in the seams to strips of black.

But when you were with me – only then – it lifted. Those days, the grey softened to silver; there were hints of pastel in patches on the walls.'

The tone is lyrical, romantic, as the female narrator describes lying awake in bed, watching her beloved sleeping, dreading the moment when he has to leave again. 'Every few seconds I would turn back to you, filled with pleasure by your closeness. In summer, your slightly bleached hair would stick with sweat to the side of your temples, your mouth would be puckered. You were rarely restless. It was I who secretly tossed and turned, plotted and schemed.'

It gradually becomes clear that the beloved is not a man but a child, the woman's own child, and the spell of their togetherness is broken when the child's father comes to collect him. '... it couldn't last. Always the earth turns too quickly on its axis, always separation faces us again... That time, the hour after your departure was the worst...'

What adds to her heartbreak at the story's end is the fact that, as they leave, the father driving the car distracts the child from turning round, and the mother is left waving to an empty rear window. This was David's strategy. When he brought Adam up to York for a weekend, he would leave him with me late morning on Saturday and collect him early afternoon on Sunday. But as soon as he collected Adam, perhaps as a ploy to stop him being upset, David would distract him, talk and make jokes, and it left me feeling he couldn't wait to erase me from my boy's consciousness.

'You never protested any more when it was time to go, you never needed consolation. There were no tears in your eyes now, no trace of them; only bewilderment. You would brace forwards, always facing forwards, while I stood on the sullen tarmac, watching the darkness swallow you.

That's how it was from then on, all those countless weekends, those irrevocable years. A few hours of reunion, then your father returning, calling you to him, pulling you away. He would say little to me – creating you was the only moment we'd converged – but as soon as you were in the car, I could see his mouth opening and closing, drawing him to you with that magnet of language, that endless voltage of words.'

Similarly, whenever I phoned Creswell to speak to Adam, there was constant static as David interrupted, distracted, told jokes. Except when we were together in person, we never had a clear two-way mother-son conversation.

Psychologically and emotionally, indeed on every possible level, the price for this alienation and exclusion was high. From childhood, I'd felt unacceptable, unlovable. Now, knowing I had failed as a mother and therefore as a woman, this was intensified. Socially, I became less confident than ever, surprised by anyone making friendly overtures. I had no confidence I would ever find a healthy relationship. And to avoid further complications or embarrassing explanations, I stopped talking about Adam and effectively pretended I had no children.

Not that I was completely bereft of new friends. Penny Florence was another of Nicole Ward-Jouve's supervisees, and dauntingly clever. She was researching relations between French poetry and art, using Julia

Kristeva's theories to link Mallarmé's poetic language with symbolist painting. I didn't always follow her theoretical work, and found her strength of character intimidating, but I admired and liked Penny enormously. Another powerful woman, Susan O'Brien, was doing a masters degree, and we had meals together or went to films. But with her solid family background and Scottish stoicism, Susan found my depression indulgent, a kind of neurosis I ought to overcome.

Inspired by their intrepid female strength, I often plotted to kidnap Adam. Once, I actually packed a bag, took money from the bank, calculated exact trains and taxis to go and snatch him from school. I raced to the station on a high, euphoric at last. I could get him back. I could be his mother. But as I approached the ticket office, reality kicked in. Where would I actually take him? We'd always be found. If I broke the law, I might end up with less access than ever. And I walked out of the station and slunk back to St. Paul's Square, staring into rooms filled with bright lights and children.

9

By Norwich Station
I Sat Down and Wept

> *Oh wearisome condition of humanity!*
> *Born under one law, to another bound:*
> *Vainly begot, and yet forbidden vanity,*
> *Created sick, commanded to be sound:*
> *What meaneth Nature by these diverse laws?...*
> *Tyrant to others, to herself unjust,*
> *Only commands things difficult and hard.*
> *Forbids us all things, which it knows is lust,*
> *Makes easy pains, unpossible reward.*
>
> Fulke Greville, 'Chorus Sacerdotum'

SATURDAY NIGHT WAS always the worst time for loneliness. But that particular evening, I was lower than I'd ever been. I sat on the double mattress on the floor of my room, reading Greville's melancholy poem – one of Gay Clifford's favourites – and listened to the sounds of other people's weekend pleasures: laughter, footsteps racing up and down stairs, jazz from an open window on the far side of the square.

I'd received a letter from David telling me he wanted a divorce so he could remarry. He'd met Jan, another school teacher, in Derbyshire; soon they would move to Birmingham to take up teaching posts there. Of course, I should have expected it, but hadn't. Now another woman would be with Adam from day to day, would effectively be his 'mother', and I felt totally eclipsed. What role would I have in his life now? *Unpossible* indeed. Far too *difficult and hard*. And with my despair knowing nowhere to go except inwards, my rage unable to find any target except my foolish self, I believed, as I had many times before, but now with renewed certainty, that I may as well not exist. I hunted out a full bottle of strong painkillers I'd been prescribed for some back trouble, unscrewed the cap and, with many forced gulps of whisky, swallowed the lot.

For a little while, I felt only the bliss of relief. *To cease upon the midnight with no pain...* I'd wanted to do this so often. David had made it clear they could all survive happily without me; indeed, my presence was more of a nuisance than anything. He'd forbidden me from ever making any financial contribution to Adam's life, and I had no idea what happened to presents I gave him. I felt totally redundant. Adam had a new mother. He would soon forget me. How could I bear to be alive with him mothered by someone else?

I started to feel drowsy. Wonderful. I was going. I didn't have to fight the suffering any more. Even the trumpet music from the flat below was growing faint. I picked up another book of poetry: the last words I would ever read. I don't recollect now where they came from, I've never been able to trace them exactly again, but what I remember reading is *(he knew) after a life so noble and so strong, that all his life he had been in the wrong...* And suddenly my mind swivelled on its dulled axis. *All his life he had been in the wrong...* What if I was in the wrong? What if all my life I'd been in the wrong? Thinking the wrong thoughts? Having the wrong priorities? What if life could be quite different from what I'd known? What if there was another way of being, one I hadn't yet tasted, yet nevertheless existed? A life that was happy, worth living? It's hard to describe this moment. It wasn't a mystical experience; more a sense of light suddenly flashing across a screen, trying to wipe out the darkness of wrong thinking.

That was when I began to panic. If this other life was a possibility, what chance did I have of finding it if I extinguished myself? By now the room was swimming, getting foggy. This was an irrevocable act. If it was wrong, if I was wrong, I needed to reverse it, needed to give life a chance. Somehow I had to crawl back to the light. I'd like to say it was thinking about Adam that called me back, but it wasn't, not directly. It was more of an instinct, as with the instinctive decision not to have an abortion: a sense of life itself insisting on survival.

I stumbled through the darkness to the usual red phone box half a mile away, fumbled at the walls until I found one that opened. I had my phone book open at Geoffrey Summerfield's number.

By midnight I was in York hospital having my stomach pumped, the desire to retch softened by the fuzzy effect of the drugs. The doctor, a handsome chap, looked down at me.

'You don't really want to die, do you? You're young and pretty.'

'Of course not,' I wanted to say. 'I'm just having a laugh.' But the fat plastic tube down my throat kept me polite.

I was kept in hospital overnight, hallucinating from the chemicals that had already entered my blood. I moved in and out of consciousness, aware of golden light on which was impressed a stark black crucifix – perhaps an imprint from the metal stands over the bed. Next morning, not having slept, I looked around the ward. There were two beds nearby, with two young women. When we introduced ourselves, I reluctantly admitted why I was there, mentioned being without Adam as one of the reasons.

The first woman, Anna, Irish, looked at me in disbelief. 'Good God. I thought it was just me.'

'Did you take an overdose?'

'I did,' she said. 'Same reason. My feckin' ex has disappeared with my two to Ireland. I don't have any idea where they are. Living in a feckin' caravan somewhere. The bastard.'

Shocked but relieved not to be alone in my folly, I looked at the second woman, Sue. She shared that she too had made an attempt on her life the day before, having lost her daughter in a custody battle. We were all three speechless. Was this a wild coincidence? Or were A & E wards all over the country filled at weekends with women wanting to die because they'd lost their kids? In a way, I felt vindicated, the shared experience making me feel less stupid. Our suicidal despair was not mental aberration, but the natural, inevitable consequence of unnecessary maternal loss. I'd like to say this sowed the seeds of a wider awareness, an ability to see personal struggles in social and political terms, but it didn't, not then. It would be years before I came to a deeper understanding.

Such thinking was, anyway, quickly dispelled by the male psychiatrist I had to see before I could be discharged. Clean shaven and reproachful, he looked at me askance as I described the events that had led to the weekend's collapse.

'How do you spend your days?' he asked.

'I'm doing a D.Phil. in literature,' I said, trying to recall some pride. 'Gothic fiction. You know, Mary Shelley, Bram Stoker...'

The consultant peered at me through cataracts of incomprehension.

'What on earth for?'

I stared back at him.

'It might help,' he went on, 'if you spent your days in a different way. Stop reading altogether and do something useful. Positive.'

I wondered what kind of behaviourist mill his training had dragged him through. Had he even heard of The Retreat?

'It's not the reading that's the problem,' I said. 'It's being without my boy. It's too painful.'

'Physical movement might help,' he said. 'Getting out of your head.'

Blistering, I thought. Cold baths. Immersion in cold water, upside down.

I damned the man further when I discovered the 'positive' action he'd taken following our interview: writing to David to inform him his estranged wife had made a suicide attempt. I suppose there was some logic to this, as the divorce was not yet finalised and David was still legally my next of kin. But a more sinister logic sketched a conspiracy theory in which NHS shrinks and ex-husbands conspired to turn Anna, Sue and me into dangerous mothers who had slid off the conventional tracks and must be shunted into sidings where they could not endanger their children. Now, my suicide attempt was not only an additional reason for my own shame and humiliation, but, thanks to the psychiatrist's wisdom, it also handed David further ammunition against me. Whatever attempts I might make in the future to reclaim Adam, or wrest back parenting, I knew now they were doomed to failure.

In the early summer of 1976, I realised in a semi-conscious way that my grant for postgraduate study would run out at the end of August. The state had paid for my courses at both Warwick and York and I'd not accumulated any debts. Apart from books, many books, and gifts for Adam, I lived very frugally. I didn't drink or socialise. I wore jeans and cheap clothes. I ate badly. The student grant had just covered these basic needs, but I had no savings. I needed to earn. I'd had a couple of review articles published by the *Times Literary Supplement*, and it was there, on the back page, that I saw a job advertised: Lectureship in English Literature at the University of East Anglia.

I'd never formally applied for any post before. My work experience was limited to Saturday jobs in Mansfield – selling meat pies in a butcher's shop and working in a woman's hairdresser's; the aborted holiday work at Lesney's Matchbox factory and a few weeks as a dresser at Drury Lane; the Duke Street gallery post-girl. I had no sense of the competitiveness of the market. I was told later that more than 400 people applied for the East Anglia job, but I was blithely ignorant of the odds stacked against me. Typing up a neat document, I quoted as references Nicole Ward-Jouve and two former professors: Bernard Bergonzi and Claude Rawson. I guessed the men from Warwick would carry more weight than Gay Clifford.

'I've been invited for an interview at UEA,' I announced in the shared kitchen to anyone who'd listen. Most of the students were duly impressed, but Clive Bell, the flautist, looked at me as if I had a terminal illness.

'Well,' he said, 'if that's what you really want. I wouldn't touch a job like that with a barge pole.'

The train journey cross-country from York to Norwich was long, with several changes. Though nervous, I was exuberant, reading and re-reading the UEA syllabus. I felt a kinship with their approach to literature, a sense of intellectual and imaginative compatibility. But I had no idea what to expect from my first proper job interview. I'd borrowed an outfit, a soft black dress, from another girl in the house in St. Paul's Square, and felt like an innocent abroad.

I was booked into the Holiday Inn on the edge of Norwich. I didn't sleep all night. Clive Bell's words kept echoing in my head. 'It's the last thing I'd want, an academic post. I need to be free to be creative.' The other Clive, from Warwick, also chipped in. 'What are you after? You'll just end up a lecturer in some provincial university.' But the thought of rejection scared me more. All night I scanned the notes I'd prepared, writing them down on smaller and smaller pieces of paper till the pointers to my memorised knowledge would fit on a postage stamp.

I was too nervous to touch the huge breakfast buffet, but I'd had the prescience to bring with me a thermos of whisky and took repeated swigs. By the time the taxi delivered me to campus, having first tried to take me back to Norwich station, I was drunk to just the right level to boost confidence without sacrificing eloquence. And as I walked into the Registry building and interview room, explaining my late arrival, someone made a joke about the station looking more like a university and the ice was broken.

It might have been a painting of the Last Supper: twelve men behind a long rectangular table. Not that I could see them clearly. I didn't wear contact lenses then, the girl who'd lent me the dress had advised me to remove my glasses, and I whipped them into my pocket at the last minute. But, thanks to the drink, the interrogation ran like a dream. There were questions I'd prepared for and batted easily, other less expected ones from random bowlers, which I bounced around before sending them to the boundary. In my blurred vision, I'd taken all twelve figures to be men, cloned figures with dark suits and beards, but a husky voice soon drew my attention to the sole woman on the panel: Lorna Sage, half hidden by a cascade of long blonde hair. I talked enthusiastically about Gothic fiction, ended with a woman to woman smile, but Lorna wasn't one for double standards, there would be no special favours, and her face remained impassive. Then linguist Roger Fowler took up the questioning, reluctant to collude with an interview he sensed was tipping in my favour.

'What languages do you know?' he asked, as if trying to catch me out.

'Fluent French,' I said. 'My first degree was in English and Comparative Literature. Spanish and Latin to O-level. Some basic German. And now I'm learning Italian.'

'You can stop there,' Roger barked, while the others laughed. 'I think that's enough.'

Outside, in the reception area, sat the next candidate. Tim, already teaching in the department, told me as I repositioned my specs that he was the inside choice, the front-runner for the job. So I returned to Norwich station with my hopes punctured, the wit and aplomb the whisky had given me fast fading away.

On the long return journey I dozed and read, weary beyond belief. Only as we approached Leeds did I became aware of a strange atmosphere around me: a sense of invisible but none the less tangible spiritual conflict. It was as if light and darkness were battling it out over my destiny and I guessed the interview panel was at that very moment making its decision, the arguments batted to and fro like ping-pong balls down the long wooden table. Roger Fowler and the traditionalists supported Tim, who had proved his worth; Lorna Sage and the radicals wanted me as an extremely bright outside female candidate. Lorna told me later it had indeed been a fight, not helped by the reference from Bernard Bergonzi describing me as unpredictable, volatile and labile. (Never send frank letters about depression to your tutors).

The spiritual battle reminded me of the recurrent nightmare I'd had as a child, the one I'd always remembered outside Coventry cathedral:

my body raised from the bed and pulled apart as if I was being crucified. God in one corner, the devil opposite, claiming me for themselves, till I was sure I would break into pieces. Now, sitting in the train as we sped north through Yorkshire, I prayed for the light to win. I knew this was a decision that would irrevocably affect my life, and thus it proved, though in ways I could not then foresee.

A few days later the letter arrived and I'd arrived, hit the jackpot: a full-time permanent lectureship in literature in one of the best new universities in the country. My mother didn't respond when I told her. Nicole Ward-Jouve and Geoffrey Summerfield were overjoyed. Gay Clifford wrote to say UEA had 'soared' in her estimation for recognising 'excellence'. But my peers at York were less generous.

'Alright for some,' one said. 'You're made for life now. You realise you'll get one term off in seven for a sabbatical, on full pay?'

In the library's coffee bar, I overheard another post-grad, an Ezra Pound aficionado, outraged at my success.

'*Lucky bitch*,' he said. 'She's not as good a teacher as me. Hasn't even finished her Ph.D. Did you hear about her suicide attempt?'

A large part of my own exhilaration came from the stability I hoped the job would provide in relation to Adam. Once I was settled in East Anglia, part of the adult world at last, perhaps I could negotiate a better arrangement. David and Jan had relocated to Birmingham, and I started planning the journeys. I'd been skidding round York first on a push-bike, then a battered red Honda 50, which left me trembling from any more than the shortest trip. Now I'd be able to learn to drive and buy a car. I could get a house and have Adam to stay, take him on holiday, treat him to things I'd not been able to afford.

Before universities broke up for the long vacation, I was summoned back to Norwich to plan my teaching commitments. As the acting head of English, Roger Fowler was expected to put me up, but he made no secret of having championed Tim's application over mine. On the same visit, I was dined by a handful of lecturers intrigued to meet me without the formality of an interview. Guido Almansi, an operatic Italian, shared with me later his disappointment at my dinner performance.

'You were *impossible* that night,' he gestured. 'You said nothing.'

It was true. No longer loose-tongued with whisky, I felt shy, intimidated by the posse of clever male brains around me, and thrown by Roger's blatant disapproval. When I left, thanking him for his hospitality, Roger gave another surly grunt from behind his beard. 'I only did it because I had to.'

Was this why, walking back through Norwich to the station, I burst into tears? Was I right to take the job? Would my super-ego enslave me even more now I was entering this enclave of confident male intellects? Was Norwich too far away from the Black Country? Would my 'success' drive even more of a wedge between me and David, make it harder to see Adam?

Wiping my face with the back of my hand, I detoured from the colour-ful market square in the centre of Norwich and down a side street. In front of me stood a small independent bookseller's, long since vanished. The shelves were packed with titles I didn't know and I searched for something to distract me on the train. One title leapt out at me straight away: *By Grand Central Station I Sat Down and Wept*, an autobiographical novel by Elizabeth Smart.

'She's a local author,' the assistant told me. 'Well, relatively. Lives in Suffolk, near Beccles.'

By the time I arrived back in York, I'd read the book through twice and sensed I'd discovered a kindred spirit. A woman who knew what love was and loss was and wrote like a fallen angel. As my underlying grief and anxiety persisted, I gripped the novel as though to squeeze from it some comfort. By Norwich station I sat down and wept. What had the lucky bitch gone and done?

10

East Anglia

*The Learned, who strive to ascend into Heaven
by means of learning, appear to Children like
dead horses, when repelled by the celestial spheres.*

William Blake

I WAS CLEARLY ADDICTED to the modern campus. First Warwick, with its mud and urinal white tiles, then low-lying York with its collegiate lawns and artificial lake. And now East Anglia, whose ziggurat-like halls of residence sat a couple of miles outside Norwich on green land once the city's golf course.

I was assigned a small office on the ground floor of the School of English and American studies, looking out to the concrete monolith of the Registry. Mike Hay drove down my hired van from York and we wheeled in dozens of cartons of books in supermarket trolleys.

The first impression was of ubiquitous greyness. No plaster on the internal walls, only raw breezeblock with its pumice stone finish. No colour anywhere: no art, no carpets on the floor, no windows in the warren of corridors, just an unerring shade of grey.

I rented a room in the Norwich suburbs, a semi-detached house belonging to Thomas Elsässer. German by origin, Elsässer taught in the school of English and European studies and would be instrumental in initiating film as a discipline at UEA. We were both inept at small talk, and I wasn't confident I could take on his impressive intellect, so our conversations were stilted discussions of rent, rubbish collection days and refectory opening hours. A few nights after I arrived, one of his young student lodgers, bleeding profusely, was rushed to Norwich hospital for an emergency hysterectomy. I visited her several times, bearing bunches of flowers fresh from the market. But I wasn't the right person to console her in her grief at not being able to have children. I was keeping as far away from them as possible.

That summer, 1976, was the hottest ever recorded in the UK. Days were the sunniest for over a century. For the first time, the government created a minister for drought as reservoirs dried up, forest fires gobbled up heathland, bath-water was tossed onto parched gardens. I heard of Norfolk's lovely beaches, of dunes tumbling down from cornfields filled with poppies to the edge of the sea, of rivers on the Suffolk borders perfect for skinny dipping, but I didn't let myself be tempted. I had to prove myself worthy of this new position, but more than that, I needed to avoid children. Term times were bad enough. At York, I'd learnt to avoid schools and playgrounds when parents were delivering or collecting, and to veer away from kids in shops, especially boys of Adam's age. Somehow I had to delude myself the universe was an exclusively adult one; if I stayed in my office working, I could pretend that children didn't exist, babies didn't exist, and I hadn't lost one. So, in the intense heat, I threw myself into preparing teaching for the autumn, over-preparing in fact, sitting in my office each day, with two secretaries a few doors away in an otherwise empty building.

I must have seen Adam that summer; I saw him in all his holidays no matter how briefly, but I don't recollect where or when. Our meetings had become so heart-wrenching, I went through them on automatic pilot. I couldn't bear to think how much his life and mine were severed, how little I knew about his day-to-day existence or his first days at school that year. The only way to survive was to put a padlock on my feelings and register nothing, virtually confining the relationship with him to the few brief hours and days we spent together.

In fact, getting the lectureship at UEA confirmed the lifestyle to which I'd been apprenticed for the past seven years: one which paid little attention to my body and none to my heart, let alone to anything as inchoate as soul. The feminine was totally denied. I ate indifferently, never cooked, took zero exercise, and, once the other faculty drifted back from their various vacations in France and Italy, began to mirror their habits of visible consumption: plentiful wine, gin and tonic, and cigarettes - roll ups, menthol or, to really impress, black Sobranies.

The University of East Anglia's reputation for literature and creative writing, and the names that have spun from its rotating glass doors, have invested it with the stuff of legend: a magical ivory tower into which ordinary mortals enter and from which literary immortals depart. Through its alchemical portals have passed many prominent and award winning writers, the most notable of them Ian McEwan, Kazuo Ishiguro, Tracy Chevalier and Andrew Miller. And although McEwan, the first M.A. writing graduate from UEA, has disavowed that he was actually 'taught' there to much effect, his success and that of the many names who've followed have transformed East Anglia's creative writing courses into the fabric of myth. Writing tutors have included Angela Carter, Rose Tremain, Andrew Motion, Sue Roe, Michèle Roberts. The success of Lorna Sage's memoir *Bad Blood* in 2000, winning the Whitbread Prize for biography, and Malcolm Bradbury's knighthood, also in 2000 –the year he died – have further added to UEA's legendary status.

But when I went there, in 1976, such myth-making was still nascent. The M.A. in creative writing was in its infancy, with only a handful of students each year. Bradbury, along with satirical novelist Angus Wilson, had instigated the course in 1970 – the first of its kind in the UK – but he himself was a relative newcomer to the dazzle of the literary limelight and, although gratified, he also seemed amused, if not bemused, by all the fuss.

Bradbury's collection of short stories, *Who Do You Think You Are?* came out the year I arrived at UEA. But it was his campus novel, *The History Man*, published to great acclaim the year before, which had put him on the map. Auberon Waugh called it 'the funniest and best-written novel I have seen for a very long time.' A.S. Byatt referred to its 'grim wit, chill comedy and new fictional energy'. The *Birmingham Post* described Bradbury's weapons as 'satire, irony, intelligence and controlled disgust, so that this immensely readable novel is comic, pathetic, mordant and serious.' I read it as soon as I got the job at UEA, and though it was set in 1972 in Watermouth, a fictional seaside town in the South of England, it bore enough resemblance to the campuses I knew for me to recognise the sharpness of its wit. It filled me with subliminal expectations as to what my new life at UEA might be, and when, at the beginning of that autumn term, I was invited to a party thrown by Malcolm and Elizabeth Bradbury in their large house off the Earlham Road, I went as the latest 'new face', half anticipating the template of the party which is so central to *The History Man*.

I felt gauche and rather clumsily dressed in a pair of black culottes and a little sweater. My wavy brunette hair was still combed in the side-parting style into which it had fallen since childhood. I stood by the fireplace in the lounge, one hand on the mantel shelf, where I could study in the large gilt-edged mirror reflections of the faculty and their wives (most of the lecturers were men) as they trooped into the room.

The Dean of the School, John Broadbent, was a Milton specialist and ex-Cambridge don. With his white hair and patrician appearance, he certainly looked the Miltonic part, a warm humanist with some Leavisite gravitas but none of Leavis' pomposity. John's wife Faith was gracious, modestly beautiful, the first person to ask me who I was and draw me into conversation. Along with many students from East Anglia and, before that, from their Cambridge days, I quickly invested John and Faith with the role of idealised parents: a rare perfect couple whose marriage seemed a tender, mutually respectful and loving togetherness.

As we sipped our wine and picked at the canapés, I tried to memorise the names of the other lecturers. Here was a handsome quick-moving Chris Bigsby and his slim wife; here another new appointment, Jacqueline Fear, to teach American history, her thesis on American Indians. Here were Eric Homberger, Allan Smith, David Punter, Ellman Crasnow, Nicholas Brooke, Lorna Sage. If we all drank a lot, as if trying to nudge the party into the debauchery of Bradbury's novel, we didn't succeed. The evening remained an urbane, moderate occasion, even a little boring.

I loved teaching and took to it immediately. Undergraduate courses were organised in modules which ran for ten weeks each, the length of a term. I inherited courses that first autumn, but thereafter devised my own. Students signed up for their favourites and I soon discovered one of the secrets to full seminars was alliterative titles or courses with multiple names: Feminism and Fiction; The Fantastic in Fiction; Gaskell and the Brontës; Tennyson, Browning, Arnold, Clough. I prepared diligently, gave generous hand-outs and ideas, felt deeply rewarded by students' responses when I saw them inspired to extra work. I was also exhilarated and excited, if a little daunted, at having such clever colleagues, the majority of them male Oxbridge graduates, from public schools. But I was still only twenty-five, closer in age to students than to the faculty, and it was to them I turned for friendship. Karen Cohen, an attractive Jewish girl from a wealthy Hampstead background, a history student, took some photographs of me for the student magazine, quickly saw past my sham self-sufficiency and became a lifelong friend.

Rich and poor students were conspicuously different in dress and attitude. Some had parents buying up houses for them half-way between city and campus off the Earlham and Unthank Roads. They talked of second homes in Skye, the Orkneys, Guernsey, France. Others, not getting the grant their parents were supposed to give, found it hard to survive. I remember Mark, having failed to attend a tutorial, arriving next day apologetic and wan.

'Whatever's the matter?' I said. 'Are you ill?'

'Don't ask,' Mark replied. 'I've been selling my body for hospital tests. Private research. You wouldn't want to know.'

But these factors didn't enter the faculty's discussions of student performance. Issues of gender, class or circumstance were irrelevant and we should pay them no heed. The intellect was all. We had regular Board meetings in the Registry, dozens of historians and lettrists from the EAS faculty sitting around a huge table like Arthurian knights, with the silver-haired John Broadbent ruling over the court. At one of the meetings a hot debate raged about whether entry requirements should be relaxed to increase student numbers. One of the elder statesmen, a renowned historian, slammed his fist down on the table. 'We are not here to care about BODIES. We are here to cultivate MINDS.' Philosophy lecturer Martin Hollis, married to historian (later Baroness) Patricia Hollis, was visibly bored at a fireworks do with his sons. Turning to me, he remarked, 'In my opinion, children are much over-rated.' If there was irony in his voice, I couldn't detect it.

If such comments were based on a premise that academic life was superior, and anything else was an unworthy distraction and aberration, I was at the time grateful for it. This was the same mythology that had informed my childhood: Athena – goddess of wisdom, the arts, civilization – is born not from a woman's body but directly from the mind of Zeus. From his forehead, his thought, his word, his Logos, a fully armed, divinely intelligent Athena is brought into being. And if our finely honed intellects sprang from nowhere but such innate intelligence, what need was there to betray my sooty origins or my troubled female history? What better place than this modern ivory tower in which to disguise the fierce heartache over Adam, or to confirm the rightness of suppressing my other human needs?

I soon moved from Elsässer's to rent a room nearer campus, in a red brick terrace belonging to Tony Gash, a lecturer in drama. Tony was another of the Oxbridge graduates, but he was one of the warmer, more accessible of the faculty, unpretentious, with a great laugh and genial sense of humour. His post-graduate research was into carnival and Bakhtin's theories of the carnivalesque, which seemed to mirror perfectly his slight penchant for chaos, and his Rabelaisian hunger for knowledge. So engrossed would he be discussing the latest book he'd read, ideas cascading irrepressibly out of him, that, as we shared the washing up, the tea towel often stayed looped round the dining plate mid-air in his hand for hours.

I quickly became involved with TUT, the Training of University Teachers, and attended courses at London's Institute of Education. Through these I met Julia Pascal, a voice coach and theatre director, and teachers from Holland. This led later to a visiting lectureship at D'Witte Leli institute in Amsterdam, and a friendship with two of the teachers there. I also linked up with the Student Counselling Service on campus, attending some of their courses on person-centred counselling, to learn the skills of good pastoral tutoring. I learned to listen more deeply and enjoyed helping students with personal issues. One colleague, newly arrived from Oxford, thought my care beyond the call of duty and dismissed it as a function gone askew.

'You're in the wrong profession,' he said, with some contempt. 'You're a frustrated social worker.'

Perhaps I was. But a genuine desire to be kind and loving was also fed by wanting to distance myself from the negative projections coming from David and his new wife Jan, and, in my paranoid fantasy, from everyone who knew my story. Angela Carter was a visiting lecturer, but not for me the luxury of her Gothic persona, her Sadeian woman. To prove that not living with my own child didn't make me a selfish monster, I had to be extra loving, extra solicitous, a visibly 'good mother', even if it was to everyone but my own child.

I still had by my bedside *By Grand Central Station I Sat Down and Wept* and often dipped into it for its passion, its lyrical sensuality. One of the mature students who became a friend told me she lived in Suffolk and knew Elizabeth Smart. She drove me down one day and introduced us, and after that I'd visit Elizabeth on my own.

Dell Cottage, a few miles from Bungay, was a lovely ramshackle old house with a rambling garden. The first time I went alone, the back door was open, but when I wandered in, Elizabeth was nowhere to be seen.

Jugs and mugs of flowers were everywhere; cook books and gardening books spilled over carpets and chairs. I called her several times, then noticed Elizabeth sitting under the kitchen table, rather pissed. As I bent down, she laughed, then crawled out to join me and I uncorked the bottle of wine I'd bought. Sixty-three then, though I believed her much younger, Elizabeth was still beautiful in a wild, eccentric way, indifferent to fashion, wearing an old fisherman's smock. Her fine blonde hair was cut in a long bob with a thick fringe, her face lined with experience, her fingers split from gardening.

'I've sorted all my books,' she said. Her voice was that of a smoker. 'Male authors on one side of the room, women on the other.'

'You think they write differently?' I asked.

'Of course.' And she quoted a few lines from one of her recent poems. '*To be in a very unfeminine/Very unloving state/Is the desperate need/ Of anyone trying to write.* Only it's hard for us to de-sex ourselves, isn't it? Impossible, once we have children. They're the real creativity, after all.' And she showed me photos of her now grown four children by poet George Barker: Georgina, Christopher, Sebastian and Rose. It was the love affair with Barker which had inspired *By Grand Central Station* and I shared again how much her novel meant to me, especially its brilliant reworking of the *Song of Songs*. Elizabeth seemed pleased to be praised, yet at the same time brushed it off by leading me into the garden, filled with roses, grasses, penstemon, plants I'd never seen.

In 1994, Maya Gallus would make a film based on Elizabeth Smart's life called *On the Side of the Angels* – an apt title for what she came to represent in my own inner world, this romantic female writer whose loves and subversive beliefs were too vibrant to be hobbled by academia. I'd never met a woman so expansive, so uncowed by people's opinions, so unfrightened of excess. Elizabeth seemed to have the same defiant licence as her semifictional character, 'I will not give up belief in true love,' her passion for life as far as it was possible to be from the hemmed-in vistas of my Puritan family and their prudishness. She had nothing small or bourgeois about her. And I returned to Norwich filled with longing for that same bohemianism, for some of her intoxication and devil-may-care attitude.

My colleagues at UEA might be impressive, but Elizabeth's sensuality in approaching life and writing alike seemed to me to represent something entirely different from their disembodied intellects. Whenever I was back on campus after visiting her, I felt I was betraying something. I'd sit teaching literary criticism, pulling poems apart, finding it hard to breathe, as if I'd stepped into a tightly boned corset. At the Dell, literature was about the heart and soul, about lived experience and embodied imagination. But on campus, writing shrank back into a cerebral thing, in the service of critical dissection and more and more an adjunct to literary theory.

I'd secretly written poetry for years, and had some published in the student magazine at Warwick. To celebrate getting the post at UEA, just before I left York, I'd treated myself to a residential poetry course at Lumb Bank, the Arvon centre Ted Hughes founded at Hebden Bridge. Rather over-estimating the capacity of my little Honda 50cc moped to judder the almost sixty miles from York, let alone my own physical endurance, I arrived at Hebden Bridge in a state of cold agitation, brains and bones literally shaking. I'd not actually heard of either of the tutors: George MacBeth and Anthony Thwaite. But at dinner, the distinguished-looking man next to me turned out to be Anthony. When he discovered I'd landed the job at UEA, he told me he taught there too.

'Very part-time,' he said. 'Malcolm Bradbury's a good friend of ours.'

Soon after I moved to Norfolk that hot summer of 1976, I was invited to visit Anthony and his wife Ann at their house in Low Tharston, about twenty miles south of Norwich. I arrived for pre-lunch drinks one Sunday, again having travelled down on my red Honda, trembling from the ride.

Their low pink-washed house fronted a small river, an enchanted *Wind in the Willows* setting complete with weeping willows, punt and gipsy caravan hidden in the trees. Any attraction towards Anthony was quickly suppressed when I met Ann, a warm, kind woman I immediately wanted as a friend. Like the Dell, though in different ways, the Thwaites' mill house was a writer's haven. Ann, a biographer and children's writer – she was to write best-selling biographies of A.A. Milne, Edmund Gosse and Emily Tennyson – had converted one of their downstairs rooms into a well-stocked library for local kids. It was a privileged setting, one where I never quite felt quite at ease, but after some initial awkwardness, we settled into regular contact. They had four daughters and sometimes, when Ann and Anthony were away, I stayed with the two younger girls, Lucy and Alice. Ann was generous to a fault. She came to my first-ever lecture, on Elizabeth Gaskell, where I spoke like a mouse, relieved Ann was in the front row so she could actually hear my whisper; she helped my house hunting in Norwich; gave me a wonderful hand-crafted cedar dining table (which, after various interim owners, I still have); let me practice on their Vauxhall when I was preparing for my driving test; invited us down when Adam visited. We took him to the coast at Walberswick and Dunwich, where a 13th century village is buried, went punting with him on the river, had day outings boating on the Norfolk Broads.

Ann and Anthony were generous hosts. They would invite me for dinner with Malcolm and Elizabeth Bradbury, where I would drink too much and eat too little, feeling the odd-one-out in their successful foursome. When Philip Larkin, a close friend of Anthony's, stayed for the weekend, I was invited down to join them for lunch and a punt on the river.

Larkin I found affable in a melancholy kind of way, completely indifferent to his fame, with no egotistical front. We talked about the thesis I was writing on Dickens and a few days later a card arrived from Larkin elaborating on a link he'd mentioned between Dickens and Grimaldi, the 19th century clown. When he was twenty-five, Dickens was asked to edit and re-write Grimaldi's *Memoirs*, which had been left incomplete on his death in 1837, then badly re-written. At first, Dickens was reluctant to agree: 'It is very badly done, and is so redolent of twaddle...' But, for a good price, an advance of £300, he did eventually take on the job. Years later, after Larkin's death, Anthony Thwaite edited his correspondence into book form. By this time, I was without an income, and hunted high and low for Larkin's hand-written card, thinking it might buy some groceries. But by then, I'd moved so often, it was lost along with so much else.

At one of the Thwaites' parties that first winter, filled with interesting neighbours, artisans and writers as well as a few of the UEA faculty, I glimpsed in their crowded lounge an extremely attractive man in his early thirties, set apart by his head of unruly curls, dark open-neck shirt and well-cut casual jacket. Someone introduced him as Roger Deakin, and we started talking about books, houses, children. I was instantly drawn to him. Roger was separated from his wife Jenny and was living much of the time without his young son, Rufus, whom he missed dreadfully. I was able to share how I missed Adam, and felt none of the usual embarrassment at being the absent parent, for Roger felt similarly compromised by circumstance. His intelligence was warm, quick and grounded, and though I later discovered he too was yet another public schoolboy and Cambridge graduate – he'd been to Haberdashers' Aske's, then read English at Peterhouse, where he was taught by Kingsley Amis – his outlook and ideas were quite at odds with the academic intellects of many of my UEA colleagues. The main love of his life was Walnut Tree Farm, a large Elizabethan farmhouse he'd bought in Suffolk in 1969, which he was single-handedly restoring – *not*, he stressed, *renovating*. He talked about beams, wood and trees, about ducks and water, and invited me down to visit.

On the edge of Mellis Common, near Diss, Walnut Tree Farm was set back from the main road and surrounded by trees. Outside, a deep red-tiled roof sloped down to 17th century walls and small casement windows. Inside were low wooden beams, wood fires, an assortment of old furniture, stripped wooden chairs and various natural objects – driftwood, shells, grasses, feathers, dried flowers – as if the outside world had migrated within. For someone brought up in post-war council houses with cardboard thin partitions, the thick stone walls of Walnut Tree Farm were wondrously ancient and solid, the whole place so full of timber beams, it was more like living in a tree than a house. It was cold, the bedrooms especially were freezing, but it didn't matter. When I stood at one of the open windows upstairs, looking out along the limbs of a tree, I felt I'd been returned to the untamed, wild creature I really was. This was where I belonged, not in the concrete labyrinth of a modern campus, but in a building still one with the trees which made it.

We sat talking by the flames of the open fire and soon became lovers. Later, I discovered Roger had been a copywriter in London for Colman, Prentis and Varley, where he coined the National Coal Board slogan: 'Come home to a real fire'. Here, at last, was a man of whom my mother might approve: not mining the black stuff like Ken, my first boyfriend, the collier from Shirebrook pit, but promoting it.

Next morning, Roger showed me round his land, past moat and copses, through woods, along hedges. I quickly lost track of what was his and what was general countryside, it all seemed one vast dream of green-land, in which he was totally at home, telling the stories of individual trees. I didn't realise then that he had a full twelve acres of land, that everywhere we walked was his: the outbuildings, stores of timber and tools, meadows, fields where an old car was rusting into a home for wildlife, a rustic shepherd's hut.

Our relationship, intermittent as it was, lasted a few months. Sometimes Roger came to Norwich, staying over with me after we'd been to a film, we especially loved Cinema City, the country's first regional film theatre. But mostly I went to him at Walnut Tree Farm. When he was away in London on work projects, I took my books into the cold bohemian lounge, sat bundled up in jackets, coats and blankets, but I couldn't study there. This wasn't a place for academic thinking. Beneath all those beams of trees, language felt humbled. Instead of working, I'd walk out into the fields, past Mellis Common, marvelling at the beauty of the timber-framed houses nearby, the romantic wooded setting.

Roger was a man unfettered, as deeply inside his lean, active body as he was inside the rural world. He shocked me by being so in touch with natural rhythms. He was the only lover I've ever known who wasn't put off by a woman's menstruation, but welcomed it as a chance to be more in touch with her natural cycles. The physical contact between us was easy, satisfying, un-neurotic. But I wasn't used to this way of being, nor to this kind of man, civilised and cultured, yet profoundly male, free, with an unabashed link to nature I had until then associated with solitude and the feminine.

'Do you think you could get me some work at UEA?' Roger asked on one of our walks, as we ducked beneath a canopy of berries. 'Some teaching?'

I looked at him, this man of the woods, tried to visualise him enduring the drawn-out minutiae of a board meeting. 'You wouldn't want it, Roger. It wouldn't suit you.'

'I need some money for all the projects I want to do here.'

'I'll ask. But I really don't have that kind of power. I'm too new.'

But I didn't ask. I wanted Roger's world to stay separate, to be uncontaminated by the sterility I was beginning to experience at UEA.

On one of Adam's visits, I took him out to Walnut Tree Farm. We drove there for the day with Tony Gash and his girlfriend Lynn. Adam, by now living in Birmingham, wasn't used to the country, and was finding it harder to make sense of all the changes and disruptions in his life. When we got hungry, Roger searched through an empty fridge, then offered us scrambled duck eggs. Adam wasn't the only one to find them over-rich – he was sick on the car journey home – and I resolved to give him a quieter time when he was with me.

In 1977, while still living at Tony Gash's, I threw a party, the first I'd attempted since my Coventry days with Gail. Tony and Lynn were also celebrating the recent birth of their first child, Anna. Roger drove up from Suffolk for the party, bringing with him Elizabeth Smart, they'd long been friends. Instead of the customary bottle of wine, Elizabeth proffered a large bottle of whisky which I immediately handed back to her, and by the end of the evening it was empty. She gave me a signed copy of her new selection of poetry, *A Bonus*. Also published that year was her second book of poetic prose, *The Assumption of the Rogues and Rascals*, a reflection on what it means to be a mother and a writer: *So between worry and action, the faces of women fall away.*

And, writing this, as I think of them both now they're gone – Elizabeth Smart died in London from a heart attack in 1986, the year her journals *Necessary Secrets* were published; Roger Deakin would die from a brain tumour in August 2006, aged sixty-three – their appearance together that night at the party lives in my memory as a kind of cameo.

Both were bright, idiosyncratic figures who lived and wrote outside the mainstream, hammering their lyrical prose into gold. I'm convinced Roger's beautiful writing was influenced by his friendship with Elizabeth; you couldn't be around her for long without wanting to give original voice to your own passion. Had I possessed more faith in my own creativity and imagination, I might have realised that I was drawn to them both because of my deep yearning for what, in their different ways, they embodied: a wilderness thinking and living and writing quite at odds with the reductive theoretical approach which dominated the university study of literature in the late 1970s, and into whose seductive pretensions I, too, quickly fell.

Roger and I were lovers, but not in love. We never argued, there was no agony, no animosity. We simply drifted apart as he pursued his work in London and on the farm, and I started house-hunting in Norwich and picked up the threads of my unfinished doctorate. Had I understood or embraced his way of being, it would have been impossible to sustain my high-wire intellectual performance; the whole neurotic edifice on which it depended would have come tumbling down. And Roger was in many ways a loner who, despite his strong friendships, loved his solitude and his time on the land – not only his own land, but any unspoilt earth. He went on to write a passionate account of swimming in wild places – moat, pond, river, leat, sea – which was published as *Waterlog* in 1999 and inspired many later champions of wild-water swimming, as well as the voice of the swimmer in Alice Oswald's prize-winning poem *Dart*.

After I eventually left UEA, I lost touch with the literary world I'd brushed against there. By the time of the millennium, I was no longer reading newspapers or watching TV; only much later, leafing through an old copy of *Resurgence* at a friend's house, did I recognise a photo of the shepherd's hut at Walnut Tree Farm, and learn that Roger had become famous as an environmentalist, that *Waterlog* had topped the UK best-seller list. I was shy about contacting him again, but eventually sat to write him a letter of congratulation. By then, it was too late. His brilliant *Wildwood: A Journey Through Trees* and equally fervent *Notes from Walnut Tree Farm* were published posthumously, in 2007 and 2008.

After his death, his notebooks and papers found their way into a permanent home in the Roger Deakin archive at UEA. Robert Macfarlane, Roger's literary executor, wrote that, 'His notes, written to himself, provide an insight into a beautiful mind and a sweet man ... This archive will capture what it was like to be a passionate, engaged, subversive country intellectual living through a time of profound change.'

Now, when I remember the walk we had in the woods, when Roger asked me to help him get some part-time teaching, I rejoice that he took a different route. To be enshrined in UEA this way, with his notebooks and jottings at the wonder of the world, is a far more fitting tribute to his vision than any academic achievement would have been. As Robert Frost famously wrote of the two roads diverging in a wood, taking *the one less travelled by... has made all the difference.*

Brief Encounters

When I dream about the children...
I dream them small-boned and wordless, as if again
I've turned my back, forgotten to come home

to feed them and need to find my way back to grace
beyond forgiving. Their dream-selves are always just-born
with their adult faces on, full of sweet anxious daylight

I can barely look at, standing here in the edge
of deep water.

Lesley Saunders, 'Particulare Care'

COMPARED WITH MANSFIELD, which boasted the highest murder rate in the country, Norwich felt safe and pretty. On Saturdays, I'd walk to the market in the city centre, the fruit and veg stalls topped with candy-striped awnings, the square surrounded by pastel-coloured buildings. Down cobbled side streets to little churches, vernacular flint houses, second-hand bookshops, delicatessens and boutiques, round past Cinema City to the cathedral. Not that I ever felt really settled; a primitive unease persisted, and the sense of missing Adam pulled me down, as if a plumb-line was tied around my heart.

At the end of my probationary year, John Broadbent told me the interview panel was 'congratulating itself' on my appointment and I was given tenure. With a £10,000 mortgage (the full cost of the house!) I bought a three-bedroom terrace on College Road, half way between campus and Norwich city centre. Contrary to rumours about university pay, the starting salary was small and by the time I'd paid mortgage, bills and basic living costs, nothing was left. To make ends meet, I took in lodgers, and a stream of students, then lecturers, started sharing the house.

First came Ruth, a lanky blonde with the clearest pale skin, who introduced into my primitive kitchen the mysteries of wholefood cooking. My own diet was erratic, increasingly soaked in alcohol, and Ruth's sprouting lentils and nut loaves were the food of pixies. She was followed by Kate, sensitive and fragile, doing the M.A. in creative writing. Kate often returned from her tutorials with Angela Carter in floods of tears.

'She's a Gothic witch,' Kate sobbed. 'She stood at the window all the time with her back to me, like a crow in her black clothes. She said I was wasting my time doing the M.A., that my writing was terrible.'

With my house given over to lodgers, I had the front box-room as a study, barely wide enough to hold a desk. A small recess with a curtain wire served as a wardrobe, ample for my handful of clothes. I had no washing machine, but made a weekly trip to the launderette on Unthank Road. It was all rather like camping.

My real home was my new office, a large room on the second floor of the EAS (English and American Studies) building, warm and light, with a panorama over campus. Having read a scientific article claiming that the colour grey induces paranoia, I was determined to fill my office with colour. I commandeered several plastic chairs the colour of Heinz tomato soup, and a red fabric swivel chair for my desk. I had shelves installed to house my thousands of books and on the rest of the walls stuck up posters by Manet alongside postcards of writers and artists from the National Portrait Gallery: Dickens, the Brontës, Oscar Wilde, Edith Sitwell; paintings by Picasso, Botticelli, Samuel Palmer, Patrick Heron, William Blake. A spare table beneath the windows took my houseplants: spider plants, *ficus*, scented geranium and mother-in-law's tongue, which grew prolifically in the perfect hothouse conditions.

I felt most relaxed there in the evenings, when the other staff had gone home and I had the whole EAS building to myself. I would sit marking or writing my doctorate until the cleaners arrived, two to each floor. We were soon sharing cups of tea and plant cuttings, and I heard about the latest in their family sagas, before they wheeled away their cleaning materials into the clever *trompe l'oeil* recess concealed in the breeze block walls.

Perhaps I felt more of an affinity with them than with my colleagues because cleaning ran in my genes. My maternal grandmother, Emma Barks, was fourteen when she went into factory work, then into service with the local lady of the manor. In the First World War, Emma lost her husband but received no widow's pension. For the rest of her life, she worked as a cleaner. Even on her days off, she'd be on her knees in her long flowered pinny, scrubbing the red tiles on her kitchen floor. Whenever I saw her, I would stare at her left hand with its pollarded fingers, sliced off at the knuckles in a factory accident.

My new office shared a phone line with David Aers. He lived in Bury St. Edmunds with his young family and had to travel up early to work, but no matter what time I arrived on weekday mornings, David was always there first, his Venetian blinds down, reading his Milton, Blake, radical criticism. David struck me as UEA's version of E. P. Thompson: serious without being dull, careful about textual readings without being pedantic, a man who cared deeply about the broad sweep of history and politics, without the fanaticism of excessive Marxist theory. We got on well, shouting through the breeze block wall to hand over phone calls.

David was the one colleague who kept trying to persuade me to step into positions of greater personal and professional power. When opportunities came to chair committees, or take on more responsibility, David would urge me to step up to the mark, but I never did. Looking back, this feels to me now rather pathetic, but I think that without a mother's or father's belief in me, I couldn't believe in anyone's. David was a coach I wouldn't heed, a champion I didn't trust was on my side. A radical thinker, he believed in the female hero, but I disappointed both of us by not being able to find her in myself.

The job had three main responsibilities: teaching, administration and research. The teaching I loved, and evaluations from my students were always glowing. The most surprising accolade, the one that meant most to me, came from a woman with sleek blonde hair who looked like she'd just walked in from Sloane Square.

'I must tell you,' she said, as we left a seminar. 'You remind me so much of a friend of mine in London. She talks about things in the same way as you. You even look a bit like her.'

'Really?'

'Yes. You won't have heard of her.'

'What's her name?'

'Gay Clifford.'

My heart leapt at the comparison. Gay and I were no longer in frequent touch, but I felt proud that in less than ten years since my first days at Warwick, I'd been identified with the woman I most admired and wanted to be.

Administration was another matter. In the days before personal computers, memos arrived in large manila envelopes tied with string for re-use, and hour upon hour was spent answering letters about students, reading minutes, attending board meetings, checking procedures.

Research was the best perk: not only sabbaticals – one term off in seven on full pay (no one checked you weren't flying to Hawaii) – but also a generous personal budget to attend conferences anywhere in the world.

My first conference, which took me back to Warwick, involved sitting in lecture theatres as scholars droned on about their favourite topic, the more abstract and abstruse the better. Restless from the start, I sat doodling flowers on my notepad, then writing messages to someone I knew a few seats away, sensing they too were blitzed with tedium. But I was next to Bernard Bergonzi, my former Professor (I'd not yet learned of the ambivalent reference he'd given me), who in turn scribbled me a little note. 'The DEDICATED academic,' it read, 'must learn to acquire a great degree of BOREDOM.'

I was definitely in the wrong job, then. I had no boredom threshold. I couldn't even bear to teach the same thing twice. Believing we teach best what we need to learn, I had no heart to teach anything unless I was encountering it anew. But now the conference was regurgitating criticism of criticism of criticism, till literature vanished somewhere over the far horizon and I shuffled from one thigh to the other, doodling hangmen and guillotines. Had I left Adam for this? Was this really better than a dead marriage?

Malcolm Bradbury was at the same conference, perhaps gathering material for his next sardonic novel. I always found him affable and pleasant enough, though we never had a profound conversation. That evening, while several of us sat round in a common room drinking, Malcolm lit up his pipe, and shared a dream he'd had the previous night, about his wife.

'Elizabeth was driving a huge juggernaut through Europe,' he said, smiling wryly as he drew smoke through the bowl. 'And I was this tiny figure in the passenger seat.'

Then he chuckled a little, as if no further explanation was needed. I was smoking heavily now too. I never really enjoyed it, but it had become a habit. Smoking was still allowed in teaching rooms, and seminars invariably started with tutors and students reaching for their fags and lighting up, till the fug already in the room turned into a Dickensian smog. With the mixture of nicotine and Norfolk damp, I was soon suffering with asthma, but I blasted my way through it with a Ventolin inhaler and carried on smoking.

I had little idea what to do with Adam when he came to visit. He was five when I got the job at UEA, ten when I left, and I never felt I provided the right second home for him. I was, of course, inwardly, still a child myself. I looked forward to seeing him, but with a mixture of foreboding, not knowing how best to entertain him and always on tenterhooks for the first few hours until we got used to each other again. It was as if he was a lover I was trying to please, unsure of his exact habits and latest preferences, not quite believing that just being with him was enough.

I didn't yet have a TV, knew nothing about football, and Adam wasn't interested in reading, walking or any of my adult activities. Mostly we went just round the corner in Norwich to Allan Smith (a colleague in EAS) and his wife Barbara and their kids, or visited the Thwaites in Low Tharston. But Adam must have been bored when he came to stay, and developed an aversion to academic life, doubtless associating it with distant parents and not enough fun.

From my own childhood, I had no notion of what it meant to play. The main toy I remember was a doll, which Mum won for me at a church fête: 'Guess the doll's name,' and Mum's devotion to Daphne du Maurier's *Rebecca* did the rest. She dressed Rebecca and me in exactly the same home-made costumes: polka dot dresses and bolero cardigans. I never had a bike, nor learnt to swim, nor mixed in with the rough and tumble of other kids. The only game my mother did ever play with me was school. She would make neat lists of names in a pretend register, and we ticked off their attendance, taking it in turns to play teacher. Mum had always wanted to be a school-teacher herself, and was particularly good at shaking her finger at bad children who had not done their work.

My vulnerability around Adam made me particularly prickly when anyone talked about parenting. I seemed to think that if I didn't refer to him, no one else would know about him, though gossip would have ensured everyone did. At one cocktail party, in the midst of small talk in which I was barely fluent, an attractive faculty wife walked up to me and asked, with a smile, 'And where does *your* son go to school?'

My mind went blank with panic. I was still swimming around in black silence when another faculty wife joined in. 'Which do you think *are* the best public schools?'

Then I realised the first wife assumed that my son not living with me meant only one thing: he was away at boarding school; it was thanks to my sending him off to a world of privilege that he wasn't by my side. To my relief, a debate quickly spread round the room about private education, not questioning the premise *of* it but the best premises *for* it. I walked to one side and lit up a cigarette, grateful the attention was distracted away. What, I wondered, would these well-dressed smiling women say, if I told them the truth? Not only had I not sent my boy to prep school, but – the real reason for my panicked response – I actually didn't have the foggiest idea where he was being educated. Perhaps fearing I might kidnap him, David shared no details, all I knew was that it was in Birmingham. And what kind of mother doesn't even know where her own son goes to school?

If it was hard to know what to do with Adam when he came to me, it was even harder when I went up to spend the day with him in the middle of Birmingham. The train journey cross country from Norwich took five hours. I'd have four or five hours entertaining Adam in the city centre, then a journey of five hours back again.

After little sleep, I'd be up before dawn to take a taxi to Norwich station. The train seemed to move impossibly slowly. I'd stare out of the window at the silvery fens creeping out of darkness, and wonder how the wings of a heron, startled into heavy rising by the train, could possibly sustain him. Books and unmarked essays would lie on the table before me, but I was too weary to read them. The train ate up the familiar names: Thetford, March, Ely. I'd keep checking my watch. The journey felt interminable. Four hours to go still. Then three. I seemed stuck in a landscape of molten Dali watches where time just wouldn't move. And every time a mother climbed into the carriage with young children, I'd pray for them not to sit near me. Kids of Adam's age simply rubbed salt into the wound.

At Birmingham New Street, I'd stand on the forecourt, shifting in the cold from one foot to another. What kind of place was this for a child to meet its mother? Then I'd see Adam and run, bend down, hold him in my arms. Each time he seemed more beautiful than ever. I'd look up at David, this stranger who was his father, and we'd agree the time he'd be back for me to hand Adam over. How had this happened? The fruit of my womb handed between us as casually as lost luggage, as gingerly as a bomb?

Then Adam and I would walk away together, hand in hand, for our brief encounter. If a suitable film was on, such as *Star Wars*, we'd spend the afternoon in the cinema. But mostly it was just shops and cafés. Christmas time was the worst, battling through the crowded Bull Ring, searching for presents in department stores. I never knew what Adam wanted and he seemed reluctant to ask for anything. In between shopping, we'd find a café, perch next to each other on high metal stools, sip chocolate shakes through bendy plastic straws.

Amidst the Christmas trees, baubles, plastic reindeer and tinsel, nativity scenes popped up everywhere, an immaculate Madonna and child reproaching me with their perfection. But if I sought a different myth to help me out, some alternative blueprint of motherhood to summon up a little comfort and meaning, there was none. Even Demeter had a whole six months with her lost daughter, half a year, not half a bloody day. I felt I was in a shadow version. I'd walked into the wrong play, the wrong poem, a badly written novel. What was I doing on this page at all, this paper that was torn down the middle?

Adam was often quiet, wistful, and I'd want to pick him up and elope like lovers to France, Italy, Spain. We could run for it, make a new start, and everything till now would have been an error, a tragedy of errors. But I knew better and was quiet too, both of us waiting for me to say something grown-up, loving, helpful.

'How are you getting on at school?'

'I'm in the nativity play. I'm one of the shepherds.'

'Great. What about football? Are you still playing?'

His face lit up and he showed me his maroon and blue scarf. 'These are Aston Villa colours. They're my favourite team.'

Then an afternoon of more shops, more snacks, more swallowed air, before David arrived and Adam and I had our final, frozen lingering hug. It would be weeks before we met again, and meantime stretched another Christmas/Easter/birthday/summer/Bonfire Night/weekend to get through without him.

The return trip on the train was the worst. Always there'd be babies, toddlers, kids of all ages spilling over seats, hurling toys, shouting, crying. If I picked up magazines someone left, they'd merely add to the agony: pictures of mothers and babies, happy families. On those crowded Saturday evening trains, no one seemed to be without a child but me, and no journey had ever been so slow, so tortuous. Adam was there too, but as a ghost, a lost limb, lost organ, heart tugging at me, looking at me through the fog of his father's jokes as he plucked him out of the station. And all the way back to Norwich I'd feel hollow, my skin on fire as if the separation was once again being tattooed into me.

By now it was dark, sky and trees invisible. When I stared out of the window, all I saw in the speeding black mirror was a blank young face staring at herself: pallid, uncomprehending. Ely, March, Thetford. Back to the endless grief of salt water fens. Back to the lovers who could never in a million years be enough. Back to the thousands of books that could never say anything.

In Norwich, I'd be one of the last in the chirpy taxi driver's shift.

'Come on, love, give us a smile. It might never happen.' But it already had happened, and my Mona Lisa grin was more of a grimace as I glanced out at the Norman castle with its neon orange light, the rows of cobbled streets, the flint terraces tucked up for the night.

One Christmas, back home, I took out the drawing Adam had given me: a Cubist portrait he'd done, my eyes huge, my nose lop-sided, earrings dangling like flowers from my skull. And underneath, the words: *'Mum. My Mum.'*

I have it still, that picture. What a perfect mouth. What a huge wide smile. What Picasso could beat it?

As soon as I passed my driving test, I bought a second hand Renault and spent my free weekends exploring Norfolk's fens and wetlands. With the help of old Arthur Mee guides, I discovered the isolated churches at Reepham and Salle; the salt marshes at Holkham; the beauty of Sea Palling, Waxham, Overstrand. I loved the Norfolk coast, the soft sand dunes that suddenly fell away to the sea, adjacent fields with flint church towers rising through the corn. I never slept well, and in summer I'd sometimes drive out to the coast before the day began, hunting picnic spots where I could take Adam. Often, as I stood watching the timid play of light on the water, I'd catch sight of seals swimming towards the empty shore.

I must have presented a strange persona to the world. In the few photos I have from that time, I look absurdly young and naïve. Emotionally I was shy and unsure of myself, but I was used to living from the neck up, tyrannised by my super-ego, a brittle cleverness trying to conceal my insecurity.

I'd long been driven to over-perform, but all my achievements rested on shifting sand. I'd not yet come to terms on any level with my difficult childhood, nor with losing Adam, though my anger should have been a clue. Less overt rage than a simmering resentment and unspoken envy I'd inherited from my mother, my anger was triggered by anyone whose passage through the world was eased by the privilege of wealth, love, or natural confidence. Of course, in some ways, I was now privileged myself. Only in my mid twenties, I had security for life: a tenured university job. But this external success had little impact on my desolate inner world.

My dreams swung between being persecuted by bad mothers and haunted by lost children. I woke in sweats of panic from dreams of Adam as an infant drowning in a canal, or riding his bike without stabilisers towards a busy main road. Or I'd surface from dreams where I was holding him close, cuddling and kissing him, telling him what infinite love and tenderness I felt for him, only to arrive back into the agony of being without him and plunged into renewed consciousness of loss. Such dreams persisted for more than forty years; even when Adam was grown, I still dreamt of him as a young child, able to touch and smell him, our bodies close.

From my Warwick days I'd written journals, but when I was at York they became fuller, essential safety valves to hold my distress around Adam. Now my Norwich journals continued to record dreams and feelings about him, but they were also veined with constant self-reproach, as if only academic success would justify my living apart from him. I was constantly whipping myself to work harder, to educate myself in the ideologies then in fashion, especially Marxism.

'Sunday. Tired but did a few hours work. Then long walk to Eaton Mill. Reorganised lounge. Determined to get more into Marxist intellectual issues. Little sleep.' I copied out quotes which are barely comprehensible to me now. 'From Hegel's *Preface to the Phenomenology of Mind*: Self-conscious mind has not merely lost its essential and concrete life, it is also conscious of this loss and of the transitory finitude characteristic of its content.'

'Feb 1978. Worked on Mary Shelley all day. Gin and tonic evening at Allan and Barbara Smith's. Shocked when X and Y stripped off and were intimate. Was I expected to do the same? No way. Made me feel old-fashioned, frumpy and Puritanical. Felt sick from drinking too much gin too quickly on an empty stomach.'

'Boost today meeting Ted Hughes, who'd come to give one of Chris Bigsby's archive talks. Somehow, Hughes was talking about menstruation. Shocked not by the subject but how anti-academic he was able to be in that context. We all had drinks and lunch together. I felt embarrassed at Z's stupid shallowness when she kept talking non-stop in an abstract away. Ted Hughes was standing directly opposite me and kept giving me a grin and conspiratorial wink, as much as to say 'You're right, this is a load of academic nonsense, but we have to eat, so what's a man to do?''

I didn't encounter overt hostility, but the whole campus seemed to me to be driven by competitiveness and mutual mistrust. People were often reluctant to share ideas lest someone steal them. I heard of several lecturers who kept their manuscripts in bank vaults. And it struck me as more and more ironic that a department studying literature should so thoroughly subordinate the imagination, let alone the heart, to the critical intellect. I felt we were meant to be robots, brains with no bodies, hollow Stepford men with no spiritual sap. It was as if the university was run by an institutional super-ego, pulling the strings of all our separate smaller egos, and we were enslaved to it, vying for its service through our various neuroses.

I was especially disillusioned when I served on the Promotions Committee. Rising up the career ladder, I discovered, had nothing to do with good teaching abilities but was crudely judged on the amount of research. Publications were literally measured by numbers of words, regardless of quality. Perhaps this accounts for the plethora of academic journals set up world-wide to provide outlets for intellectual mincemeat which would otherwise have no home and little meaning.

I discovered on the library shelves periodicals with acronymic titles like PMLA (Proceedings of Modern Language Association), housing articles on vital subjects such as 'The Function of the Semi-Colon in Keats' poetry.' I leafed through them in disbelief, amazed at the pedantry Western scholarship had reached. But I was part of the same system. I wanted to belong, and went to great lengths to yoke myself to the current ways of thinking.

One weekend when I wasn't seeing Adam, a frantic knocking at the front door revealed two friends, a post-grad and his partner, asking to come in.

'We're wondering if you'd store something for us,' he said.

'Of course. What is it?'

'A few books.'

When would I say no to books? But it was more than a few. As they unloaded their car, box after box of pristine books appeared: hundreds of them, on contemporary theory, cultural studies, literature, theatre.

'Are you moving or something?' I asked. 'This looks like your whole library.'

The pair looked embarrassed.

'I was caught stealing books this week,' the man said. 'We're worried the police might come to the flat to see what else I've lifted.'

'You're saying all these are lifted?'

He squirmed and nodded.

'Good Lord.' I remembered Clive at Warwick with his pilfered collection, and how I'd recently seen an older female lecturer slide a new publication under her newspaper in the university book store. How many academics were secretly book thieves? Later, this same post-grad became an eminent Professor.

The only other woman in the English Studies section was Lorna Sage, but she never became the ally I needed. For the first couple of years, we barely spoke to each other, the veiled demeanour and long blonde hair I'd encountered in the job interview still in place. Lorna rarely wore trousers; mostly dark suits with shapely skirts and always high heels. When eventually we did talk, or found ourselves drinking together at parties, Lorna never shared anything personal. In fact, I had to wait another twenty-five years to discover in her autobiography *Bad Blood* the striking similarities of our stories: teenage pregnancy, shotgun wedding, a determination to get a degree with a baby in tow, a lectureship in English at UEA. By another uncanny coincidence, her daughter Sharon's birthday was 29th May, the same as Adam's.

Yet throughout my five years at UEA, even when we spent more intimate time together, and I met the teenage Sharon, Lorna's story remained unknown to me, this parallel part of our female lives totally invisible in the patriarchal world we inhabited. God knows what other dark secrets were concealed behind the breezeblock walls, but this particular silence, and the fact I knew of it only after Lorna died, strikes me as especially poignant.

Sharing those earlier chapters of our lives, and our intellectual victory over them, might have brought us closer. Knowing Lorna's history would certainly have assured me I need not hide my own, need not feel shame about it, and might have made my standing at UEA feel quite different and thus altered my subsequent decisions and destiny. Reading *Bad Blood*, I was also unable to suppress my envy at Lorna's good fortune in having a mother who completely took over Sharon's care while she and Vic completed their degrees at Durham University. Had her mother not stepped into the breach, they might have had less success in 'breaking the rules and getting away with it'; like mine, Lorna's options might have been more compromised.

12

A Lover's Discourse

An intellectual is all the time showing off.
Lovers dissolve and become bewildered...

Some intellectual tries to give sound advice to a lover.
All he hears back is, I love you. I love you.

Love is musk.
Do not deny it when you smell the scent.

Jelaluddin Rumi, 'Low in the Roots'

I N 1977, TWO NEW LECTURERS arrived at UEA on temporary contracts. Both doing Ph.D.s at Cambridge, they were strong characters who would, in their different ways, change my life forever.

Linda Gillman was a striking looking woman who wore colourful Frida Kahlo outfits: long red skirts decorated with dozens of tiny mirrors, ethnic jewellery. If, at Warwick, I'd projected onto Gay Clifford and my flat-mate Gail the gorgeousness and sophistication I felt I lacked, so now, as we became friends, I invested Linda with maturity and wisdom in the ways of the world. She talked about the Eleusinian mysteries, about her research into French literary theorists such as Georges Bataille, and I was in thrall. I would take her advice on anything.

One morning, as we sat in the smog-filled 'fishbowl' on campus, amid dozens of students consuming coffee and cigarettes, Linda picked up my dog-eared copy of Jung's autobiography *Dreams, Memories, Reflections*.

'This is why your life's not working,' she announced, as she tapped her ash into silver foil piled high with cigarette butts. 'You're too bogged down with Jung and his soggy ideas. You should be reading Freud. That's the way forwards now – psychoanalysis.'

And, just as I'd followed where Gail led, even if it meant poisoning my brain with LSD, so now I jumped to Linda's order. Jung was immediately dumped and I became staunchly devoted to Sigmund Freud. I annotated my way through the Penguin paperbacks of his works and went on to consume French theorist Jacques Lacan. I read Juliet Mitchell and started to offer courses on psychoanalysis, feminism and psychoanalytic literary criticism. In the late 70s, women's studies courses were still finding their first footholds in academia. Lorna Sage taught women's social and political history with Labour historian Patricia Hollis, and my feminist modules ran parallel to theirs. Thomas Elsässer said I was turning into UEA's version of Jacqueline Rose, a brilliant academic at Sussex, and though I doubted the truth of the comparison, I was flattered.

The other new arrival that year, Allon White, was taken in by these seemingly high-flying credentials. Fresh from Jesus College, Cambridge and before that from the Ecole Pratique des Hautes Etudes in Paris, and Birmingham's Centre for Cultural Studies, Allon was devoted to contemporary literary theory. He'd soon instigated a small Marxist reading group for the left-wing faculty. Allon, Linda Gillman, David Punter, Jon Cook, historian Logie Barrow, Walter Bachan, Jon Cook's partner Diane de Bell and myself met in each other's homes to discuss Adorno, Althusser, Engels, Marx, Walter Benjamin, Michel Foucault, Wilhelm Reich. It was heady stuff, the texts all male, and I felt as I had as a teenager, accompanying my dad to the vicarage in Shirebrook to sit with a group of men debating the niceties of New Testament doctrine. A different kind of religion, of course, but my ego was boosted by a similar intellectual pride in belonging to such a clever cartel. No one touched on anything personal. We were there to concentrate on higher issues, and we sat back on our Marxist sofas, as the vicar's men had relaxed in their Christian ones, and put the Western world to rights.

What struck me immediately about Allon was his intellectual generosity. While many of the faculty at UEA seemed reluctant to share ideas, as if they were in short supply and could be pilfered, Allon never succumbed to such pettiness. He behaved as if he were tapped into an infinite wealth, confident that whatever knowledge he gave away would be returned a hundredfold. He was profligate with ideas, his latest reading and enthusiasms spilling out of him unstinted.

Stuart Hall, who had supervised Allon's M.A. at Birmingham, talked later of his 'generous, branching intelligence,' his 'rich sense of humour', the breadth of his reading, the subtlety of his critical sensibility, his 'passionate intellectual curiosity.' This exuberance was part of Allon's appeal. He was full of zest and sap, not only with learning but in all areas of life.

According to my journal, the final Marxist reading group took place in the summer of 1978, in the midst of a hectic week in June, perhaps the closest I came to something from Malcolm Bradbury's novels. On Monday evening, 'we were all at the Sainsbury Centre for Angus Wilson's farewell do, a late and alcoholic night'; on Tuesday, 'I worked madly on my thesis but work is getting less coherent'; that same evening 'had meal out at French restaurant with Nicholas Brooke (another, older lecturer), and was plied with brandy at his house but at 4 a.m. managed to escape home in a taxi'; on Wednesday, 'worked on thesis all day' before hosting the Marxist group at College Road. 'So tired, I can barely concentrate, yet feel I must reorient to Marxist scene and understanding... All this theory about the human being as a liberal construct, the human subject having ceased to exist. How on earth, then, am I to learn to become one?'

That night, after the others had left, Linda Gillman stayed behind. We both felt uncomfortable at not studying any women writers and lamented the lack of female theorists.

'Even here,' Linda said, 'the feminine is out on a limb.'

Then the doorbell went. Allon had returned. He'd driven Logie Barrow back to Thomas Elsässer's, where they were both lodging. 'But I couldn't bear to stay in on a lovely summer's night like this.'

Linda soon left to cycle home, and when I came back into the lounge Allon was standing, waiting.

'The real reason I came back,' he said, 'is that I want us to be lovers. I've wanted to say so for quite some time.'

I was shocked. This wasn't on my agenda. Not that Allon was unattractive. He was slim, dark haired, with a contagious laugh behind his neat moustache. But he was a long way from my craggy Ted Hughes ideal. I hesitated, wondering what to do, when Allon moved forward and kissed me. And as I tasted his vivacity and passion, I suddenly sensed the possibility of a more than walk-on part in life. Moments later the doorbell rang to reveal a stranger telling us Linda had sailed over her bike's handlebars at the bottom of the hill and an ambulance was on its way. We rushed with her to Norwich hospital and by the time we'd checked X-rays and settled Linda back home in bed, it was nearly midnight. But the closeness to hospitals and mortality only made the passion sweeter.

In the reading group, one of the texts we'd studied was Wilhelm Reich's *The Function of the Orgasm*. Now, as we made love in my mocha chocolate bedroom, with its Victorian brass bed and framed Chagall print on the wall, we joked how many orgone boxes we could fire up. We had no desire for sleep, and when I confessed I often went to the coast in the early morning, we drove north to Overstrand, standing in the chill air as light returned over the North Sea. I can still see the grey-green waves breaking beneath an orange-tinted sky, hear the gulls cawing as they wheeled overhead. We stopped to marvel at huge rhododendron bushes in full bloom, as if the purple pink flowers were the first things in creation. Like others newly in love, we felt we'd crossed the threshold into another realm, where all the love poems in the world suddenly made sense, and we couldn't stop quoting them to each other. *And now good morrow to our waking souls,/ Which watch not one another out of fear;/ For love all love of other sights controls,/ And makes one little room an everywhere.*

When I visited Linda later that day, she was appalled by the news.

'He's married,' she said. 'Or did that fact escape you?'

I must have known, in a vague way, of Allon's wife, but he'd never mentioned her. He spent so little time in Cambridge, I wasn't even sure they lived together. Anyway, the fact of George Barker's marriage had not stopped Elizabeth Smart from falling in love.

'He's using you,' Linda persisted, 'incorporating you into his system. Why do you think he's left it till the eleventh hour? To the end of his contract, when he's about to leave Norwich and go back to Cambridge? It's safe for him. You're an adjunct, an extra bit of pleasure before he leaves.'

When I shared with Allon what Linda thought of his behaviour, for a few hours he was sheepish. But he could never be subdued for long. He told me he wasn't happy in his marriage, that they weren't physical any more. ('That's what they all say,' Linda scoffed). His wife wasn't an academic and what he craved was a sparring partner, an intellectual equal who would keep him in the fast lane. I was to be Beatrice to his Benedick, Simone de Beauvoir to his Jean-Paul Sartre. He seemed proud to be in public with me. He insisted we invite Malcolm and Elizabeth Bradbury to College Road for dinner, had me cook the best food for them, buy the best wine. He was unabashed by any moral qualms; he needed to be public, visible.

The only photograph I have of us together is from a weekend when we rented a cottage in rural Norfolk, but for all the beauty around us, we barely went out. We were obsessed with each other. 'You've got me,' he said. 'I'm yours.'

In the photo, we're standing on a patio with a large garden behind us. I'm wearing pale blue cord dungarees and a white shirt Linda had bought for me. Allon has one arm draped casually over my shoulders, a smile of irrepressible joy on his face. He always looked cheerful, jubilant even, his sense of humour one of the most irreverent I've ever encountered, aware of life's absurdities but never overwhelmed by tragic circumstance.

He split his time between Norwich and Cambridge and on each return visit, Allon would dip into his briefcase for books he'd bought for me at Heffers'. A beautiful facsimile of a 17th century edition of Donne's poetry; Norman O. Brown's paperback *Life against Death*; Roland Barthes' *A Lover's Discourse*, charting the various stages of rapture, blindness, illusion and disillusion that mark the progress of 'love'. Later, having discovered we both loved George Barker, he gave me hard-back first editions of his poetry.

The pleasure of the text rivalled the pleasure of the sex and with both we were in ecstasy. Allon was a great conversationalist and though we talked mainly about books and ideas, he was not the total highbrow I'd imagined him. He read fiction voraciously, especially women writers – Fay Weldon, Beryl Bainbridge, Elaine Feinstein – and loved reading out loud to me. My father had read books to me as a young child in bed, so I felt especially nurtured as Allon and I lay curled together on the blue chaise longue at College Road, beneath a poster from a recent Millais exhibition which showed a girl reaping. He read to me the whole of Ursula Le Guin's *Earthsea* trilogy, then *84 Charing Cross Road*. We laughed at the funny bits, wept at the moving bits, Allon's quickness to humour and tears quite at odds with the ambitious, intellectual persona he presented at UEA.

Just before the end of term, he put on at the university a short play he'd written, a fast-moving satire set in a supermarket, and I remember my excitement at his energy, my envy at his unstoppable confidence. He went to great lengths to drive up his piano from Cambridge to donate it to a charity which would make good use of it. It was this generosity and passion for life, so at odds with my life-denying upbringing, which most drew me to him.

'*Lustleben*,' he said. 'Why don't we have a word for it like the Germans do? *Lust for life* just doesn't carry the same intensity.'

Enthusiastic about his own research and endlessly encouraging of mine, Allon urged me to complete my D.Phil. thesis and I wrote it at breakneck speed that summer. It wasn't difficult, the notes and research were already there, it was simply a matter of weaving things together. This was the time before computers; a near illegible hand-written manuscript went in chunks to the school typist, who, apart from turning 'fantasy' into 'factory' and 'divided self' into 'divided serf', produced a perfect text.

Later that year, in a strange combination of the different strands of my life, Allon, my mother and I stayed together in the Mill House in Low Tharston, house-sitting while the Thwaites were on holiday. Mum, flattered to be asked and efficient in execution, had been persuaded to make use of her long-distant secretarial training to help sort the hundreds of footnotes to my thesis, while Allon arranged the extensive bibliography. We made a strange trinity – my mother, my lover, myself – kneeling on the floor of the beautiful Mill House lounge, with hundreds of sheets of paper strewn around us, beneath shelves housing Anthony Thwaite's collection of antique bellamine jars.

Although Mum was unable to listen or empathise (Linda Gillman said she had never met such a narcissist: 'she's incapable of real dialogue with the *other*'), she liked to talk to a captive audience. Now, in the evenings after our day-long labours, ignoring me entirely, she talked endlessly *at* Allon with her stories of the Second World War. The ancient mariner tale which needed repeated airing centred on her younger brother: what a wonderful man he was, how he gave her away at her wedding, what a tragedy it was to lose him when he died from emphysema after serving in Pompeii in 1944. I always felt she was less in love with my father than with this idealised lost brother (she named my own brother after him), and the story was endlessly replayed. Allon indulged her beautifully, never betrayed boredom, smiled frequently and asked the perfect questions to keep stoking my mother's unquenchable monologue.

When Adam had come to stay that summer, we'd again spent time with Barbara and Allan Smith and their children. We took them all to the north Norfolk coast, to the beautiful flat sands at Holkham, where I caught sight of Chris Bigsby, building the most impressive castle on the beach for his children. Adam was now seven, remarkably stalwart and unquestioning of my unpredictable life. That autumn I took him down to Cambridge so he could meet Allon, who was decorating his house, painting a bathroom ceiling. Of course, there is nothing so gullible as a woman in love. Despite all the evidence, I still persuaded myself Allon meant the promises he kept repeating about leaving his wife, and just needing the right moment to tell her. But when I noticed that, with Adam, Allon was polite but lukewarm, not really engaging, I drove back to Norwich flat and depressed. Why would I draw Adam along into a relationship that wasn't one? Why would I let him be ignored? I might deceive myself, but Adam deserved better.

Looking back, I realise that psychoanalytic theories of our 'being in love' state are probably right. What we fall in love with is more often than not our projection, some missing part of ourselves that we are trying to find in the other. Allon (and other men I've loved since) embodied aspects of myself I had not yet realised: a strength, power, ebullience, ('masculine') ability to negotiate the world, that I then lacked. At the time, I simply envied his abilities and longed to absorb them by osmosis: the way he could leap from one achievement to another, with an assured sense of entitlement, lacking any of the self-doubt that plagued me and held me back. Impatient when I was diffident about my own success, he often told me how important it was not to hide one's light under a bushel and, perhaps influenced by his time in Paris, he frequently lamented the English habit of excessive modesty.

'The French have two words for pride,' he reminded me. '*Orgueil* and *fierté*. *Orgueil* is the seventh deadly sin kind, closer to false pride and vanity. But *fierté* is a seemly pride, dignity, a due sense of self-esteem, the opposite of false modesty. This is what the English lack. We're meant to enjoy our achievements, to celebrate our success.'

With this kind of philosophy, it wasn't surprising Allon was alienated by my failure to put myself forward and my increasingly low moods. He hated illness of any kind and depression especially he found anathema, responding – as many did – with contempt, as if darkness was something a strong human will and right thinking could readily banish. For Allon, depression was a waste of time and human potential, threatening to pull him back from what he felt was his due: life at its fullest and most shining.

When he arrived at College Road to find me lying on the lounge floor in front of the gas fire, he took my low mood as a personal affront.

'What's got into you?' he asked crossly.

'I'm not feeling well,' I said. 'My asthma's really bad. I spent most of the night awake, unable to breathe. Maybe it's the damp. But sometimes I just can't bear being without Adam. When I do finally manage to fall asleep, I wake from dreaming about him and the loss is unbearable. I can't bear being without you either. I feel paralysed with sadness.'

But this woman was not the feisty intellectual equal Allon craved and had put energy into fostering. Had he driven all the way from Cambridge for this lethargy?

'I'm not here to be your doctor,' he snapped. 'I'm not looking for a patient.'

The exact chronology of our contact after he left Norwich is muddy in my memory, though Linda's original forecast was proving right, as an age-old plot of seduction and betrayal moved steadily towards its denouement. I was too blinded by love and a desperate longing to see any of this clearly enough to extricate myself at the time. What I remember are meetings planned and cancelled, Allon's impulse to see me squashed as appointments in Cambridge took over. He was now back at Trinity College as a research fellow, and enjoyed recounting menus of the multi-course dinners he had there.

I would wait in for his promised arrival, excited as always at the prospect of time together, only for the hope to vanish with a thirteenth-hour phoned apology. On the occasions Allon did drive over, the miraculous joy at our togetherness was harder to find. It became a predictably vicious circle. The brevity and infrequency of his visits increased my feelings of loss; my bereft state made me less and less the woman he desired; and as his equivocation increased, and he retreated still further, so the more lost and abandoned I felt.

Linda too, now her contract was over, had returned to Cambridge and after the intimacies we'd all shared, I felt orphaned, all my closest human connections gone. My thesis was finished, but no new project had yet entered to fill the gap. In the autumn, I went up to York for my D. Phil. *viva*, stayed overnight with Penny Florence and next day sailed through the interview with external examiner Gillian Beer, who was generous with her praise. But though I now had the title 'Doctor', and a navy hardback copy of my thesis would henceforth gather dust in York University library, I felt little sense of victory. It was the exactly the same as it had been with the other milestones in my academic career – A-Levels, first degree – as if the external success simply exacerbated the inner sense of emptiness and lack of self-worth it was meant to bolster, and I sank into ever greater darkness. But Plath-like despair was not something Allon had signed up for and he wanted none of it. His visits grew less, love's visitations declined, and I grew ever more bewildered why the love he'd evoked, and claimed he wanted, was now spurned.

I turned for help to the counselling service on campus. In my first year, I'd been to Paris to attend a residential workshop with Carl Rogers, the founder of person-centred counselling. A handful of us went from Norwich, including Brian Thorne, subsequently professor of counselling at UEA. We were among nearly two hundred international delegates, who arrived to find the conference in Paris had no planned activities. Out of this nothingness, we were meant to evolve our own timetable. It took two days to shape the inchoate hours into meaningful structure, by when it was nearly time to go home anyway. I should have known from this that person-centred work wasn't entirely for me. But it was the only free option on offer, and now, feeling my heart was breaking over Allon, let alone permanently splintered over Adam, I began seeing one of the counsellors working under Brian Thorne.

M was a kind, deep-feeling man, well-meaning and sincere. He followed the tenets of Rogerian counselling to the letter, rarely stalling in the required 'unconditional positive regard'. I had nothing against Carl Rogers' philosophy, indeed I was immensely grateful to have somewhere to go and talk each week, to unburden myself. But it soon became clear to me that person-centred counselling would have a struggle unravelling my knotted psyche.

Early on, I took to M a dream in which my mother died. She was in the shower and I was walking across the room towards her and found her dead on the white tiled floor. When I recounted this dream to M, wanting him to hear the huge relief, if not triumph, at being released at last from her sinister presence, he looked at me with some reproach.

'But you don't really want your mother to die, do you?'

For M this was a rhetorical question, and I felt disappointed. Of course

I wanted the old witch to die. Hadn't I also shared a recurrent dream of seeing a full breast sliced open to reveal thick black jelly instead of a mother's milk? What I needed was help to get rid of this dark mothering. Why else was I pacing across the concrete walkway to M's office every week?

But it would take years, and the depth of a more psychoanalytic approach, before I understood that what I wanted to die, to see the end of, was not my literal biological mother, but an internalised symbolic version of her: the figure who had become so oppressive and sadistic in my inner world, whose hostility drove me to long for suicide and its oblivion. How else to be rid of that oppressive demonic figure who *was* me? But at that time the two figures – literal and symbolic mothers – were still inseparable for me; indeed, they remained so, sadly, virtually until my real mother's actual death thirty years later.

The Rogerian counselling with M never addressed this intra-psychic complexity which had me in such a tangle of despair. We never discussed the body at all. Food, sex, violence, all visceral things, seemed out of the frame of Rogerian 'niceness', as if unconditional positive regard could be sustained only by keeping bad blood off the map. But then, if M had been a rigid psychoanalyst, what came next – an event which changed my life forever in ways I had neither consciously sought nor foreseen – could not have happened.

I was in the windowless women's loos in the EAS building, applying a careless streak of lipstick, when a student I'd not seen for a year walked in.

'Eileen!' I said. 'How great to see you again! How are you?'

Eileen, an Irish redhead with tumbling pre-Raphaelite curls and freckled skin, had been a student on my Feminism and Fiction module.

'I've not been well, actually,' she said. 'I've had hepatitis. But I'm so glad to bump into you. I was going to leave you a note.' She paused. 'Would you come to my wedding?'

'*Wedding?*' Eileen had been one of the more outspoken feminists.

'I know! I can't believe it either. Me! A renegade Catholic, advocate of women's rights! We're getting married next month. You will come, won't you?'

'Well...' What would I be, a skeleton at the feast? But I was very fond of Eileen and agreed.

'The other thing,' she went on, pausing even longer, '... he's a Muslim. It'll be a Muslim wedding.'

I had no idea what this meant.

'His name's Abdullah. He used to be called Nigel. And I'll be Nefissa.'

Curiouser and curiouser.

I drove to the wedding, about an hour north of Norwich, one fine Saturday afternoon, crisp and sharp. It was held in a village hall which was being used as a school by a group of Muslim converts, mostly American and English, who'd set up a small community nearby. I parked on the edge of a verge, made my way to the school hall and pushed open a pair of double doors.

The hall was already full with a few dozen people, but there were no chairs. Apart from two middle-aged couples, presumably parents of the bride and groom, conspicuously uncomfortable as they perched on a window ledge in their well-pressed conventional suits, everyone was standing and dressed in robes. But what struck me, the moment I opened the swing doors, was something – as palpable as fragrance in the air – that I could only describe as a rush of love: love as I'd never encountered it before. Love that was fully human yet at the same time something more, an unconditional love that words could not convey. This love was larger than any one person in the room, yet it felt anchored through them all, as if each one had caught the fire of divine love (what else could it be?) by contagion.

Nothing changed visually, there was no unexpected light, but it was as if everyone in the room had been caught up in a cyclone of unfathomable love that now marked them. I knew nothing at all about Islam at the time, I didn't even know the name. But as my eyes travelled to the children's art on the walls: mystical scenes of night skies, stars and crescent moons, then back to the women and men moving round the floor in their loose robes, I felt I was privy to a way of seeing, of being, of loving that I hadn't known existed. It was like discovering a new dimension. Even in my many years of Christian devotion until I left home, I'd never experienced such inner tenderness before, a kind of quiet rapture, a conscious serenity. I felt as if I'd found the threshold to heaven; as if, after prolonged exile in the desert, I'd at last stumbled on an oasis and could kneel and drink my fill.

Eileen/Nefissa, her glorious red hair covered now, arrived with another bride for their joint weddings. Someone read Arabic prayers from the Koran, followed by music from harmonium, tabla and drone, incense burning, more prayers. When the ceremony was complete, the men (yes, men) brought in a banquet on large collective plates: lamb, spiced vegetables, exquisite sweet dishes, dates, non-alcoholic drinks. We all sat on the floor to share the food. There was neither cutlery nor individual crockery, we simply ate with our fingers from the large dishes. And after months, years, of trying not to eat, trying to starve myself into the requisite female ideal, suddenly I was hungry, famished, and relished every mouthful. A woman sitting near me introduced herself as Irene. Audibly American, she told me her first marriage had collapsed when her husband, in the pop music industry, started screwing around. Now she'd converted to Islam and was about to marry a man from the community.

'I could only marry a Muslim now.' She eyed me curiously. 'You're not happy, are you?'

Well, I thought, it hardly needs the CIA to detect that.

'Al Ar's calling you,' Irene said. I was about to ask her who Al Ar was when she moved away, and another woman, conspicuously beautiful even in her *hijab*, took her place. Her body had the kind of grace I'd always wanted to emulate: upright, serene, dignified, sexy, sacred, confident, fluid, all at the same time. Her deep set eyes were lined with dark kohl, her exquisite lips and skin didn't need make-up, her Persian profile strong and perfect. She asked how I knew Nefissa, and as I explained I'd taught her, she too leant towards me, reading my face.

'You look sad,' she said. 'You have a lovely face, but very sad. You need Allah. You need God. Allah is calling you.' Ah, I thought, so that's who Al Ar is: God Almighty. And as we stood up, Irene in her elegant loose robe and *hijab*, me with my embarrassingly over-tight clothes and ragged shoulder length hair, I guessed this was how Mary Magdalene must have felt, newly arrived from walking the streets into a crowd of piety.

I'd gone for Eileen's sake, fully expecting to feel sorry for her as she regressed from being an independent free-thinking woman to someone shackled by two repressive ideologies: first marriage, then Islam. Islam!! I had no idea what it really was, but I knew it would be as suspect as Christianity to the likes of Allon and my UEA colleagues. 'God is dead. Religion is the opiate of the masses.' But as I drove my gold VW Beetle along the country roads back to Norwich, trying not to lose the miraculous feel of the gathering, I felt only one thing: envy.

When I unlocked the red front door of College Road, I regretted being in between lodgers. The lounge felt cold and hollow, the lecture papers on the long wooden table scattered like dead leaves. On the shelves were books I'd once coveted. Now I suddenly felt guilty about the trees felled to make them. I couldn't sit on chairs, they were too uncomfortable. I wanted only cushions on the floor. And in the kitchen, the metal cutlery looked like weapons. I ate supper with my hands. For the rest of the weekend I felt as if I'd stepped into another world and couldn't get back to the old one; all I possessed seemed to have been emptied of its previous meaning and was seeking something new.

It was the same when I went back to campus on Monday morning. I felt I'd been turned inside out. I stared at the shelves of books in my office, trying to remember what they were for. When I opened one, I started reading it backwards, as if it should have been an Arabic text where the pages went from back to front and the lines from right to left. I looked out through the window. Armies of men were marching from the car park to the Registry like a scene from John Cleese, his Ministry of Silly Walks. Chris Bigsby was hurrying along the walkway as if he was on ginseng. If we were in a Muslim country, I mused, they'd all be wearing floor length robes. If Al Ar was God, then perhaps he was calling them too. He. At the wedding, God was definitely a he. But where did this fit with my feminism?

'God doesn't have to be conceived of as male,' Linda would say. 'That's man's projection.'

Allon would be even more scathing. 'God doesn't have to be conceived at all. That's human projection.' And once his voice was in my head, I couldn't get rid of it. 'You've seen *The Stepford Wives*. It's like that. They're religious robots. They brainwash you. It's a conspiracy. They're mostly Americans, you said? Think Moonies. They want to replace your hard-won reason by dogma. Don't trust it. Don't forget how hard you've fought to get where you are. Don't you want to think for yourself? Don't you want to be yourself any more?'

But I couldn't let a mere pronoun snag me. Something irrevocable had happened that Saturday afternoon and now I wanted what that group had, what Eileen/Nefissa had. That tenderness. That heaven.

At my next counselling session with M, I told him the details of the wedding and its effect on me: how a lid had been taken off a hunger I hadn't known was there, how the usual manhole cover wouldn't fit back on.

'So the upshot of it is,' I concluded, 'I've decided to become a Muslim.'

M's face lost its Buddha-like beam.

'I want what they've got,' I repeated. 'There was a feeling in that room

I've never known. I can't go on living like this. I come back to campus and it's all sterile. Meaningless. I'm in an academic rat race.'

'Do you...' M paused. 'Do you know how Muslims treat women?'

'They looked pretty happy to me,' I said.

'If they divorce, for example, the man gets the children.'

'Ah.' I raised my eyebrows. 'You're forgetting my history.'

'But... you're a feminist.'

'I hope I always will be. But look how it's being interpreted. Power dressing, high heels... the illusion of newness, but still having to spout the same nonsense as men. It's not changing how gender is actually lived. It's not about men learning to be more feminine. It's about women becoming honorary men.'

I looked round at the breezeblock walls of M's office, the calendar, the photo of a man sitting on the ground beneath a tree. 'Maybe this is why I had to come to Norfolk,' I reflected. 'Not to be a successful academic. But to convert to Islam. I shall go and see Nefissa's teacher.'

M looked non-plussed. 'You really are seriously thinking of –'

'I am,' I insisted. 'You know how depressed I've been. I've got to find something worth staying alive for. Something worth following.'

M seemed to be carefully weighing options, casting around for a way to save me from my recklessness. 'Look,' he said at last, 'before you make a final decision, why don't you explore some other spiritual perspectives? Islam isn't your only option.'

'Don't suggest Christianity. Please. Christian mysticism's OK, but I can't stand the church. I did eighteen years of it.'

'No, I was thinking...' M hesitated. 'Well... I have regular meetings at my house... about an Indian teacher. You might find it interesting.'

I'd worked with M long enough by now to know he observed all the boundaries and ethics. He wouldn't break the counselling rules and invite me to his house unless he thought the situation exceptional.

'I don't know,' I said. This wasn't the first time in our sessions I felt I'd brought a tempest into a room used to dealing with fair weather. Was this 'Indian teacher' another way of trying to quieten my despair, of deflecting the terrible storm?

I had no intention of going to M's that Sunday at all. But it had been another long weekend missing Adam, no contact from Allon, a time of inventing tasks, going for walks, seeing other people with their kids, feigning interest in the Sunday papers. In the early evening, I found myself cycling to Earlham Road, climbing the path to the redbrick house where M lived with his artist wife Caroline, crossing the Persian carpet, settling on the floor with my back to one of the cream sofas in the lounge. A tall avocado plant filled the bay window and the walls were covered with Caroline's paintings, the large diamond shape canvas opposite me a Bridget Riley look-alike with red and blue stripes.

Not knowing the handful of people in the room, I felt shy without my academic role to protect me. M told us he was going to play a video with background music by Pete Townshend of *The Who*: a film called *Parvardigar*, edited shots of M's spiritual teacher; Townshend too, apparently, followed him. M pressed the play arrow. And a slight man in a faded pink coat over a white sadhra walked across the screen, lithe and quick for all his limp, against a backdrop of cultivated Indian gardens in full sun – Guruprasad, Pune, 1962.

Within seconds of first seeing that moving figure, my life changed irrevocably. It was the same feeling I'd had when Adam was born, of love unexpectedly flooding into the world; the same feeling I'd had during the Muslim wedding, that sudden blossoming of unconditional love; except these loves were now magnified a thousand-fold. Logic told me I'd never seen this man before, but he was someone I instantly recognised, someone who evoked a love greater than I could imagine. No one needed to tell me anything. I knew I'd come upon a being who embodied the greatest love, truth, purity and beauty I could conceive.

The film continued with images from different phases of his life. Some were prior to whatever accident caused the limp, for in younger shots he was walking swiftly, as if on water, his feet barely touching the ground. In some of these, his long hair was loose, but mostly it was tied back and plaited. His eyes were endlessly animated, one minute full of mischief, the next serious, even pained, as if he endured more suffering than the world could hold. Then he was smiling again, his face emanating compassion. What shocked me was the sense of intimacy, as if we were the oldest companions who had just re-found each other. But most of all I was struck by the exquisite beauty of his human form and I could hear John Donne's words: *If ever any beauty I desired and got, 'twas but a dream of thee...*

Silence enveloped the room as the video ended. Everything in the world seemed to have changed, to have revealed itself as total illusion compared with the figure we'd just seen. I had no idea what his teachings were, I'd barely registered his name. But, again with a sense of shock, I realised that I loved him utterly, that I'd fallen irreparably in love in a way I never had before, that even the experience with Allon was no real competition for this, but its foretaste, the start and preparation for something so much larger.

I wondered if everyone in the room felt the same way. No one said much. How utterly bizarre. Were we all in love with the same man? What a strange notion. But I didn't really care. You only had to glance at that face, those eyes, to know he had love enough to spare.

I cycled the short distance home in a daze, went to bed and set the alarm. For years I'd not slept well or easily and for some time I lay absorbing the evening's film and its impact on me. My bedroom fronted College Road and, when I switched off the light, the few street lamps were a pale glow filtering through chinks round the floral curtains my mother had made. But tonight, as I lay there, as awake as ever, the darkness began to shrink and the room became preternaturally bright. A light, diffuse, ineffable, white-gold, had appeared in the centre of the room, small at first but spreading steadily outwards until it engulfed me in its radiance. It was shaped in a sphere, like a huge sun or star, so beautiful, I barely dared breathe.

What followed was how people often describe a Near Death Experience, but I was alert, fully conscious throughout, still aware of the room, the sound of occasional cars. Slowly, the light expanded until it enfolded me. Or, rather, it absorbed me so I wasn't looking at the light but had become it. Not that I had ceased to exist, though on one level I had, but somehow my identity was no longer limited to my small human self. I expanded into the light, or it expanded me into itself, and I understood, or rather experienced, that this light was simultaneously all existence. I felt no longer differentiated from the rest of the universe, but caught up in the love, the unity which the light carried, embodied, and which I too now tasted, carried, embodied. Words are useless to convey all this. Even the usual terms radiance, brilliance, ecstasy, bliss, fail to capture the luminosity, the profound love, unconditional love, joy, the beauty of being inside, no, of actually *being* the light. I was aware I was still conscious, but I felt simultaneously suspended outside time, expanded beyond my body and mind, suddenly knowing myself to be both human and infinite and eternal.

The light was so perfect, the bliss so complete, the love so unconditional, I wanted it never to leave. This was the home I'd always been seeking. I wanted to live in it forever. But gradually the intensity started to fade, and the more tightly I tried to hold on, the more elusive it became. I had no idea how much time had passed. When I eventually checked the alarm, it was 2 a.m. The experience probably lasted between one and two hours, but I took it to be a seal on what had happened earlier that evening: a visitation from love itself to confirm the rightness of this particular spiritual path for me, a sign that it would take me home. The guide on this path, Meher Baba, the man in the video, I took then, and still take, thirty-eight difficult years later, to be an embodiment of divine love. I was resolved to follow wherever he might lead.

I knew this would make me a new kind of madwoman in the eyes of my secular colleagues, an unfashionable heretic. Like all the new universities, UEA favoured materialist thinking. I was working in the very epicentre of secular culture; Nietzsche's famous boast that 'God is dead' was sustained through a long line of intellectual denial in the so-called 'Masters' of modern thought – Chomsky, Freud, Sartre, Heidegger – even up to Angela Carter's contemporary motto, 'Nothing sacred'. I knew it would be unwise to share this unexpected revelation with my peers; even sharing it in this memoir (Oh *Guardian* readers!) makes me vulnerable to scorn and cynicism from Richard Dawkins think-alikes. ('How can someone as intelligent as you believe in *God*? Let alone follow a *guru?*') One friend urged me to exclude the explicit spiritual story from my memoir. 'It's not fashionable. It's not new. It will make people think you're flaky.' But my inner experiences, that precious night and in the months and years following, were too strong for doubt. As Jung answered, when asked if he believed in God, 'I don't believe. I *know*.'

Life would never be the same again. I'd crossed a threshold and could never travel back, no matter how uncomfortable or unpopular it made me. From that Sunday night onwards, after so many years of staunch devotion to the intellect, I was being offered a new way of knowing. A way of unknowing. A glimpse of that same Love which Dante invokes at the end of the Divine Comedy: *L'amor che muove il sole e l'altre stele*. The Love which moves the sun and the stars.

13

The Gretchen Question

The conflict of faith and scepticism remains the proper,
the only, the deepest theme of the history of the world
and mankind, to which all others are subordinate.

Johann Wolfgang von Goethe

OVER THE NEXT FEW MONTHS, I read extensively about Meher Baba's life and work. As well as the meetings in Norwich, I went to Twickenham where, alongside his recording studios, Pete Townshend had set up Oceanic, a London centre for Baba gatherings. Here I met Adi K. Irani, Baba's secretary since 1944. Everything I discovered confirmed what my intuition had told me about Baba's purity and selflessness.

Born into a Zorastrian family in Pune, 1894, as Merwan Irani, he'd had a conventional education and loved English poetry, Shakespeare and Shelley in particular. Then, in 1913, Hazrat Babajan, a female mystic or 'Perfect Master', reputed to be one hundred and twenty-two years old, living under a neem tree in Pune, kissed him on the forehead. He immediately entered a state of bliss, where 'all created things ceased to exist.' It was nine months before Merwan started sleeping and eating normally again, then several years of training with other 'Perfect Masters' to return fully to human consciousness while remaining simultaneously aware of infinite consciousness. A group of friends became followers, named him Meher Baba (Compassionate Father) and gradually his number of disciples grew. He had an equal number of male and female *mandali* (close ones), who shared his life of celibacy and renunciation and joined his early ashram at an old British army camp at Meherabad, in the Deccan plateau.

I was particularly struck by Baba's silence, which he began in July 1925 and maintained unbroken for the rest of his life, even in the midst of intense activity and travel. At first, he communicated through an alphabet board, later through his own language of hand gestures. The world, Baba claimed, has been given enough words, enough teachings; the time has come to live them. On his tomb slab at Meherabad, where he was interred in 1969, are engraved the words: 'I have come not to teach, but to awaken.' At his tomb shrine, he claimed, his presence would remain as strong as when he was in physical form, and would enable the same inner connection with him, for one hundred years following his death.

I felt I was rediscovering a language I didn't know I'd forgotten, connecting with my spiritual mother tongue. Ideas about karma and reincarnation, the ego and its dissolution, all made perfect sense. The impression I'd always had of the material world as a transparent, illusory realm, was no longer a mental aberration from my built-on-sand childhood, but the recognition of well-established spiritual truths: that this world *is* an illusion, and our task is to see through the deception to a reality beyond.

Even when I read about the details of Meher Baba's life and close ones, everything seemed familiar, mirroring what I somewhere, somehow, already knew. I didn't have to twist my mind to persuade it of anything. Baba had visited the West several times, including England and the U.S., making a special link with Sufism. A Sufi Order had been established in the States in 1910 by Hazrat Inayat Khan, whose successor as Murshida or leader was Rabia Martin, then Ivy O. Duce. Through Duce, Meher Baba instigated in 1952 a new Order called Sufism Reoriented. Its central tenets were love, longing for God, and selfless service.

Trying to share this new enthusiasm with my colleagues at UEA was, predictably enough, a mistake. The last thing they wanted was an Indian guru stirred in with their secular cocktails. When I told David Punter about my new-found love, he raised his eyebrows.

'But what did Meher Baba *do*? As far as I can see, he didn't actually *do* anything.'

'He served the poor,' I said. 'He renounced money and possessions. He embraced lepers and worked with the untouchables. He inspired Gandhi. They met on the Rajputana, when they were both travelling to England in 1931. Gandhi knew Baba's status. He asked to be one of his disciples.'

'*Gandhi* followed him?'

'No. Baba said it would mean giving up his connection with politics. And they both knew that wasn't possible. Gandhi's task was to liberate India.'

'Gandhi was right,' David said. 'If you abdicate politics, there's nothing left worth fighting for.'

When Linda Gillman read a couple of biographies of women who'd spent time with Baba, she admitted she envied my certainty, but couldn't share it. Penny Florence seemed to read my devotion to Baba as not only an intellectual lapse, but a betrayal of my feminism. A *guru? Male?* In fact, my over-frequent references to Meher Baba led her to forbidding me to utter his name in her presence and, as a result, our friendship died for several decades. But topping all this was Allon White's 's total disdain.

For Allon, my 'magical thinking' was not only an apostasy on my part, but an affront to his rational mind and ego. He was more interested in getting me to pay my dues to the gods of ambition and worldly success and couldn't understand why I hadn't immediately started turning my thesis into a book. I think he was more delighted than I was when, a couple of months after my doctorate was finished, the next rung on my career ladder appeared in the form of a book contract with Methuen. Janice Price, one of their senior editors, was on the hunt for 'bright young things' to write for their New Accents series, being overseen in Cardiff by Terence Hawkes. Janice arrived at my office door one day and offered to take me to lunch. A few minutes later, we were walking down the concrete walkways, past science labs, to the Sainsbury Centre for Visual Arts, which sat on a sloping site at the far end of campus.

Opened the year before, in spring 1978, and still shining with newness, the Centre was rightly hailed as something of a marvel, both for its architecture and for the art it housed. Norman Foster's first public building, it was a huge prefabricated structure, its factory-made parts assembled on site. I loved walking into the vast open space, the size of an aircraft hanger, filled with light and giving off a buoyant sense of transparency. I particularly admired the collection of artefacts from the ancient world: tribal art from Africa, Asia, the Pacific Americas, alongside modern art by Giacometti and Henry Moore. These were the objects I imagined in Freud's consulting room: primitive sculptures of the human figure given new meaning by their modern context.

'This place has really put UEA on the map,' Janice said.

'Yes. It's amazing Sainsbury's chose to put the collection here. It was something like three million for the building alone.'

Janice gave an ironic smile. 'That's why my groceries have gone up.'

A couple of hours and two glasses of wine later, I returned to my office having agreed I'd deliver a book for the New Accents series on fantastic narrative from Gothic fiction onwards. The advance of £1000 seemed to me generous, half on signature and half on delivery.

I wrote the book from start to finish in my first sabbatical term (ten weeks) in the autumn of 1979. I made sure I had no lodgers, and worked in the lounge at the long cedar table the Thwaites had given me. Feeling overweight – since Allon and Linda returned to Cambridge I'd been comfort eating – I existed for the three months it took to write the book on slimming biscuits (chocolate Limmits), cups of tea, glasses of gin and tonic (Slimline). I worked with a steely will, taking no exercise, barely seeing anyone. For twelve or more hours each day I sat there, ignoring my rumbling stomach and equally ravenous heart.

Allon was more excited than I was. Half the material for the book was adapted from my doctorate, but the rest was fresh, much of it injected from Allon's irrepressible bank of ideas and theory. Until then, I'd known next to nothing about Todorov, Julia Kristeva, Hélène Cixous, but suddenly I was bouncing around on their fashionable intellectual trampolines. Allon turned up on his next visit with Todorov's structural study of fantasy in his case, and as we walked to the park, he thrashed out a possible theoretical approach.

'What you need is a new phrase for the weird perspective found in the fantastic,' Allon said. 'Something that locates it alongside or behind the real. How about *paraxis?*'

We rushed back to College Road so he could draw a diagram, like something on an optician's wall, as if this conferred scientific veracity. I knew he'd recently read Fay Weldon's *Praxis*. Did the word slide, Edward Lear like, from there?

'You can draw on Todorov, but you need to extend his ideas.'

'I thought I'd use more psychoanalysis,' I said. 'Explore what the fantastic represents in terms of unconscious drives.'

'Yes. You need Julia Kristeva,' Allon went on. 'You could argue that the fantastic exists outside the social, in Kristeva's realm of the pre-symbolic. It's where culture breaks down into non-meaning, the 'non-thetic'. Which is why it can dissolve language and form.'

I knew this was where, more and more, Allon located me too: in the 'non-thetic,' a place that was not fully socialised. When I'd failed to attend a board meeting in the Registry, and evaded other important university events, Allon said, 'You know, you're the most a-social person I've ever met.' And while this wildness had initially been part of my attraction for him, it now turned into a source of frustration and difference.

Allon belonged very clearly in the social realm. He was a left-brain hero, ambitious to rise to the top of the academic hierarchy. But I was already slipping away from it, increasingly indifferent to its values. This made me perfectly equipped to write a book about a literary form which was on the edge. Fantasy writing was at a tangent: it evoked an underworld, a surreal and often unknowable landscape on the far side of the mirror.

Janice Price was thrilled when I sent her the manuscript. It needed no revisions. I helped choose the cover, a black and white reproduction of a painting by Hieronymus Bosch, his disturbing 'Garden of Earthly Delights'. And, knowing Allon's part in the book, I placed him along with Linda at the top of the Acknowledgements. The heavy weight of theory, that is both the book's virtue and vice, even its title and subtitle, *Fantasy: The Literature of Subversion*, would not have existed without him.

If I was expecting similar reciprocity in Allon's publications, I was mistaken. In 1981, the same year my book came out, Allon published *The Uses of Obscurity: The Fiction of Early Modernism*. This grew out of his own doctoral thesis, a study of George Meredith, Joseph Conrad and Henry James. We'd discussed it in detail, he'd read passages aloud and absorbed my comments. But I didn't figure in his Acknowledgements. Instead, a footnote mentioned my book, without pointing out the borrowed arguments. By the time I got a copy, we'd definitively broken up, and when I saw this omission, alongside the inclusion of eminent names more useful to his career, I became the woman scorned whose fury hell doth not contain. I opened the volume at random, found some text that was especially pretentious and, like a vengeful figure from one of Grimm's fairy tales, cut up the offending page with a large pair of kitchen scissors, then another, till much of the book lay in shreds. I had to buy another copy on Amazon to write this memoir.

Allon was to publish just one other book in his lifetime, *The Politics and Poetics of Transgression*, 1986, which he co-authored with his friend Peter Stallybrass. His collected essays *Carnival, Hysteria and Writing* appeared only posthumously in 1993, with an Afterword by Jacqueline

Rose. This also contained Allon's fragment of autobiography, 'Close to the Bone', written just before he died, also published in the *London Review of Books*. This personal piece referred back to the time he'd spent in Norwich, describing how he'd been sleeping badly and how, in his rented room at Elsässer's - the same room I'd had when I first came to Norwich - he used his insomniac hours to start writing a novel.

'It was when I was breaking up with my first wife. One night I was in my room at Norwich and, pained beyond endurance by the break-up, I suddenly began to write - in extremis, you might say... fast and fluently, pages of the stuff, and though my eyes were full of tears and I normally write with pedantic care and exquisite self-consciousness, this time a coherent story sprang from the end of my pen already formed...'

He'd shared some of this novel with me at the time: a double narrative, one strand set in the 17th century during the Civil War, about Nicodemus, a self-absorbed mystic; the other strand based in the late 1950s, about a hydraulics engineer engaged to drain the malarial swamps of the Sardinian coast. But Allon's account in 'Close to the Bone' makes the break-up of his marriage sound like a car accident coming out of nowhere, as if he was living as a monk in Elsässer's hermitage. All that happened between us has vanished. Indeed, this wasn't when his marriage broke up at all, for he subsequently went back to live with his wife and they had a child together. No wonder he openly confessed he didn't 'believe in biographies', and warned the reader to be 'especially sceptical' about his own.

Death is a strange rear window. I'm looking back now down a road more than thirty years long, with Allon dead for more than twenty of them. Yet even at this distance, I can feel his remarkable energy. I feel I've neither romanticised him nor invested him retrospectively with more life than he had. He did possess a rare exuberance, and its loss from my life seemed to take some of my own brightness with it.

Despite the difficult context and all our differences, our love and passion were hard to extinguish and our affair persisted, on and off, for some time after his return to Cambridge. But following my spiritual awakening, when Allon discovered my new inner path was there to stay, he became in turn disbelieving, scornful, outraged and, finally, rejecting.

Among the photographs I'd gathered of Meher Baba, one was an Indian postcard, tinted pink, stuck to the dark chocolate wall above my bed. It was a head and shoulders shot, Baba smiling above heavy garlands of rose and jasmine.

At first, as we were getting into bed, Allon made a joke of it.

'He looks like a cross between Gandhi and Salvador Dali,' he laughed. 'How do you know he's not a charlatan? I'm sure India has its fair share of false gurus.'

'Of course,' I agreed. 'But the existence of margarine and imitation spreads doesn't mean there's no such thing as butter.'

Allon looked at me as if I'd gone potty. Losing my brains to depression was one thing; losing them to an Indian master was so much worse.

'You're not who I thought you were, Dr Jackson. I never thought an intelligent woman like you would be following a guru. You know this is pure regression. Wishful thinking.'

'No,' I said. 'Just anti-Cartesian thinking. Less I *think therefore I am*... than I *am therefore I am*. Even I *am that I am*.'

I wanted it not to matter that we believed different things. Even with all the stops and starts of our relationship over the past few months, the physical ecstasy had not diminished. Our bodies knew each other well enough to pleasure each other, regardless of what was happening in the rest of our lives.

That night, though, it was different. For the first time since we'd become lovers, Allon was impotent. He was shocked, more disappointed than I was, and angry. After several vain attempts at being intimate, he switched the bedside lamp back on and gestured to the tinted postcard.

'It's this bloody picture,' he said. 'How can I be myself with that staring down at me? It goes against my whole belief system. I don't know how you can be so credulous. I've invested so much in helping you be successful and you just want to throw it all away. It's insane. You're going back to the dark ages.'

I glanced at the rose pink portrait. I should have taken it down before Allon came. But why apologise for my beliefs?

'He's brainwashed you,' Allon said.

'How could he?' I replied. 'He's not in the body any more.'

'Not in the – what kind of discourse is that? You mean he's dead.'

'If you must be crudely literal about it.... Yes, he's physically dead. *There are more things in heaven and earth, Horatio, than are dreamt of in your philosophy...*'

'You're worshipping a dead guru!' Allon's voice was thick with contempt. 'Isn't this a bit passé? The Beatles discovered the Maharishi a decade ago.'

'It can't be that passé,' I said. 'He's Pete Townshend's guru. Anyway, I'm not doing it because it's fashionable.'

'Well, let's hope it's a need you grow out of.'

'Don't be so patronising. I won't grow out of it. He's got me for life. Many lives, I hope, not just this one.'

'Good God!' Allon sighed. 'Who needs a glass ceiling, when there's this one in your head? And you're supposed to be a feminist! What *does* a woman want?'

'Look,' I said, and put my hand on his arm, 'this is just my path. It needn't impact on you, on us, at all.'

But I hadn't reckoned on Allon's male pride. 'It's got everything to do with me,' he said. 'You expect me to lie here making love while we're overseen by some supposed 'higher power'? An Indian Big Brother watching my every move?'

'I can't believe you're getting so incensed by a... a postcard.'

'If it's only a postcard to you,' Allon said, 'then kindly take it down. And we might be able to get on with making love.'

It would have been so easy to do. Pluck the postcard from the wall and hide it in the old chest of drawers. Why should I be attached to a bit of tinted paper? But something in me felt stubborn. I was tired of kowtowing to values in which I no longer believed.

'He's not going anywhere,' I said. 'It's non-negotiable. I'm not giving him up.'

'A projection? A father figure? You're happy to give away your own authority?'

I looked between them, these two different loves. Allon was all I wanted as a man. I'd loved him more than any other man in my life. Even with his prevarications and the hurt he'd caused me, I couldn't imagine wanting anyone more. The sex was perfect. The talk was inspiring. I loved the brilliance and passion for life he embodied. *Lustleben* indeed. But Meher Baba was, to me, of another order altogether: not only a manifestation of life but a link to its source and meaning. How could I explain what he evoked in me?

By now Allon was standing on the bed, still naked, waiting. 'You've got to decide,' he said. 'One of us has got to go. I mean it. It's either him or me. You can't have us both.'

Would I really run the risk of losing a man of such energy and brilliance for the sake of keeping a postcard stuck to the wall? A picture of someone I'd never met? Yet I heard myself speak without hesitation. 'You'd better pack your bags then.'

Allon looked at me in disbelief. Was this what he'd risked his marriage for? Was this the return for his generosity, for giving me so much?

'You can't be serious.'

'I've never been more serious about anything.'

'If you mean that,' he said slowly, 'you need to understand I won't be coming back. Not this time. Not at all. Be very careful.'

I looked again at the smiling face on the wall. I could almost smell the jasmine.

'I understand,' I answered, equally slowly. 'You'd better pack your bags.'

Within minutes, his books and belongings stuffed into a holdall, Allon was gone. I stayed in the bedroom, listening, as he pulled the front door firmly behind him. Then his car revved up and for the last time he drove away from College Road down the midnight route back to Cambridge. I didn't cry. I was too stunned. I almost wanted to laugh. I looked at Meher Baba again. How could a picture have such power? How did he manage it? Ousting one of the cleverest intellects in the country through a mere photo?

For the rest of the eight years between the end of our relationship and Allon's premature passing, we had little contact. The first was a phone call out of the blue one day, Allon's unmistakeable voice on the other end, full of jubilation. 'I'm a father! I've got a beautiful baby girl!' And when I calculated backwards, I knew Linda was right. I'd been a credulous idiot, an adjunct; even when we were together, marital relations had not been as sparse as Allon claimed.

Another time, when I was visiting Linda in Cambridge, I bumped into Allon in the street. His face lit up with unfeigned delight and he took me to see the gardens of Trinity Hall, where his favourite flowers, dark blue delphiniums, were in full bloom. He was unchanged, as buoyant and optimistic as ever, seeming to know nothing of the heartache I'd been through at losing him. Not that he was mean. He was far too curious about the world beyond him to be a narcissist. But he was ambitious, with a vaulting ambition that resented any attempt to slow him down.

In worldly terms, Allon got some of what he wanted. He nimbly climbed the rungs of the academic ladder – his doctorate, his first book, a lectureship at Sussex University. He gained international renown with his academic work, aligned himself with the big intellectual gurus: Derrida, Adorno, Gramsci, Foucault, Chomsky. He had visiting lectureships in the States. And when his first marriage did eventually break down irretrievably, he found a lovely second wife, also not an academic, a therapist, in Brighton. His professional reputation remained impeccable.

But by the time our paths crossed again at a conference in Oxford in the late 1980s, Allon was already fighting a losing battle with leukaemia. We absconded together from the conference to a quintessentially English tea shop and sat on opposite sides of the white clothed table. Who would have thought these smart professionals sipping their earl grey tea from willow pattern cups had once sweated their naked bodies into one?

Allon told me about the new research he was doing into tombs and memorials, and the visualisations he was practising to defeat the cancer.

'I'm the Emperor on the throne,' he said, 'and the white blood cells are rebellious subjects I'm banishing from the court.'

I wanted to remind him of the night he stood on my brass bed, trying to push away an Indian mystic. Had he learned nothing about the impotence of the ego?

He invited me down to Brighton for a weekend to meet his second wife, Jen. She was the perfect choice for him, bright and lovely. Allon told me how supportive his Sussex colleagues were, especially Jacqueline Rose. But none of them could help him win his 'battle'. I was living in Bristol by then, not far from the Cancer Help Centre run by Penny Brohn. And when conventional medicine and bone marrow transplants failed, Allon phoned to ask if he and Jen could come and stay with me while they visited the Centre.

'You'll have to do a major spring clean,' he said. 'The slightest infection and I'm done for.'

But they never made it. On 15 June 1988, while working in my study at home in Cliftonwood, at 11 a.m. I was suddenly overcome by an inexplicable feeling of nausea. I was too dizzy to stand. The whole room felt caught up in a vortex, as if a whirlwind was tearing into it. It was an hour or more before it subsided, a sickening sensation of something unravelling inside me, being wrenched away.

When I next phoned to find out how Allon was, Jen's voice on the answer machine said he'd passed away on 15 June, at exactly the time I'd had my bout of nausea. How, I wondered, would Allon account for that? Like me, he was thirty-seven. We were the same vintage.

First novels are often semi-autobiographical and when I started writing fiction in the early 1990s, I found myself returning again and again to the drama with Allon. I wanted to write a story about contemporary university life, not in the satirical vein of Malcolm Bradbury and David Lodge, but in a way which named the cost of ambition and academia both to women and to the 'feminine' side of the psyche. Logically enough, given my background, it took the form of an updating of the Faust myth.

Ever since Gay Clifford alerted me to its importance at Warwick, Faust, who sells his soul to the devil in return for infinite worldly knowledge and power, had been a major obsession. I wrote about the legend in undergraduate essays, then as part of my doctorate. I consumed all the major versions, from the original *Faustbook* in Germany in 1587, through Christopher Marlowe's haunting drama *Doctor Faustus – O Ile leap up to my God: who pulles me downe? See see where Christs blood streames in the firmament* – then Goethe's brilliant *Faust* of 1808 and Mann's 1947 masterpiece of a novel, *Doctor Faustus*.

Jung thought the Faust myth enacted a central dilemma of the human psyche: the battle between ego fulfilment (represented by a pact with the devil) and ego denial (represented by love). And I came to read it as a perfect parable of what was happening in modern academia: the way that lust for worldly success and renown can eclipse the values of love and simplicity. I invented the University of Wessex, a new campus set in rolling Dorset countryside near Abbotsbury, where a contemporary male scholar, my own fictional Dr Faustus, was ambitious, learned, prepared to push open heaven and earth to satisfy his appetite for life and the power that comes with knowledge. He was based on the figure of Allon, whom I also made into a brilliant jazz pianist, while I put myself into a young woman, based on Gretchen, whom Faust seduces, gets pregnant and betrays, scorning her for the simplicity of her affections and her religious faith. It was poetic licence, of course, to give Allon a demonic pact behind his worldly success. But for all his convivial manner and charm, a ruthless ambition did persist in him, one that his physical body, perhaps, could not sustain. (How he would have hated this reading of illness as metaphor).

It was Goethe who introduced the character of Gretchen into the myth. Goethe's Faust kills Gretchen's mother with a sleeping draught, then murders her brother, Valentine, when he tries to avenge Faust for Gretchen's illegitimate pregnancy. Gretchen, driven mad with grief when Faust leaves her, drowns her new-born baby, is imprisoned and sentenced to death. Faust offers to save her with a Mephistophelian pact of her own, but Gretchen, unable to deny her simple but strong faith, refuses the demonic deal.

The question she poses to Faust at this point became famously known in German as the *Gretchenfrage*, the Gretchen question, and can be seen as the whole crux of the play; indeed, Goethe saw it as the 'deepest theme' facing civilisation. What, Gretchen wants to know, are Faust's true values? Does he believe in God? Does he have any faith or love at all? 'Now tell me,' she asks, 'how do you take religion?'

Until I started writing my novel, Gretchen hadn't much preoccupied me. It was Faust who had been my main obsession. But now the young mother who had lost her child (the parallel to my own life is obvious), and whose faith gave no relief to her suffering (ditto), came to haunt me. Whenever I sat down to write, Gretchen was at my side, urging me to include her. I would see her through my study window, bending over the garden pond to search for the baby she'd drowned in her grief over Faust's neglect.

At first, I thought the story of my novel was simply an allegory born from the drama between Allon and me, and the different options we finally chose: the male academic whose ruthless ambition drives him to ever greater achievements and premature death, the young woman who stands for values of faith and the heart. Our scene in the bedroom at College Road, where the naked Allon gave me an ultimatum over Meher Baba, and I refused to betray my faith, I saw as our own version of the *Gretchenfrage*.

But as Gretchen entered my waking and sleeping hours, leading me in dreams through dark alleys and over narrow bridges to walls of old houses where some secret was kept, I slowly came to realise that the whole story could also be read as a parable for what had happened in my own psyche. Was I not also Faust, who had put scholarship and ambition before love? Had not I, too, effectively 'abandoned' my child for the fruits of worldly knowledge and success? Why else did the myth feel so peculiarly and painfully my own? Of course Gretchen kept pointing out to me the dreadful secret of the dead baby. Didn't I have a baby I'd left behind? Wasn't I haunted by frequent nightmares of Adam drowning?

I understood then that I found the Faust myth so powerful because it embodies a split between 'masculine' and 'feminine' sides of the self: the 'male' ego which puts ambition above love; the 'female' heart which puts love before ambition. Gretchen represents that side of the self which is not afraid to assert spiritual experiences, even if they are at odds with worldly success, and even though they do not remove human suffering. Faust, by contrast, represents the power and arrogance of the human will which likes to believe itself omnipotent.

In 1996, at a brilliant production of Goethe's *Faust* by the Royal Shakespeare Company, I found myself wishing contemporary faith was as straightforward as Gretchen's seemed to have been. If only I could find the same triumph: 'she is saved' (*sie ist garettet*). But I was still torn between the two worlds, ambitious to have my newly written Faust novel published, still wanting worldly success. It had a near miss with Penguin, but in the end they found it 'too harrowing': too serious for the popular zeitgeist of campus comedies or chick lit romance.

Sometimes I've fantasised about the lives we might have had in a parallel universe, if both our egos had enjoyed the success Allon envisaged for them: lives in which we became professors and got brilliant reviews in the *New York Review of Books*. I even fantasised that, in his state beyond the body, Allon might help get my novel published. It was about him, after all. But wherever he was now, doubtless such things no longer mattered. As it was, both our careers were prematurely dissolved, Allon's by death and mine by a kind of wilful embrace of 'failure', which he found so wasteful.

But without my plummeting into heartbreak over Allon, I may never have embarked on my spiritual path, certainly not in the absolute way I did. This has always struck me as ironic: that one of the legacies of such a complete atheist should be the opposite. Until I met Allon, my life, like his, was unashamedly in the service of the ego; but from then on, mad as it seemed to him and everyone else in that secular world, I embraced a path which deliberately seeks the ego's annihilation. Far from drawing me further towards the laurels and rewards of university life, my time with Allon levered me irrevocably away from them. As in a game of snakes and ladders, what had been my painstaking climb towards academic heaven changed through our connection into a slide downwards towards obscurity, one which I tried to invest with nobility by quoting Yeats to myself: *I must lie down where all the ladders start,/ In the foul rag and bone shop of the heart.*

Other human loves eventually came into my life, but the inner link with Allon was never completely severed. I remember our last phone call, in May 1988, a month before he died. Despite his illness, he listened to me generously and understood my depression in ways he never had when we were together.

'You were too wild a person for me,' he said, 'but I did love you. I love you still. You're an extraordinary woman, Rosie Jackson. You're powerful, beautiful, sexy, energetic. You've really lived. You must go on really living and writing. You must leave the negativity behind.'

On my desk I have still the few objects that carry Allon's presence: books of George Barker's poetry; a postcard of one of Picasso's ceramics inscribed, 'For my love at Christmas time'; a bloodstone pendant mounted on a silver chain, its dark green stone striated with one single vein of crimson –'the most expensive present,' Allon claimed, 'I've ever bought anyone'; a handwritten letter from his hospital bed, fighting till the end against a gentle surrender to that good night.

And here he is, in black and white, on the back cover of one his books newly arrived from Amazon: a jaunty hat, a light tie on a dark shirt, the wicked smile of a man filled with fun and *fierté*. A man who declares in every pore of his being, 'I am alive.'

14

A Walk-On Mother

I have given away my son,
And all the years of patience and of love...

The truth is, I gave away my son
Being young myself, having ambition

To enter a harder race. I was not wise,
And harnessed neither burden nor remorse.
I stumble from success on to reverse,
And even if I win, you are my loss.

John Wheway, 'Success'

ADAM WAS EIGHT OR NINE when the inevitable question landed on the table between us. Inevitable, yet even so I wasn't ready for it. We were in the lounge at College Road, sitting doing some art work, one of the few things I could think of to do together. Adam spoke casually, without actually looking at me.

'Why don't I live with you, Mum?'

I felt my heart stop, then race faster. The moment when the villain is caught: nowhere to run, no alibis.

'Everyone at school lives with their mum,' he went on. 'Why don't I live with you?'

From his point of view, it was the most obvious and essential question. From mine, the most impossible to answer. I wanted him to know, as if by magic, the ins and outs of the situation. Did he not remember, in his blood, what had happened when he was a child? How could I vindicate myself without damning his father? How could I protect his father without damning myself? I was panicking, but knew I must tread carefully, must only say what was true and loving. I wanted to say I'd always wanted him to live with me, ever since I took the tracks in the opposite direction. It was true, but I must be responsible, mustn't blacken his dad.

'It's complicated,' I began. 'Your dad and I weren't getting on, and we both wanted you with us. One of us had to lose, and,' I took a deep breath, '... it was me. It doesn't mean I don't love you or don't want you with me. We both love you very much.'

Still Adam didn't look at me. His hair was short, with a slightly longer lock at the front. Did Jan cut it for him?

'So I could live with you?' he persisted. 'If I wanted to?'

I felt like a river dammed up for years, suddenly given permission to flow. I wanted to run in all directions at once. Yes! Yes my darling, you can live with me forever if you want to. But I mustn't gush, mustn't make false promises.

'Well,' I said, 'in theory, yes, you could live with me. And of course I'd love that. It would be lovely. It's what I've always wanted. But we have to wait till you're old enough to decide properly. Perhaps in a few years' time, when you're a teenager, if you want to come and live with me, you can. We'd have to discuss it with your dad, of course. But I don't see why you can't choose what you want, when you're a bit older.'

Adam nodded at that and seemed satisfied. We had a hug, and the conversation changed. For a whole week after he'd gone, I allowed myself to almost enjoy the possibility of looking out on a different landscape: a future with Adam in it more fully, a teenage son in the house. How wonderful. I could be normal. I could have a life with my own child in it.

The following weekend I'd set aside for writing a lecture. On the Saturday morning I was late up, slobbing round the kitchen getting coffee and opening mail, when the front door bell rang. I slouched to it in my navy tracksuit, my tousled hair uncombed. There on the doorstep stood David, looking stern. I was rigid with fear.

'My God! What's happened to Adam?'

'Could I come in?'

'Is Adam alright?'

'Of course.'

I stepped aside to let David enter the narrow hall with its dado rail, white wallpaper below, magnolia walls above, ridged beige carpet. At the sound of footsteps upstairs – the current female lodger – David, perhaps assuming I had a live-in lover, raised his eyebrows.

'Did you drive here?' I wondered.

'How else?' My IQ fell to zero.

'Would you like a coffee?'

'No thank you.'

Now we were in the lounge, with its dark brown carpet. The previous owner had knocked the two front rooms into one and beyond the dining table, through the French windows at the back, grew white Japanese anemones beneath a straggling Schumacher tree.

'Do you want to sit down?'

'No.' And David proceeded in a solemn manner to deliver his speech, to the effect that I was never again to offer Adam the choice I'd mentioned the previous weekend, that he might one day live with me.

'But,' I said, unusually defiant, 'he *can* have a choice, when he's older.'

'No he can't,' David said. 'There's no choice. You made your decision, made your bed, and now you have to lie in it.'

'I don't see why he can't...'

'If you ever broach anything of that nature to Adam again, you will never see him again. Never. He's been in a terrible state all week, confused, wetting the bed... It's not a choice he is able to make.'

'No,' I agreed. 'Not now. But later, when he's older...'

'Not ever,' David repeated. 'Do you understand? *Never. Never.* There is no choice to be made any more. The choice was made long ago. Do you understand?'

Somewhere, in a far-off region of my brain, swam a dim thought that there must be ways of standing up for myself, but I couldn't access them. I felt like the school dunce, always wrong-footed. I had no weapons and David had them all, or at least the only one that mattered: the threat of stopping me seeing Adam. I didn't even try to argue that this had all come from Adam's own questions, that maybe he needed to believe we both wanted him. Again, retrospectively, I can see that David doubtless thought he was doing what was best for Adam. And maybe he was. But it put me in the position where Adam grew up thinking I hadn't fought for him, didn't care. With the threat of never seeing Adam again hanging over me if I said no, I had little choice but to agree to this new condition and once I'd done so, David walked to the front door. In the entrance hall, there was a picture in a thin wooden frame: one of Adam's very early drawings, much treasured, of a cat, with his just-learning-writing beneath: three crooked letters – C a t.

'I suppose,' David said, 'you want to show off to people that you've got a child?'

I pushed the door to behind him, sank to the mat and sobbed. From then onwards, whenever I was with Adam, David's shadow was somewhere in the room with us, listening to conversations. I never dared get too close, in case I might lose Adam completely. I had to pretend I didn't want what I did. I had to not claim too much, not play too much of a role in Adam's life, though already I barely had a walk-on part as a mother. I wasn't told when he was ill and had a small operation on his ears. I didn't know when he changed school. It would have been easy for Adam to read this as my indifference, as being passive, giving up too easily. But I couldn't complain; that would merely risk forfeiting the small amounts of time with him I did have. So, despite being more settled and secure now, I was forbidden from offering Adam a home with me. It seemed I was damned if I tried to be a real mother, damned if I didn't. And because it all seemed my fault, I must take whatever blame that David, his family, and even in time Adam himself, might throw at me.

Small wonder I became split. Small wonder I identified with the divided figures of Gothic literature, half one person and half another. But there was no supernatural device here. I didn't need the magic vial that turned Stevenson's Dr Jekyll into Mr Hyde. I was Dr Jackson by day and a depressed, sorrowing, angry woman by night, her mothering hidden, surfacing only as something embarrassing, to be apologised for and concealed. Small wonder I hunted the double to its intellectual lairs, tried to fathom its secrets, made research trips to London and sat in the beautiful dome of the (then) British library copying out by hand great swathes of Otto Rank's psychoanalytic study, *The Double*. I was a divided self who yearned to be put together again.

I'd like to say that my spiritual awakening changed everything, that it flooded love into my parched being and lifted me out of the misery and conflicts I'd endured. Surely this was the answer, at last, to my sense of division: a spiritual path that offered the promise of unity? But it only exacerbated my feeling of not belonging at UEA. I already felt an outsider in the department, and embarking on a spiritual path devoted to an Indian guru merely confirmed I had no home in this mostly male, middle class and secular intellectual milieu which was at the forefront of all the then fashionable-isms: modernism, post-modernism, Marxism, materialism, structuralism, feminism.

It felt ironic to be working in a department of literature where literature itself was largely ignored, and the author (like God) was (in a famous essay by Barthes) also declared dead. Ted Hughes, in a fine foreword to John Moat's *The Way to Write*, lamented the 'fashionable culture' which was inimical to the nurture of those very values which literature had traditionally espoused and were certainly, for me, the reasons I turned to it the first place. Hughes talked of it as 'that strange hostility to literature' which is 'called everything but high treason of a most effective sort.'

Secular thinking was not only the norm in left-wing circles but seemed a requirement, a benchmark of intellectual sanity. All the giants of modern thought were agreed on it: for Marx, religion was an opiate of the masses; for Freud, God was a projected father figure. When Bob Dylan brought out his album *Saved* in 1980, following his conversion to Christianity, several men from the Marxist reading group loudly lamented his apostasy. This was an ultra-secular milieu; any form of religious belief put you out on a limb. Looking back, it appears to me now as a kind of intellectual Stalinism, and I became terrified of losing whatever little credibility I had by admitting my belief in anything spiritual. Like my maternal love, my spiritual love was something to hide, apologise for and be embarrassed about.

One cold day early in 1979, Tony Gash came to my office asking me to play the female lead in a drama production he was putting on: Georg Büchner's *Woyzeck*. It was a relatively little known play, still in fragmented form when Büchner died in 1837. Expressionistic in its short spliced scenes, it had a filmic structure: 1979 was also the year Werner Herzog made his film of *Woyzeck*.

The play was based on the true story of Johann Christian Woyzeck, a wigmaker from Leipzig. He was pressed to join the military and, in 1821, in a fit of jealousy, murdered the woman with whom he was living. He was later publicly beheaded. But *Woyzeck* was more than a drama about a crime of passion; it was also a portrait of working class poverty and, as in Shakespeare, exploited the comic and grotesque elements that so often lie on the margins of tragedy.

Tony wanted me to play the role of Marie, Woyzeck's doomed partner, mother to their illegitimate young son. I needed persuading. I'd only been on stage twice before. Once as Mary in the nativity play at infants' school in Leeds, wearing a floor-length blue cloak and pink dress my mother ran up on her sewing machine. Then in an amateur production in Shirebrook's church hall in a play about a stranger Michael, visiting a small town. To most eyes, Michael was human, but I was the child sitting at his feet, who knew he was an angel.

I had no delusions about my acting ability. But somehow Tony got me and other faculty on board. Vic Sage was the showman complete with horse; Nicholas Brooke was the Doctor; John Fletcher from English and European Studies was the Captain, 'grotesque, grotesque!' Alan Pulverness was Woyzeck, while my lover, the army's drum-major, was played by Philip Bird. Years later, whenever I caught sight (on other people's TVs) of Philip's face in adverts or dramas such as *Casualty, Doctors, The Bill, Midsomer Murders, Holby City*, memories of *Woyzeck* returned.

We performed to a packed house of faculty, students and public in Norwich's Theatre Royal Studio in March 1979. Allon White promised but failed to come, but Linda Gillman travelled up from Cambridge, and my mother arrived with a boxed presentation orchid. As usual, Linda was unimpressed by my mother. 'I don't know why you bother with her at all. I've never met anyone so self-engrossed. She talked about herself non-stop all evening.'

Apt mirror for my own life at the time, Marie's role centres on a spiritual conversion. Poor and ill-educated, she's seduced by the handsome drum major when the army is billeted in town, but immediately regrets it. In a short but crucial scene, Marie reads out the New Testament passage where Mary Magdalene is saved by Christ from stoning by a hypocritical male crowd. 'Let him who is without sin cast the first stone.' Like her namesake, Marie determines to sin no more. But her repentance comes too late to save her from Woyzeck's rage and revenge. In a carnivalesque finale, perfectly fitted to Tony Gash's theatrical genius, Woyzeck murders Marie at the front of the stage. In my moment of gory glory, I bit into a capsule of artificial blood and collapsed over the edge of the stage, hair cascading towards the floor while blood spurted from my mouth. Presciently enough, the UEA carnival continued at the back of the stage without me.

A few days after *Woyzeck*, my confidence buoyed by good reviews in the local papers, I ventured into the Senior Common Room. This was unusual for me, for it was always filled with a phalanx of men, and I felt an odd one out. That morning was no exception: dozens of male historians, lettrists and philosophers, mostly bearded and bespectacled, sitting in their suits drinking freshly percolated coffee served by the only other woman in the room, in pale blue overalls. I was just taking a cup when one of the senior lecturers shouted my name from the far side of the room.

'Rosemary!' he yelled, loud enough to make everyone else stop their talk and listen. (I'd not yet shortened my name). 'Rosemary! I must say, you make a first-class whore!'

After a second's shocked silence, the whole room exploded in a collective male guffaw. It went on and on, grew louder and louder, *ha ha ha*, a viral infection of gentlemen's toilet laughs. The word *whore*, the worst word of all in my family's lexicon, threw me into demented confusion. It was what my brother called me when I first experimented with lipstick. Now, I felt a blow torch had been aimed straight at me. First my face went hot, then my blood. Had I been faster thinking, I might have thrown back a clever riposte. 'Let him who is without sin cast the first stone.' There were several Don Juans in the room, whom I was sure had never received this kind of insult. Had it happened a generation later, I would have known to report it as abuse.

As it was, I left the coffee on the table and walked out of the room, titters rippling behind me like chortling schoolboys. From then on, I knew I had no home with such people. I never crossed the threshold into the Senior Common Room again. The lecturer in question became a prominent name. Years later, when I heard him on the radio, I would remember that incident and wonder if it ever crossed his mind. Probably not. Adrienne Rich, I decided, was right: women can never be full insiders in institutions fathered by masculine consciousness. And if we deceive ourselves into thinking we can, we are likely to lose touch with parts of ourselves which that consciousness defines as unacceptable: what Rich calls our 'vital toughness' and 'visionary strength.'

Soon after that, I had a dream which recurred until I left Norwich. In the dream, I'm in the School of English and American studies, climbing the stairs one grey concrete step at a time. All the walls are bare, pock-marked breeze-block. I walk up the stairs to the first floor, turn and climb the steps to the second floor, then the third, on and on. I'm wanting to climb as far as is possible, floor after floor, but just when I think I'm about to reach the final one and turn at the stairwell to the top, there's no way out. There's a concrete wall in my face. I can't go any further, and I can't turn back either. It's a nightmare of futility; stuck in a narrow stairwell, unable to move. *All dressed up and nowhere to go.* Only instead of being the title of one of Malcolm Bradbury's comic novels, this is now a statement of the utmost gravity. The university steps lead to a blank wall. There is nowhere to go.

15

The Palace of Tears

While the east slept in the arms of the west
each house broke into two divided houses,
& concertina rolled out across dead of night
to cleave a full moon. Doors were nailed shut
between the two...The bird emissaries flew higher.
The mole burrowed deeper. Seven crows called
from a windowsill: What's a wall for?

Yusef Komunyakaa

I DROVE OUT TO BERLIN at the end of the Easter holiday 1980 for a term's teaching exchange set up by Thomas Elsässer. Ignorant of world politics, unaware that West as well as East Berlin was effectively a police state, I packed my little VW beetle as blithely as if I was going on holiday. The car was gold, its metal polished like the coaches of fairy tales to protect me from harm. I motored from Norwich to Great Yarmouth, took a ferry to Holland, then steered my way across West Germany till I hit the straight no-man's land corridor that cut through East Germany towards the enclave of West Berlin. I spoke no German, the whole enterprise a trusting to magic more than reason as I somehow navigated motorways and heavily armed checkpoints.

When I discovered the student quarters to which I'd been assigned, a rabbit hutch of a room on one of the main arterial ring roads, too noisy for sleep, I telephoned Elizabeth, the exchange lecturer. Not yet left for Norwich where she would take over my teaching, she invited me to stay with her and her husband in their apartment that night so we could arrange somewhere new the following day. I drove over, parked my gold VW on the road outside their block – a smart middle class suburb – and kipped in their spare room.

Next morning, needing some toiletries, I went down to the car to retrieve one of my cases. It had been late when I arrived, and as I intended to move on quickly, barely worth unpacking my three-month supply of books and clothes. But where I thought I'd parked, the space was taken. Perhaps I'd been further along the block than I remembered. I walked up and down the street several times, lace curtains twitching, round the corner and the neighbouring streets but the gold beetle was nowhere in sight. I ran back up to the first floor apartment.

'Elizabeth! Did you or Siegfried move my car last night? It's not where I left it.'

Siegfried, a tall stolid German, moved towards the window.

'It's not there,' I repeated.

'Not there?' Siegfried echoed. 'How could a car disappear? Let me see.' A man who seemed to inhabit a world where the unexpected must not happen, he removed his glasses, gave them a polish, then went down to the road and looked in all directions. Elizabeth followed suit.

'We must call the police,' Siegfried declared, and dialled the number.

Minutes later, I was in a police car being accompanied by heavily armed men to the local station. Not as an innocent visitor whose car had been nicked, but as a suspected terrorist, for my car had been found abandoned in the early hours on the other side of West Berlin, in a district renowned for harbouring terrorists.

A stream of German buffeted me like machine gun fire as I entered the station. Over the burly shoulders and weapons of my guards huge posters of wanted suspects were plastered on the walls: black and white photos of the Baader-Meinhof gang with triumphant red Xs over the faces of those who had been killed. Adrenaline shot through me like a year's supply of caffeine. I was ordered to sit at a desk for interrogation and though I neither spoke nor understood German, I caught the gist. If I wasn't linked with Baader-Meinhof, it must be some other terrorist group, my golden beetle a front for smuggling in explosives. I'm in a story by Kafka, I thought, or trapped in one of my recurrent nightmares where I'm pursued by Nazis, forcing myself to wake before the gas turned on. But the dream would not be dispelled.

It took a couple of hours for Siegfried and Elizabeth to argue their way into the station and produce papers which convinced the police of the authenticity of the teaching exchange. I'd never been so grateful for anyone's pedantry. While they were talking to the chief officers, I was left in a room with bars at the windows, staring at more dead terrorists. Then Elizabeth slipped back to me.

'Because they found the car in a district where there's a lot of militancy,' she explained, 'they thought there might be a bomb in there.'

'A bomb?'

'With the GB number plate, they thought you might be the IRA. Your things were all over the road. So they had to search the car from top to bottom. I hope nothing was stolen. Did you leave anything valuable in there?'

I tried to remember what I'd packed. One case of summer clothes. Another filled with books for teaching – *Frankenstein* and other Gothic stalwarts. A large envelope with my favourite photos of Adam: one sitting on the grass in the back garden at College Road stroking a neighbour's black cat; another standing on a windy beach at Walberswick; a third eating a large sweet, a mischievous grin on his face, his cheek bulging.

We got the car back later that week, but it was never the same: dented and bruised, the gear-stick malfunctioning where it had been wrenched. Everything inside was soiled. My underwear was torn and tangled, the few books that remained hurled in a heap. I never enjoyed driving the car after that and, as soon as I got back to England, sold it at a huge loss.

That was the prelude to three months of hell. I've felt alienated by many places, but nowhere more so than West Berlin. I hated its bourgeois values, embodied in legislation such as the *Berufsverbot*, which forbade government jobs to anyone with radical sympathies. I was convinced that if I stayed in the country I'd be compelled to join a guerrilla group myself. None of my colleagues at the *Frei Universität* offered friendship, and students were too scared of crossing boundaries to do more than smile.

The very name of the *Frei Universität* was a misnomer in a city and system where nothing was free. Nothing that is except FKK – Freikörperkultur – the peculiar practice some Berliners had of wandering around their city free of clothing. I discovered this on my second week there. When the university showed itself indifferent to my accommodation problems, I hunted privately and spent the next week in the basement of a large villa in one of the ostentatiously wealthy suburbs. From here I walked to the park on the edge of the Wannsee, a lake which, unbeknownst to me, had been turned by rich Berliners into an area for naturist sunbathing. When

I saw wrinkled bodies, all male, sauntering casually under the trees, then walking towards me, I thought I must be having another acid flashback. Had I unwittingly stepped into the frame of Manet's *Déjeuner sur l'Herbe* with the sexes reversed? Didn't they know that in the civilised UK, exposure was illegal?

The villa too was no safe haven. Its owner, Otto, in his late 40s, was threatened by my not belonging to anyone. Every time he saw me, he shouted out, 'Wo ist dein Mann? Wo ist dein Mann?' Where is your husband? Perhaps he feared I might subvert his wife's subordinate role. With her perfect body and long blonde hair, Angelika was a mermaid out of water in his fairy castle. One afternoon when Otto wasn't there, Angelika confided to me that she lived in a 'golden cage': its price too high, but that she dared not bid for freedom.

I soon understood why. That night, after dark, perhaps worrying I was spending too much time brainwashing his wife, or perhaps simply wanting to bash out my own female brains, Otto bundled me with the whole family into his VW estate. He insisted I get into the front seat – no mistaking the spirits on his breath – and drove us out to a forest. Here he raced the VW at top speed towards a tree, braking half a centimetre away from the trunk. Then he laughed, reversed and repeated the operation like a kid in a fairground, threatening to bash into every tree he could see. The two children in the back were screaming. Angelika tried to feign an obedient laugh. I kept yelling at him to stop, but Otto just repeated the suicidal manoeuvre with more gusto than before, time after time, until we all felt sick from the near death experience. Next morning, after a sleepless night, I departed the villa with my packed bags and when I reached the university called Siegfried, who agreed I could have their spare room for the rest of my stay.

It puzzled me, how much I hated Germany and how it seemed to hate me. I'd been looking forward to staying in a foreign country and learning a new language. I went to German lessons for two or three hours each afternoon, but as I struggled to memorise the grammar I kept hearing Sylvia Plath's *Daddy*, where the tongue stuck in her jaw, as if in a barbed wire snare, *Ich, ich, ich, ich, I could hardly speak... the language obscene*. Every moment I spent in Berlin turned into psychic torture. I couldn't sleep. My body hated the heavy diet of dense bread and meat. My soul could find no lightness of being.

I kept myself sane by writing long letters to John and Faith Broadbent, turning them into surrogate parents. I wandered into toy shops looking for something I could send Adam. I bought a box of oil pastels and drew still lives of sliced-open peppers and tomatoes. Most evenings, I escaped to a small arts cinema which showed English speaking films. When I turned round in my seat, Siegfried was sitting there too, on the back row. Unsure whether he was stalking or protecting me, I barricaded the door of my bedroom each night.

Don Ranvaud, a film lecturer who shared College Road for a while, had recommended the cinema and he also gave me contact details for Helke Sander, a radical filmmaker. I'd seen her feminist portrait of a woman photographer, *The All-Round Reduced Personality*, (*Die Allseitig Reduierte Persoenlichkeit* 1977) in Norwich. It was a brilliant vision of what it meant to be a woman in a patriarchal society, so close to my own experience of the world, I fantasised Helke might be a soul-mate or at least a friend while I was in Berlin.

I arranged to visit her one afternoon, wandering for two hours through a maze of concrete in Berlin's back streets and parks before I found her small modern flat near a children's playground. Helke made two black coffees and I offered her the volume of Maya Angelou's poetry I'd taken as a gift. But one of our personalities was clearly too reduced for socialising, for after barely half a dozen sentences, Helke announced she had to go to the bank to pay in some cheques and led us both to the door.

I had more luck with another couple of Don's friends – his social network seemed to span the globe – who invited me for dinner a few times. They had the kind of relationship I'd always dreamt of, loving and conscious. While he cooked dinner, she danced barefoot to African music in their large uncarpeted flat. They quoted Brecht and Rilke at me and were concerned for my unhappiness.

'You can't possibly bear three whole months of this,' they said. 'It's like being in prison for you. Solitary confinement. Why don't you just leave? Go where you feel at home.'

But I had my contract and needed the money, especially now I had to buy a new car. It would be another year before I heeded their words in a deeper way, and made a decision to walk away from places where I didn't feel I belonged.

While in Berlin, I became obsessed with the wall. In York I'd lived near the city walls, but they were picturesque medieval ruins, their golden stone matched by myriads of daffodils in spring, their military role long since eclipsed. Berlin's concrete structure, twelve feet high, imprisoning West Berlin by a boundary of ninety-six miles, and making a border between East and West of nearly twenty-seven miles, could not be disguised. Day after day I walked as near to it as I could along the perimeter, as if just being there, looking at it, had some kind of meaning.

Die Mauer (why make a wall feminine?) was dubbed by West German Mayor Billy Brandt a 'wall of shame' and in The All-Round Reduced Personality, Helke Sander had made of it a symbol of patriarchal oppression. Perhaps it was seeing her film before I went that drew me to the wall, as if by staring at it long enough, I might solve the mysteries of my own experience. The wall rose like something summoned from the unconscious: a blank screen of hostility, irreconcilable difference. What place on earth could offer a better metaphor of the divided self than this split city, with its rift of friends and families, its pitting of one world against another? This was where the Cold War was at its most arctic, the Snow Queen's kingdom at its deadliest.

I wandered to Checkpoint Charlie, peering over to the so called 'death strip' behind the wall where small crucifixes and withered bouquets of flowers marked spots where people trying to flee from East to West had been shot. Between the wall's erection in 1961 and its demolition in 1989, an estimated five thousand people attempted to escape over it, the official death toll of one to two hundred masking an unofficial one far higher. And I became intrigued by what might lie on the other side, the terra incognita, as mysterious as the far side of the moon. A couple of weeks before I left Germany, I procured a tourist visa to the East, travelled again to Checkpoint Charlie (Friedrichstrasse station) and checked in at the so called Palace of Tears (Tränenpalast), the place of so many poignant farewells.

But I was not prepared for what I found in East Berlin: the far side of the moon itself could not have been stranger. I emerged from the Unterbahn into a half city, a place from which life had disappeared. The handful of people leaning on the station barrier looked haunted. Their clothes were jumble, their faces harrowed and ashen. Outside, the streets were eerily deserted, pallid, as if washed with white dust. I felt the wall was a looking glass and I'd walked through it into an invisible city. The Alexanderplatz, a large pedestrian square, was totally without sign of life. Against the utilitarian buildings, the only human presence came from armed guards and police patrolling the streets. The whole of East Berlin felt evacuated, all passion and humanity drained away. No colour anywhere. Concrete seemed to have been poured from the heavens and erased every distinguishing mark.

What astonished me most was that I didn't need to look at my street map to know my way around. I found myself walking north up Friedrichstrasse with the confidence of a local, turning into Chausseestrasse, then treading a route I knew by heart to Bertolt Brecht's theatre, the Theater am Schiffbauerdamm. Everything was familiar, everything I looked at – church, bridge, stone walls, trees – gave me shock after visceral shock of recognition. I wandered further into the streets in the vicinity, trying to lose myself, to prove I *hadn't* been there before, but without success. Not only was I walking through an invisible city, I was treading on the heels of my own invisible lives – who knew how many? – their doors opening as I approached them. It was as if I'd entered a different layer of reality, one which wouldn't let me forget this larger memory that had been mysteriously poured into me: the memory of someone who had lived in this place before me – someone who, it seemed, had been me. I even walked up to a house and had to refrain from knocking on a door I recognised.

This was my first experience of déjà vu in any sustained way, and I found it terrifying. I didn't want to be this floating, potentially multiple being. I wanted to wake up and return to my current self, no matter what her pain. In some panic, I turned and headed south, hoping the harsher shapes and buildings of the GDR would fit me into their linear reality. I found the Eastern side of Brandenburg Gate, the neo-classical architecture of the Unter den Linden – university, opera house, museum, government buildings – but still things were dream-like, softened and dissolved as if I was underwater.

I kept blinking, trying to shed this sense of double vision, of being inside another life, one which I was unwillingly inhabiting. But when it persisted, sooner than planned I fled the place. I passed to the Unterbahn to head back to West Berlin, conscious of many sad, envious eyes on me, and the pearls of great price of my passport and papers.

Siegfried, who had by now proved himself a harmless housemate, offered to show me some of the country. He suggested we go for a weekend to the holiday chalet he and Elizabeth owned in the mountains, visit Austria and Salzburg. En route, he said, we'd take in a concentration camp. 'It's important to keep that memory alive.' I don't remember clearly which one it was, but it was most likely Buchenwald. My knowledge of the war and of post-war European politics was shamefully thin. In A-level history, I'd learnt by rote the causes of the French Revolution, but we'd studied nothing after 1900. I had only the vaguest sense of the enormity of events in 20th century Europe.

Buchenwald had held a quarter of a million prisoners and exterminated fifty-six thousand, of whom eleven thousand were Jews. I followed Siegfried into rooms where starved bodies had been lined up ready for death, looked at wooden shelves where families had been slotted to sleep. I imagined my mother lying there with me.

Years later, reading the work of Eckhart Tolle, I found a possible explanation for the heaviness I felt in Germany. Born there in 1948, playing as a child in the ruins of buildings destroyed by allied bombers, Tolle was consistently wretched in his homeland. He came to believe that in countries ravaged by war, the memory of suffering continues on a psychic level, lingers as what he called 'pain in the energy field of the country'. For some reason, while I was in Germany, I couldn't shield myself from this pain. I felt linked to it in a mysterious way, needing to honour it. This was why I liked the writing of Christa Wolf and Primo Levi, literature that spoke lucidly of the darkness.

Another, more personal, explanation for my unhappy time in Berlin came as a post-script two years later, after I'd moved to London. A new friend, who knew nothing about me, took me for a drink and we chatted about life for a little. Then, à propos of nothing, he suddenly said, 'You know, you must be careful where you go.'

'Sorry?'

'Some places aren't good for you. Some countries, I mean. France is OK. You've had lots of good lives in France. I expect you can speak French well, can't you?'

'Well, not bad. I'm fairly fluent...'

'It's easier to learn a language if you've had good lives there. But promise me you'll never go to Germany.'

I looked at him in bewilderment. It was one thing me believing in my own past lives; it was quite another someone else having access to them.

'You will walk into a shadow,' he said. 'You had a terrible life there. Your most recent one. You were Jewish. Your whole family was taken. You would feel a sense of the horror again.'

I remembered the concentration camp. I remembered East Berlin, the shock of recognition I'd felt there. I remembered the relief with which I'd driven away in my battered beetle, down that long armed corridor.

'Too late,' I replied. 'I've already been.'

16

Lost Faculties

I shall not commit the fashionable stupidity of
regarding everything I cannot explain as a fraud.

Carl Gustav Jung

WHEN ADAM SAW photos and books of Meher Baba in the house, he was at first interested, perhaps relieved to see me so engaged in something, my underlying sadness banished. He leafed through a large book of photographs of Baba at different stages of his life, pointing out one where he was dressed as Krishna, seeming to know without being told his spiritual importance. He asked to borrow a book to take home with him and, though surprised, I felt happy at the thought of not having to suppress this new found love in the way I had to suppress my love on a motherly level.

The next time Adam visited, he glanced scathingly at the pictures of Baba. 'Dad says it's all nonsense.'

'What's nonsense?'

'This Baba stuff. He says gurus like this are ten a penny in India.'

I refrained from pointing out that David knew nothing about Meher Baba and had never been to India.

'I told my friends at school about him,' Adam went on. 'How you follow him. How he never spoke. They all laughed at me.'

I tried to imagine them, in the playground of the school I'd never seen, taunting him. I thought of his innocence, his willingness to share something so precious to me and being mocked for it. I put my arms round him. 'I'm sorry, darling. This is what happens when people judge something they know nothing about. It doesn't mean Baba's a fraud. Some of my friends are the same. It's just outside their usual frame of reference.'

But the wound had gone deep and, from then on, Adam refused to talk about Baba again. Logically enough, he trod ever more firmly in his father's footsteps, aligned with the sceptics and cynics who assumed I was subject to some kind of Moonie-type brain-washing, my spiritual path less a mark of strength or integrity than stupidity and weakness. It repeated what had happened with Allon and the irony of the same vicious circle did not escape me: that the path I clung to as the only means I knew of surviving the pain of loss – of Adam, of Allon, of anyone close to me – merely alienated them further, driving me in turn to cleave ever tighter to the only love that never went away.

I held some of the Sunday evening gatherings for Meher Baba at College Road. My knocked-through lounge could easily accommodate the dozen or so people in Norwich who followed Meher Baba, plus any visiting speakers. One of the first meetings I hosted was for Tom and Dorothy Hopkinson. Tom, in his late seventies, was newly knighted. He'd edited *Picture Post* from 1940 to 1950, one of the first magazines to use photo-journalism to present graphic pictures of social inequality. In South Africa, he worked on *Drum* magazine with photojournalist Peter Magubane, publishing harrowing anti-apartheid coverage of the 1960 Sharpeville massacre, which slaughtered sixty-nine black protesters.

Tom had been married since 1953 to Dorothy Kingsmill, one of Meher Baba's early followers in the UK. In 1974 they published a book they'd co-authored called *Much Silence*, whose title derived from an African proverb: 'Much silence makes a mighty noise,' referring to the absolute silence which Baba elected to observe.

Suited and slightly hunched, Tom recounted the time he met Meher Baba in person in London in 1952. He seemed to animate the humane, practical, love-in-action quality so visible in Baba's film presence. Dorothy, white-haired and indomitable, was more flowery in her tributes, but the sincerity of her commitment to Baba was unmistakable.

For a time, Tom Hopkinson's educated and liberal if not left-wing credentials lulled me into thinking my two worlds of head and heart could be woven together, but they quickly moved further apart again. Whether it came from a family history in which the word 'love' was rarely heard, or simply from an intellectual context in which anything mystical was a cause for contempt, I was embarrassed about my new spiritual life. I feared I was seen as Dylan was by my colleagues, a born-again Christian, pilloried for being so gullible. Far from making life easier, the association with Meher Baba exacerbated a sense of conflict, of incompatibility, as if I'd stepped into a brave new realm which simply did not belong on the old planet.

By now Donald Ranvaud, appointed as a lecturer in film studies at UEA, was a lodger at College Road. Looking older than his twenty-seven years with his beard and glasses, Don had an encyclopaedic knowledge of film, literature, culture and politics. It was impossible not to like him. Bilingual (at least), with an Italian mother, he had a fast mind and endearingly warm manner. In no time I'd given him the best bedroom in the house and was living with domestic chaos, cigarette smoke, late night coffee, phone calls to his mother in Florence and friends all over the world. Before long I'd also agreed that his friend, Ben Gibson, a postgraduate film student, could move in and the house on College Road transformed from a lonely brick terrace into a hive of cultural activity.

Don, who'd also studied at Warwick and knew Gay Clifford and Germaine Greer, was the founding editor of *Framework*, a radical journal for film theory, television studies and international cinema. Some weekends his girlfriend Jo joined him, and the lounge turned into a *Framework* office, with Don arranging articles, Ben cross-legged on the floor under the long cedar table and skinny Jo munching chocolate bars instead of meals.

Don's vivacity and enthusiasm for film was contagious and I was soon caught up in it. I wrote an article for *Framework* on the film *An Unsuitable Job for a Woman*, stuffed envelopes with the latest issues for mailing (a suitable job for a woman), got involved with a film-making co-operative in Norwich, joined a group of women making a feature film in the fens, taught film studies courses with Don on Hitchcock.

He was a genius at networking. *Framework* featured directors such as Godard, Rosellini, Pasolini; writers including Umberto Eco, Peter Wollen, Ricciotto Canudo, feminist film theorist Claire Johnston. But I was never quite at ease with their cosmopolitan confidence and theoretical panache and my sense of inner division intensified. I knew how religion was viewed in that radical world.

Don's friend, Paul Willemen, who worked for the BFI and was later one of *Framework*'s editors, described film as 'the primary focus for theoretical work in the cultural arena'. Its task was to oppose 'the solid victory of Leavisism as the ruling set of discourses in academia since the fifties.' Anything that smacked of 'essence', any 'truth' that claimed to be timeless, or 'independent of its cultural formation', was seen as the result of being hoodwinked by 'dominant ideology'. And here I was devoted to an Eastern guru whom I took to be the very embodiment of truth. What a dupe I must have seemed.

Framework's main offices were in the Other Cinema, a radical distribution group in London. I tried to ensure the spiritual gatherings at my house happened when Don and Ben were down there. But one Sunday evening, they returned earlier than expected, when a Baba meeting was in full throttle in the lounge. That night we had no guest speaker, just the Norwich group with the usual tea and cakes and a few happy-clappy sing-along songs with self-taught guitarists and primitive percussion.

Don and Ben entered the room as the group bashed out a jangly chorus: 'Meher Baba's love, Meher Baba's love, Meher Baba IS love.' A large coloured poster of Baba was propped over the gas fire, with a maxim saying 'Don't worry, be happy.' Ben Gibson's handsome jaw dropped and he looked round in bewilderment. Who could imagine anything further from the politics of radical film theory? I was already squirming in embarrassment at the singing – not exactly Bach, let alone Bowie – but with Don and Ben in our midst it was a hundred times worse. I wanted to be accepted, respected, and here I was presiding over a kind of Sunday school hymn session in my front room.

Another photo showed the *Samadhi*, Baba's small tomb shrine, whose white plaster dome carried beneath it in black capital letters the words 'MASTERY IN SERVITUDE'. I prayed Ben would look the other way, but he was too perceptive and, eyes popping, took it all in.

This was the era of a book series with snazzily patterned covers published by Fontana, called 'Modern Masters'. The masters in question were not spiritual but intellectual gurus, an A-Z all male canon: Adorno, Barthes, Chomsky, Engels, Fanon, Freud, Gramsci, Heidegger, Lévi-Strauss, Lenin, Lukács, Marcuse, Mailer, Nietzsche, Popper, Reich, Sartre, Saussure, Trotsky, Weber, Wittgenstein. One of the members of our Marxist reading group, Walter Bachan, had attacked this notion of mastery in a lecture on campus.

'Where there is a master,' he thundered, 'there has to be a slave. That is the dialectic.'

And now I was a slave with a master I hadn't even met.

I knew from repeated readings of the New Testament as a child that, according to St. Matthew, 'No man can serve two masters: for either he will hate the one, and love the other; or else he will hold to the one, and despise the other. Ye cannot serve God and Mammon.' Yet I was trying to hang on to the idea that I could buttress my academic career on the one hand and climb up a spiritual ladder on the other. My ego wanted the same worldly success that Don and Ben were pursuing and that proved to be lying in wait for them, but my spiritual life had something else in mind.

When Don Ranvaud left UEA a few years later, he entered the film industry. In Hollywood, he produced Oscar-nominated films including *Farewell My Concubine* (1993), *Central Station* (1998), *City of God* (2002), *The Constant Gardener* (2005), then pioneered Latin American film production, especially in Brazil and Bolivia. Ben Gibson headed production at the British Film Institute, before becoming Director of the London Film School.

My own path, I was soon to discover, required the opposite: an unknowing and undoing of all my old ways and beliefs, including the loss of the illusion that the rational ego is in control. The result was that, in contrast to Don, Ben and many colleagues at UEA and since, my life went into relative obscurity. My mind has often judged this as my 'failure', which it certainly is from the vantage point of the ego. But a genuine spiritual path pays no truck to the human ego; on the contrary, its prime task is to smash it to pieces. Thus, pursuing the metaphor of the master and slave, my own 'fall' from worldly ambition might be read less as the slave's failure than the master's success.

When Adam stayed with me for his summer holidays, I took him to Edinburgh, where Don Ranvaud had arranged for me to have a small flat, for free, near the castle during the Edinburgh Film Festival.

One of the new independent features at the festival was by German feminist film-maker Claudia von Alemann. *Blind Spot*, originally called *Die Reise nach Lyon* (The Journey to Lyon), was about a woman historian, Elisabeth, researching the little known life of 19th century French socialist and feminist Flora Tristan. Elisabeth abandons academic approaches and leaves her family to visit Lyon where Tristan worked. Here, instead of word and image she uses sound to evoke and recall the past: first through music, then water, footsteps and voices that would have been heard in a similar way by Tristan a century before, from which Elisabeth has a glimpse of a potential new future. I found it deeply affecting and it impressed on me a sense of urgency to change one's own life.

Claudia Alemann was at the festival with her young daughter – she and Adam were the only children – and we spent time together, taking it in turns to see films in between child-minding. I discovered Claudia had made a short documentary film about Germaine Greer; she discovered I was writing my next book on Mary Shelley and suggested we collaborate on a film about her, inviting me to spend two weeks with her in Tuscany.

Once Adam was back in Birmingham, I flew to Rome, my feathers fluffed out. I felt I'd finally made it. Film, feminism, a little fame, a fortnight with a female director I admired, re-framing *Frankenstein*. What more could my ambitious ego hope for? At Rome station, I climbed into a railway carriage crammed with tourists, waiting for the train to depart north. For some reason, we were delayed. Italians around me gesticulated and swore. And in the hour or so of delay, I sat thinking about Mary Shelley.

Why was I so obsessed with her? What did *Frankenstein* really mean? All this sewing together of a human being from severed remnants, the *disjecta membra* of the dead... Why did I keep poking around the old corpses? Mary Shelley had based the story on a dream she had, of her dead baby coming back to life. Why did that image haunt me so? It was the same image as in the Faust story, Gretchen pulling her poor drowned baby from a stagnant pond, wanting to restore it to life, but not being able to. Could the real female meaning of this be translated into a film? Was it possible? I sensed something in the story was about me, the deepest part of me, but I couldn't define exactly what. Would Claudia understand? Was I equal to the task of working with her? By now, in the hothouse of a crowded railway carriage in Rome in August, I was dizzy and flushed. Sweat pooled in the small of my back. Then, as renewed commotion suggested the train was about to depart, to my utter astonishment I saw the person I thought I was frantically scoop up her bags and leap off the train just as it was leaving.

This was another major turning point: not a conscious decision, but a visceral compulsion, as if it was a matter of life and death to stop, to get off the tracks I'd been on for so long. Looking back, I realise it presaged my departure from UEA a few months later, but at the time it also felt a form of breakdown. I knew it was ridiculous, absurd, to say no to something so potentially ambitious and exciting as working on a film with Claudia, but instinctively I knew I had to. Something deep inside had gone on strike. All my inner batteries had finally reached the end of their life; the voltage that charged my old way of being had died.

For a while I stood trembling on the platform, melting in the heat, then I found a phone to send a message to Claudia saying I was ill and couldn't come. I returned to the airport to try to get a flight home, but the earliest was in three days' time. So I went to the cheapest hotel I could find in Rome to wait it out.

They were a long three days. I stayed at the top of a cramped *pensione*, with no air conditioning, no shower, a tiny window with a view onto adjoining roof-tiles. It was the middle of August; a heat-wave threatened to bake Rome to a cinder. I was in an inferno, so frightened by what this stranger inside me had done, I couldn't eat and barely drank. My head was full of voices telling me I was stupid, I'd wasted a great opportunity. What a child I was, what a fool. Yet I knew I'd had no choice but to step off the train. My body and psyche had come to a definitive full-stop.

On my final day, I ventured into Rome. I hated it. Everywhere I went stood carvings of war heroes and gladiators. I came across endless statues of Romulus and Remus, the two babies suckling beneath the teats of a wolf. How appropriate, I thought, that the city's founding myth featured no human mother, only a she-wolf and Mars, god of war. Aggression, fierceness, patriarchy, militarism seemed to define the place. I stumbled after tourists into the Pantheon and stared up at the *oculus*, an eye with no pupil. I felt sick and dizzy, terrified at not being able to understand what was happening to me, only knowing that the way of life and identity that had been running me for nearly three decades had come to some kind of end.

Those days and nights of heat and panic in Rome felt interminable, the closest I'd come to complete breakdown since my fragmented time in York. Only a steely will somehow manoeuvred me back to the airport, then Heathrow and Liverpool Street station, where I had three or four hours to wait before the early morning milk train to Norwich.

In the station's coffee bar, a dozen or so men were sitting out the night. No tables were free, so I opted for the most respectable looking man. After a few minutes of tea drinking, and exchanged glances, he started up a conversation.

'Are you on your way back from holiday?'

'Yes,' I lied. 'I've been to Italy.'

'Lovely.' He asked what I did.

'I teach.'

'Let me guess. English.'

'How did you know?'

'You remind me of the English teacher I had at school,' he smiled. 'There's something about you that's the same. I'm Ian by the way.'

'Pleased to meet you.'

Ian had no luggage with him, so I asked where he was going. He gave me an inscrutable look. 'I'm in between things. Don't have anywhere to live at present.'

'You've not got any work?'

'Not at the moment, no.'

I put him in his late thirties or early forties, good-looking, lean, his hair combed back from his face, his jacket not yet shabby.

'But how come you're spending the night here? You must have somewhere to go.'

'It's complicated,' Ian said. 'I was married and we split up. I don't have the money for a house, and it's hard to find work.' No self-pity in his voice, just a matter-of-fact shrug that sometimes life was a bitch.

'Maybe you should get out of London.' Suddenly I wanted to rescue him, to offer him a room in my house. 'I'm sure you'd find work then.'

Ian smiled again but shook his head. 'I can't leave London.' He said it with such finality, I didn't ask why. I tried to buy him another cup of tea and something to eat, but he refused. 'I'll get them,' he insisted.

He seemed to want to talk more about his English teacher and his love of reading than his challenging life situation, and for the next couple of hours we chatted about Shakespeare, Steinbeck, Brian Patten, our shared love of Wilfred Owen. When he recited the opening lines, '*Strange friend, I said, here is no cause to mourn....*' I replied in kind.

'*None, said that other, save the undone years,/ The hopelessness. Whatever hope is yours,/ Was my life also...*'

When the time came for the milk train to arrive, Ian warned me there were no toilets on the train. 'You'd best go to the ladies' now if you need them.'

I started to gather my bags, but Ian made a gesture to leave them. 'I'll look after these for you.'

Feeling it would be churlish to refuse, I smiled gratefully, picked up nothing but my shoulder bag, and departed for the ladies', where a loud running commentary ensued between my mother and myself. She was always more garrulous in my head than in person.

'You're so stupid, trusting a stranger. Before you can say Jack Robinson, he'll be off with your bags, sell your Canon camera and all those lovely bits and bobs.'

'*Mum*. Ian's a nice man. He's just down on his luck. Men often get short shrift, you know, with housing. Councils give priority to the woman with the kids.'

'*Ian!* How do you know that's his real name? These men sit there all night waiting for gullible girls like you. Poetry indeed! It's a wonder he didn't ask you to sleep with him.'

'You don't trust anyone.'

'By the time you're out of here, he'll be hawking that stuff down the King's Road.'

Determined not to succumb to her cynicism, I protracted my washing of hands and applying of lipstick. When I got back to the café, only five minutes remained before the train was due to leave. Ian was nowhere to be seen and my heart lurched.

'See,' my mother gloated.

But Ian was walking towards the Norwich platform, my cases in tow, beckoning me to hurry. 'Come on, you don't want to miss it!'

I didn't tell anyone in Norwich about the Rome experience. I didn't feel anyone would understand. Ever since I arrived at UEA, I'd been pushing myself beyond my natural limits: teaching new courses, finishing my D.Phil., writing my *Fantasy* book. I'd organised a lecture series, inviting prestigious contemporary names: Marxist critic Terry Eagleton; film-maker Claire Pajackowska; art historian Griselda Pollock; writer Elizabeth Wilson; social historian Rosalind Coward. I'd hosted a visit by American academic Elaine Showalter. I'd taught Victorian fiction with Jon Cook, film studies with Don Ranvaud. I'd done my stint in Amsterdam teaching at D' Witte Leli institute. Now Virago were about to commission a book on Mary Shelley. All against a backdrop of insufficient sleep, poor diet, ill health, no exercise, the new heartbreak over Allon, perennial heartache over Adam. I was burnt out.

But I didn't dare ask for concessions. Sometimes I fantasised changing my teaching to writers who were spiritually more compatible. Perhaps I could try Milton and Spencer, confess my love for George Herbert, R.S. Thomas, John Donne. But I felt too embarrassed to 'come out' with my new found spiritual life. It felt the new taboo: easier to talk about sex than about spirit. Guido Almansi came to my office one afternoon and invited me to teach courses with him on fantasy writing, but I found the prospect terrifying. What did I know about his interest in 'the aesthetic of the obscene'?

Once, when Lorna Sage was Dean, and I was particularly exhausted, I got as far as the doorway of her office. She turned round from her filing cabinet in her pin-striped suit. Her high heels seemed taller than ever.

'Yes?' she said.

But how could I ask for mercy from the relentless teaching and research demands when she allowed no double standards for herself? Lorna worked harder than anyone I knew, teaching, reviewing for the *Observer*. She barely slept. It would have been shameful to admit I couldn't cope.

Had I been less seduced by theoretical intellectual giants, creative writing and comedy might have been the answer. This was Malcolm Bradbury's solution. I liked Malcolm. He was wry and unpretentious, his voice always sounded as if it was about to crack into urbane humour. He'd escaped his own northern working-class background – his father, like my grandfather, was a railway worker – and dealt with any feelings he had of not belonging by channelling them into satire. He parodied the pretensions of campus life, turned the groves of academe into the stuff of comedy. But his targets, I knew now, were easy ones. Satires of universities, whether by Bradbury, David Lodge or Tom Sharpe, didn't change a thing. They might feed off the intrinsic absurdities of academic pretension, but they also validated them, kept them running. They didn't envision anything better in their place. And the myth of university life they helped construct – glamorous, erotic – was quite at odds with the pedantic reality.

When a TV version of Bradbury's *The History Man* appeared in 1981, Don Ranvaud and I watched it in the lounge at College Road. (One of the lodgers had bequeathed a TV). It was less subtle than the novel, unable to capture the narrative irony, and we were both annoyed by its trivialising of serious issues, especially the sexist portrayal of women as one-dimensional.

Don, never one to waste time watching bad films to the end, left the room to make his international phone calls and I sat penning a feminist riposte to *The History Man*: the start of a novel I would call *The Hysterical Man*. Later I renamed it *Lost Faculties*.

But irony isn't ascribed to the devil for nothing. The writing didn't engage my heart, merely caught me in the same distorting hall of mirrors I was trying to escape.

According to Horace Walpole, the world is a comedy to those who think, a tragedy to those who feel. Perhaps my humourless upbringing, then my painful experiences over Adam, stopped me being able to make a joke of life. Doubtless I was still someone who felt too much and thought too little. But I couldn't find much to laugh about. I wanted novels which engaged my heart and imagination, not cerebral wit.

The funniest thing was when I took Linda Gillman up north to show her where I came from. We went in winter, when snow was on the ground.

'Oh,' Linda exclaimed. 'You didn't tell me you had ski-ing up here.'

'Ski-ing?'

'Yes. There's the ski lifts.'

I looked over to where she was pointing. Against a white mountain the suspended wires with metal shapes hanging beneath did indeed look like chair lifts.

'They're coal buckets,' I said. 'Under all that snow lies a slag heap. Welcome to Shirebrook pit.'

17

The Stones Start Spinning

When I see your face, the stones start spinning!
You appear; all studying wanders.
I lose my place...
In your presence I don't want what I thought
I wanted, those three little hanging lamps.

Jelaluddin Rumi, 'The Great Wagon'

NEARLY TEN NOW, Adam was starting to shrug off my attempts at mothering. David and Jan had a child of their own and, with a new step-brother, Adam clearly felt his real family was back in Birmingham. Despite the belated presence of a TV, the illusion of College Road being Adam's second home was never very convincing. Because I still needed lodgers to pay bills, he didn't have a room of his own or leave things behind to mark the place as his. When I bought him a football, he took it home with him. Barbara Smith tried to reassure me I wasn't the only woman who didn't know how to entertain a near pubescent son. 'It's not because you live apart, it's just how it is, being the mother of a boy,' but I found this hard to believe. Adam seemed reluctant to demand anything, or ask for too much. Rarely did he betray anger, as if being polite would keep an already volatile world steady. I still had no washing machine, so he took his dirty clothes back home. How strange this seems to me now, never to have washed my own boy's laundry.

When I drove Adam back from Norwich to Birmingham, four or five hours each way, I was conspicuously unwelcome. Perhaps not wanting to betray conflicting loyalties, Adam turned his back on me as soon we reached the house and the door was then closed in my face. I never saw his bedroom. Only once, on a hot summer's day, did I ask to use the loo and request a drink. Jan showed me to a small room and handed me a glass of water as if I'd got leprosy. I heard David return to the house and ask what the matter was. Jan replied, '*She's* here. She invited herself in.' I hurriedly left for the long drive home.

With their new child, they seemed more than ever a solid family unit and I felt ever more conscious of my isolation and exclusion. I knew I wouldn't be able to see Adam over Christmas – always a heartache anniversary of our separation – and in December 1980, desperate to escape the lonely festivities, I surrendered to the pull I'd been feeling for over a year towards India. I wanted to visit Meherabad, where Meher Baba was buried, and Meherazad, where his close disciples still lived.

I travelled out to India with Aude Gotto, an assured counsellor from Norwich who'd also learned about Baba through M. We flew from Heathrow on a cheap Gulf airline, a long flight which stopped to fuel at desert watering holes – Dubai, Abu Dhabi – and left us exhausted when we finally disembarked in Bombay (now Mumbai).

A mesmeric coral pink dawn broke around us as we descended into the beauty and mayhem that is India: kids in rags, women in saris, turbaned Sikhs, barefoot boys, men in frayed pyjama suits, dozens of hands fighting for our cases against a cacophony of shouts, shrieks, horns, traffic chaos, a Babel of various Indian languages. In the midst of a jam of cars, lorries, rickshaws, our tired taxi shunted us a few yards at a time through the crowded back streets and slums of Bombay, past thousands of families housed under sheets of hessian or plastic stretched over sticks. As if they were invisible, men and boys stood or squatted by the roadside to pee and shit. Children thrust their arms, often stumps, through the open car windows begging for money. I'd never seen such an ocean of humanity. It was easy to believe the predictions that by 2050 every seventh person on the planet will be Indian.

That first night, we stayed in Bombay in the home of Nargis Dadachanji, a woman in her fifties, whose whole family had devoted their lives to Meher Baba. Since Allon's indignant departure and my colleagues' left-wing bewilderment, I'd been apologetic about Baba's presence in my life, holding back when people saw his photo or asked who he was. But now, as we stepped from the dusty chaos of Bombay into the welcome cool of Nargis' house, it was a shock and relief to see on the turquoise walls not only photo after photo of Baba, but fresh flowers balanced on their frames.

Nargis herself, who had spent time with Baba, emanated a sense of peace and calm, as if she'd found a way of obeying his dictum to not worry, be happy, and all needless anxiety had been tamed.

Our journey next day, one hundred and sixty-six miles by car and rickshaw, saw us crossing the tall ghats and dusty plains of the Maharashtran plateau. Maharashtra (*maha* = great, *rashtra* = nation) is the third largest state in India and the second most populous. On paper at least it claims to be the richest, but Aude and I stared wide-eyed at the deprivation in village after village we drove through. From the broad ochre plains of the plateau rose sudden hills, with small white shrines and temples hidden behind trees. Women thrashed clothes on rocks at the edge of rivers, or bent down to fill brass water pots, their coloured saris – fuschia, turquoise, yellow, orange, lime green – bright against the dusty earth. Water buffalo plodded as fast as their hobbled feet allowed. Solitary goatherds waved their sticks. Roadside stalls sold chai and sweets to handfuls of men in white pyjama suits who sat around with their drinks. Overloaded lorries with exquisite painted decorations carried injunctions to 'Horn Please'. Fat banyans, the national tree of India, stretched down roots from their top branches to the earth like the rope hair of giants. Bony bullocks carried *daimons* of moon-white egrets on their backs.

As we drew closer to Ahmednagar, a burgeoning industrial town a few miles from Meherabad, we found poverty similar to the horrors we'd seen in Bombay. Gipsies camped in a field amid municipal litter. Tents of plastic bags and twigs ran along the roadside. Stick-thin kids stood barefoot outside dwellings little more than mud huts with no water or sanitation. Rubbish and excrement from human and animal lay everywhere. Nowhere is such a land of extremes as India: a simultaneous barrage of all that is most repugnant with all that is most radiant. Every sense seemed more intense: sights more vibrant, sounds louder and more abrasive, tastes hotter on the tongue, smells more pungent. While one nostril took in fragrant perfumes of jasmine, rose, frangipani, cardamom, the other inhaled pee, sweat, death, oil, diesel. India thrust in your face a fullness of life which would not be refused. It defied being put away and I soon discovered that whatever invisible protection I'd tried to wrap around myself for so long could not be sustained.

We stayed in a newly opened pilgrim centre at Lower Meherabad, a beautiful building designed by Harvard trained architect Ted Judson.

Dormitories for men and women were on opposite sides of a central dining room, round quadrangles and archways reminiscent of a mediaeval cloister. The rules required being in bed by 10 p.m., restricting bathing to one bucket every three days to conserve water, never stepping into any of the other gender's rooms, observing a vegetarian diet and taking no alcohol or drugs. As ashram life goes, this was not particularly stringent. Food was delicious and plentiful. No compulsory programmes, no meditation or yoga; morning and evening prayers were optional. A free bus into Ahmednagar several days a week allowed shopping trips for luxuries such as fruit, chocolate, toilet rolls, coffee.

If my spiritual awakening had been dismissed in the West as regressive, magical thinking, in India I soon discovered I was in the company of veterans for whom spiritual life was the most serious and worthy of human pursuits. Most of Meher Baba's closest followers, or *mandali*, were still alive then and through them we had a glimpse of what real discipleship is. They'd been with Baba for many years and devoted every aspect of their lives to him.

The first to greet us when we arrived at Meherazad, Baba's home, was Eruch Jessawalla, Baba's right hand man. Eruch had come to live with Baba in 1939 and his whole family had followed. A good-looking man, with sparkling brown eyes and a Rhett Butler moustache, Eruch was well-educated, fluent in several languages – as were most of the *mandali* – and humorously self-deprecating. His baggy white T-shirt, given him by an American resident, proclaimed 'I SERVED GOD FOR FORTY YEARS AND ALL I GOT WAS THIS LOUSY T-SHIRT.' Meher Baba sustained until his death in 1969 the absolute silence he'd begun in 1925, and it had fallen to Eruch to interpret Baba's messages, first from an alphabet board, then from an idiosyncratic sign language. But his closeness to Baba, far from boosting his ego, had left him well aware of his own fallibility and limitations.

On the porch behind Eruch sat Baba's cousin, Pendu, who had been severely injured in 1956 in the second of two car accidents Baba endured. The first, in the States, in Prague, Oklahoma, 1952, smashed the left side of Baba's body; the second in Satara, India, broke the right. Hence Baba's limp in the films I'd seen. Pendu laughed and made light of his injuries, though he could barely stand and was in untreatable chronic pain. One day I witnessed him visit the *Samadhi*, in visible agony as he bent down to kneel and rose again. But the *mandali* never moaned about their suffering; they'd learned it was part of the spiritual package.

We sat by Eruch in *Mandali* Hall, once a garage, where Baba used to deal with correspondence and meet followers, the hall's concrete floor covered now with Indian rugs and cushions for our Western backsides. Eruch sat cross-legged on the floor, the light from a small window streaming in behind him and, in English far more eloquent than ours, talked about the spiritual path in a way which deftly turned upside down the world-view still peddled in the secular West.

'People always ask me,' Eruch said, 'what have I gained, following Meher Baba for nearly half a century? And I say to them, you are asking the wrong question. Do not ask me what I have gained. Ask rather what I have lost. Ask what he has taken away. This is his service to us in letting us serve him. Not to aggrandise our egos. But to strip us away. There is no point coming to Baba if you are looking to gain anything. If you want this and that favour, this and that gift, you have come to the wrong master. This is the losing game. Isn't it? This is where you will find everything, but only at the price of losing all.'

Such ideas weren't entirely new to me. I knew from my years of church-going and my love of Christian mysticism that the goal was 'the pearl of great price' which the seeker must sacrifice everything to reach. But now I was meeting people whose lives embodied this search in earnest. None of them owned a thing. They shared small bedrooms (invaded by pilgrims as we dumped bags and scarves) and ate communally. They had no money of their own, no luxuries, but lived on a small stipend administered by a charitable trust entirely dependent on voluntary donations.

Behind *Mandali* Hall the lovely gardens of Meherazad led to the women's quarters. Here, on Christmas Day, shaded by awnings from the intense afternoon heat, a couple of hundred people gathered for carols and an open-air cabaret with music and skits. The gardens, created out of near desert conditions over the previous thirty years, were filled with flowering poinsettia trees, trailing jasmine, terracotta pots of geraniums and marigolds, while all around us prolific bougainvillea showed off tissue-thin petals shaded pink, crimson, mauve, lilac, salmon. I couldn't help thinking ruefully of Adam, opening his presents in his new family, and wished he could have been with me, but there weren't many young children to tug at my heart, for Westerners were discouraged from taking children under seven.

I sat on the ground in front of rows of chairs holding Baba's closest women disciples: Mehera, Mani (his sister), Mehru, Goher, Katy, Arnavaz, Naja, barely yet able to match names to faces. Their life-time devotion to Baba left me awed and intimidated, though their manner was always modest, warm, unpretentious. They spoke English with much greater skill and vocabulary than most of the Westerners – the Americans' casual bluster seemed crude by comparison – and I never heard any of them preach or patronise. They'd been well trained. Even the invasion of their home by loud gum-chewing foreigners, all too often opinionated and arrogant, met with a loving response.

My favourite time was visiting Meher Baba's *Samadhi* (tomb shrine) for prayers, or *arti*, at 7 a.m. and 7 p.m. In the evening, the sun set so rapidly I could count the seconds as it sank against a mango coloured sky, then we'd stand in a line of pilgrims from all over the world, waiting to enter the tomb and have *darshan* (blessing). As we came out again, we were handed *prasad*, a symbolic love gift, usually small orange boiled sweets in the shape of a crescent moon, or sticky balls of *bundi ladoo*. I never wanted to leave. For the first time in my life, I was where I wanted to be. I was home.

Electricity was not yet installed on the hill, so the *Samadhi*, a small stone building with a white domed roof, was lit by a couple of kerosene lamps which softened the atmosphere inside. After the prayers, which we all said out loud, the queue inched slowly forward, while music was performed by any musicians or singers present. Sometimes there'd be a professional Indian sitar player, or an American cellist playing one of Bach's suites. Kids from Arangaon village sang in Marathi. Guitarists strummed a well-known chorus – 'Welcome to my World', 'Forever Young' – or someone would give a rendition of Cole Porter's 'Begin the Beguine', one of Baba's favourites, which he'd instructed to be played at his interment. *To live it again is past all endeavour,/Except when that tune clutches my heart...* Then, at last, as the music was playing, it would be my turn to step over the threshold and kneel down. *What moments divine, what rapture serene...*

The marble slab of Meher Baba's tomb, covered with hundreds of roses and garlands, gave off a fragrance of ineffable sweetness, somewhere between frankincense and whatever purity smells like. But just kneeling, bowing my head to the edge of the raised shrine, never felt enough. So I did the same as some of the longer-term devotees and prostrated myself fully, lying flat on the floor, pressing my skull as close as it would go to the edge of the tomb. Now nothing remained but a few inches of marble between me and the greatest Love I knew in this world. I stayed there as long as I dared, greedy for all I could absorb despite the queue still waiting, before I forced myself away.

Even though we were only in India for two weeks, it was enough to pull me ever further away from my life in Norwich. Flying back to a wet, grey England was like being sentenced to a black and white film after a world of colour. I stepped back over the threshold at College Road shivering with cold and shocked by the profligacy. My house was simply furnished, even austere, but after seeing so much poverty in India, it felt absurdly luxurious. Who were all these rooms for? Why all this paraphernalia, this more than one of everything? Who could read so many books? I heard the young Paul in *Dombey and Son*, asking his banker father, 'But what is money *for*, Papa?'

And over the next weeks and months I couldn't help looking round at the well-appointed homes of colleagues, the luxury of campus, the extravagant Sainsbury centre, with an increasing sense of alienation. This, surely, was what Marx meant by 'surplus value.' Everything in excess of need, yet still the mouths were chewing, colleagues fighting to publish and be damned so they'd get promotion, pointing out the inequitable rate of pay for lecturers compared with other professions such as medicine or law. I'd felt uneasy before, but now the whole of Western materialism and its aggressive secular values were under permanent question. All these properties, possessiveness, career ladders, avarice, ambition, intellectual marksmanship, ego gratification... what *was* it for?

I kept hearing the question George Barker posed when I'd invited him to UEA to give a poetry reading. He'd arrived early and wandered through three floors of airless corridors, past notices of meetings, deadlines, exams, pompous questions about literature on the walls before he found me in my office, ploughing through piles of paperwork. He looked me straight in the eye and, with no preamble, said, 'How can you bear it?'

The question had pierced me through, as if he were Hermes carrying a message from the gods. Perhaps reading my silence as incomprehension, Barker gestured again to the ubiquitous concrete, the phallic tower of the Registry, and repeated his words. 'How can you bear it?'

In the reading which followed – to a shamefully small audience – I sat musing to myself, wishing Allon was there to share it. Here was George Barker, T. S. Eliot's protégé, Elizabeth Smart's lover, a man who'd devoted his life, in his own way, to literature. This was what I'd originally entered the world of writing for – poetry, a love of words that made life meaningful. Why, then, had I let myself be so bludgeoned and intimidated by intellectual fashion? Why was I still trying to enter the left-brain landscape of the theoretical boys? I'd come for poets like William Blake and Ted Hughes, and instead I'd got theorists like Jacques Lacan and Louis Althusser. I'd come for inspiration and got deconstruction. Instead of Keats' fluid sense of life, his 'negative capability', I'd got what he called this 'irritable reaching out after facts and certainties.' How *could* I bear it?

A few colleagues commented on the change in my appearance that January after India. They were used to me wearing mostly black, but now huge flowers had bloomed on my floppy Indian jacket. Guido Almansi gestured to me as we walked past students in the corridors.

'Where did this colour come from? What's happened to you? *Lei è nell'amore?* Have you fallen in love?'

Perhaps I had, but I couldn't say so. All I knew was that I was in a cocoon of transformation, over which I felt I had little control.

My life was now divided into pre- and post- India. I still went to the free drinks and lunches at faculty functions, sat through feasts and vintage wine at dinner parties, but I no longer wanted to consume anything. Not that I hadn't asked questions about Western capitalist values before I went. It was one reason I'd joined the clever Marxist reading group, to try to get a handle on the meaning of it all. But after India, the questions became more visceral and absolute. They were no longer posed by armchair Marxists whose sentences were ever more difficult to understand and whose left-wing ideas were exploited to get them further in the rat race of promotion. Now the questions came from bodies living under scraps of plastic in Indian slums, from the near-naked man I'd seen lying on a rusty old bed-frame in the middle of a Bombay roundabout, from walking skeletons who could neither read nor write.

My book on *Fantasy* came out early in 1981. I was gratified – I'd always wanted to be a writer – yet also strangely embarrassed. I carried the book under my arm to meetings, half of me wanting to be congratulated while the other half feared contempt, as if I'd secretly delivered another baby and once more didn't know whether to be proud or ashamed.

Critics and peers were generous in their response. Terry Eagleton, Kate Belsey, Laura Mulvey and other well-respected left-wing figures sent Methuen enthusiastic appraisals. Gay Clifford covered it for *Encounter*, while the TLS and other literary reviews were positive enough to promote the book for undergraduate courses. It remained a critical classic on the subject for over three decades and was translated into Italian, Spanish, Korean. It seemed I'd captured the current zeitgeist: Gothic fiction took off as one of the most popular literary fashions and moved from a marginal position to being central to many English degrees.

But I felt awkward about the book and even now remain ambivalent about it, strangely reluctant to own it as fully mine. When I open it, I find the voice of a ventriloquist, Allon White perhaps, speaking through me. Clever confident sentences; a huge weight of reading; an adaptation of arguments from Georges Bataille, Julia Kristeva, Frederic Jameson, Tzvetan Todorv; a peppering of polysyllabic words like 'dialogical' and 'subjunctivity.' All signs of a woman driven to placate her super-ego and its insatiable appetite for achievement; and behind that, signs of a child whose failure to have any response from her own mother now yearned for an impossible equivalent in impressing an academic audience.

Beneath the intellectual parroting, though, are some ideas which I believe remain true. As I came to understand it, 'fantastic narrative' from Gothic fiction onwards could envisage the world only in broken dystopian forms. From Mary Shelley's *Frankenstein*, through Stevenson's *Dr Jekyll and Mr Hyde* and Dostoevsky's *The Double* to Kafka's *Metamorphosis*, Gothic is a dark form of imagining, a sign of the imagination unable to reach less horrific forms of transformation. I wrote in my book: 'Whereas fantasies produced from within a religious or magical thought mode depict the possibility of union of self and other, fantasies without those systems of belief cannot realize absolute truth or unity. Their longings for otherness are apprehended as impossible, except in parodic, travestied, horrific or tragic form.'

What I came to see by the end of the study of *Fantasy* was that Gothic is a negative version of spiritual longing. It's the desire for another world frustrated and turned upside down. Because of being trapped in a secular world, it can reach neither hell nor heaven, only *this* world broken and made strange. In the words of Frederic Jameson, whose work on magical narratives hugely influenced my thinking, the fantastic 'seeks to convey the sacred, not as a presence, but rather as a determinate marked absence at the heart of the secular world.' Elsewhere, he wrote that 'never in any previous civilization have the great metaphysical preoccupations, the fundamental questions of being and of the meaning of life, seemed so utterly remote and pointless.'

But by the time *Fantasy* was published, I'd been to India for the first time, and such questions, far from being remote or pointless, were close, urgent and answerable. I knew I no longer had to approach the sacred in an inverted, if not perverted back-to-front way, but could instead experience it directly. I'd found what my heart was looking for, though sadly I didn't know how to incorporate my new way of seeing into the highly secular intellectual milieu of the time, and felt compelled to remove myself from UEA. Had I understood then what I have understood more clearly since, and had I been less diffident or cowardly about my own beliefs, maybe I could have found a different resolution.

I also realised that fantastic narratives, the fictions of Poe and Kafka, of Dostoevsky, and all those places in Dickens and Victorian fiction which erupt into Gothic sequences, explore a peculiar psychological state. Unable to experience the empirical world as fully real or reassuring, yet equally unable to reach any other metaphysical realm, they give a sense of not belonging, of being stranded between this world and the next. This was the place I'd always inhabited. Not quite fully real and alive, yet not quite disembodied. Perhaps this was another reason I was reluctant to show off the book.

That spring, I was invited to give a paper in Florida, at the University of Boca Raton, at a conference on 'The Fantastic in Literature'. Two male lecturers from the School of European Studies also attended, and on the first afternoon, I escaped our high-rise Holiday Inn with one of them, a lovely, sensitive man. We walked along the beach at Miami talking about Brecht and Handke, laughing as we trudged through sand in our dark suits, our leather briefcases stuffed with lecture notes, while bikini-clad girls peered at us as if they'd spotted dinosaurs over their sunglasses.

My paper, well received and subsequently published, was called 'Narcissism and Beyond: A Psychoanalytic Reading of *Frankenstein* and

Fantasies of the Double.' But as I watched earnest Americans scribble down my words in their frantic quest for tenure, I realised that the only part of this title that meant anything to me was the word 'beyond' – beyond narcissism. How I longed to get rid of the ego, to transcend the limitations that keep us bound on the wheel of life through innumerable incarnations and ignorance.

I followed the time in Florida with visits to South Carolina and California. Myrtle Beach in South Carolina housed Meher Baba's 'home in the West', a beautiful centre donated by Elizabeth Patterson, one of his early followers: five hundred acres of dense forest and virgin woodland hidden away from the town's rapidly expanding golf links and malls. I stayed in one of the small cabins and spent hours walking by freshwater lagoons then through woods of long-leaf pines, cedar, cypress, live oaks covered with lichen and tangled with hanging moss, to a beach of pristine white sand bordering the Atlantic. Here, for a few days, my relationship with Meher Baba was filtered through Americans of all ages, and I was struck by their quiet conviction, their intelligence, their humour, their commitment to give over their lives to something larger than ego-bolstering. The house of Kitty Davy, an indomitable Englishwoman from upper-class Kensington, then in her early eighties (she would live to see a century), was the hub of the Myrtle Beach centre. When I walked in to greet her, Kitty lost no time in ticking me off.

'You're disobeying Baba's instructions.'

I racked my brain. Should I have recited some mantra? Removed my shoes?

'You look depressed,' Kitty went on. 'Baba said you should always strive to look happy. *Though your heart be cut to bits, let there be a smile on your lips.*'

Puzzling how this could be reconciled with Baba's equally strong injunction to avoid hypocrisy, and reluctant to betray my perennial feelings of loss over Adam, I nevertheless attempted a grin.

'That's better,' Kitty conceded. 'What can I do for you?'

'I want to change my job,' I found myself saying. 'Change my work.' I explained my situation at UEA and we discussed options. Psychotherapy emerged as the favourite, and Kitty advised me to talk it through with the friend I was visiting in California, a man I'd met in India who was training as a psychotherapist. This was Bruce, tall and handsome, rather like Monty Don, his dark hair in tiny curls. But by the time we left San Francisco airport to drive to his home in Oakland, any potential intoxication we'd imagined in India had already been dispelled, and we took it in turns to sleep on the floor in his tiny studio.

I loved the spaciousness and quick golden energy of California, the physical beauty of Big Sur, the different faces of San Francisco, tram rides up and down the steep hills. Bruce introduced me to the work of Ken Wilber, who was bringing together psychotherapy and spirituality, challenging the Freudian reading of spiritual quest as an evasion. Wilber's book *The Atman Project* offered a new theory of human evolution towards spiritual wholeness and as Bruce and I sat with some of his friends in a café in Berkeley (they were all on diets that excluded alcohol, caffeine, sugar, fat, salt, wheat, dairy or anything remotely edible), we discussed the evolution of the soul. Someone uttered the word *authentic*, and I could hear Allon White's outrage in one of our arguments.

'You can't use the term *authentic* in relation to the self, as if there's a lasting, unchanging essence. There's no such thing as a real self. Everything is a role, a construct. That's how new age quacks make their money. Pursuing the illusion of a real you.'

'But the *soul*...' I insisted. 'Doesn't the soul constitute an essential you?'

'What is the soul?' Allon asked. 'Another term for the psyche? The unconscious?'

And now I found myself wishing I could stay in California, where there were clever intellects who didn't rubbish my faith, but were as convinced as I was that the soul's union with the divine was the highest possible ambition and ideal.

18

Buying Bewilderment

Sell your cleverness and buy bewilderment.
Jelaluddin Rumi

RETURNING TO NORWICH from California repeated the sense of not belonging I'd had after coming back from India. I felt I was sitting with an acquaintance I knew was going to die. I had no idea exactly how or when the end at UEA would come, but sensed it was only a matter of time. I had nightmares that I was standing giving a lecture in a hall where the audience sat in stepped rows rising in front of me. Someone had let loose bloodhounds who were racing down the gangways between the rows, their teeth going for my throat.

I started drawing unearthly women with elongated skulls on my bedroom walls, balloons coming out of their mouths saying 'I WILL leave UEA.' But with the place growing in prestige more and more, I felt mad, everyone else battling to get IN to UEA while I was battling to get OUT, putting me in a torture of indecision where I couldn't actually deliver the resignation letter I'd drafted.

Linda Gillman had by now abandoned her research in Cambridge and was involved in bio-energetics, a form of bodywork. When I met up with her after returning from the States, her hair had been cut short and her visible stamina gave her added authority.

'The reason you're unhappy,' Linda said definitively, 'is because of UEA. The world's so much bigger than Norwich. You should just leave. It's not the right place for you.'

'You really think so?' I asked. 'But where would I go? I've no idea what to do.'

'Go to London. There's lots going on there. Just take the plunge and leave.'

I sat in my office, the usual piles of books around me, but they'd lost their meaning. I was still trying to work my dutiful way through Jacques Lacan, but it now struck me as the complete cul-de-sac of Western thought. Everything I'd been taught to think felt bankrupt. Someone told me that Louis Althusser, the French theorist I'd included in my book on fantasy because Allon expected him there, had murdered his wife a few months before, on 16 Nov 1980. Perhaps thanks to Gay Clifford's lasting influence, I couldn't help but read this allegorically. How could the murder of Althusser's wife not be read as a symbolic event, his mental health not-withstanding? Wasn't this what sophisticated theory was doing to all of us? Killing off the female side?

Above my desk was a quote from Karl Marx: 'What, then, constitutes the alienation of labour?... First, the fact that labour is *external* to the worker, i.e., it does not belong to his intrinsic nature... in his work, there-fore, he does not affirm himself but denies himself, does not feel content but unhappy, does not develop freely his physical and mental energy but mortifies his body and ruins his mind...' What better description could there be of my working life misery?

And next to it on the wall was a small photo of Meher Baba. I remem-bered some of his messages I'd read at Meherazad. 'Love can help you unlearn all you have learnt intellectually.' 'Things that are real are given and received in silence'. 'Love is no game for the weak and faint-hearted'. Maybe this was what I had to find the confidence to do: unlearn every-thing, abandon this life of ideas and go for something quieter. Maybe seriously pursuing a spiritual path meant summoning the courage to leave behind what was familiar and jump into the unknown.

David Aers, in the office next to mine, was one of the few lecturers not to be dashing off to Italy or the Aegean at the end of the summer term. He was the only person I told.

'What do you mean, you're thinking of leaving? Why the hell would you do that?'

'I've had enough.' I looked out of the window at the Registry tower and the distant ziggurats of the halls of residence. 'I can't do this any more.'

'Stop then. Take a break. Have a holiday for a few weeks.'

'You don't believe in holidays.'

'It's true, they're a post-industrial invention. If people actually enjoyed their work, they wouldn't need them. But you don't want to make a bloody fool decision just because you're tired.'

'I suppose. But I'm too unhappy.'

'You could be the next head of English Studies. You can't let the side down. You owe it to other women. Think about it carefully, for Chrissake.'

But I still didn't really *think* about anything, let alone carefully. I did request a meeting with a senior administrator in the Registry to see if I could get some form of redundancy, which I'd heard might be in the wings, but he told me I was several years premature. When I got back to my office, a phone call from the current Dean, Howard Temperley, summoned me to him.

Howard, a professor of American history, had a slow, lugubrious way of speaking. 'I hear you're thinking of resigning.'

'Yes.' My answer was quick but sullen.

'That's rather a rash thing to do, isn't it? Shouldn't you be talking this through with someone?'

You, probably, I thought.

'But you've got tenure and your first book out. This is a secure job in one of the best universities in the country...' Howard leant back. 'There are people would kill for that, you know. Couldn't you... I mean... Why can't you just coast along like the rest of us?'

What was his salary, I wondered, for 'just coasting along'?

'It's not in my nature, Howard, to coast. I drive myself. That's the whole trouble. That's why I've done so well.'

I was so angered by what I took to be his complacency, his failure to understand, that when I got back to my office, I signed the resignation letter and took it by hand to the Registry.

Next day, David Aers tried one last time to rescue me from career disaster.

'You didn't deliver it, did you?'

'Yes.'

'It's not too late, you know. Just go over there, say you made a mistake and ask for the letter back. Say you've been under pressure and had a mental aberration or something.'

I sensed the genuineness of his concern, and for a few seconds it countered Linda's instruction to leave. David Aers had always been kind, urging me to go further. Perhaps I should do what he said, race over to the Registry and beg for my letter back. Maybe things weren't as bad as I thought. Maybe I was being paranoid and some colleagues liked me.

Maybe I could ignore the sexism, the intellectual bullies. Maybe it was the situation with Adam which kept wrong-footing me, making me feel judged. Maybe I was valued at UEA, without my knowing it.

'David,' I started. Then the coincidence struck me. He had the same name as Adam's father. Why hadn't *he* spelt out the consequences of leaving? Why hadn't *he* tried to persuade me to stay? And suddenly I was back again on that winter's day just before Christmas when we separated, David standing on the station platform in Leeds with three year-old Adam in his arms. Once more I was thinking, please ask me to stay. I need only the slightest crumbs, no grand gesture. If you just ask me to stay, show some sign you love me and want us to make this marriage work, I will. I'll give up my D.Phil. I'll drown my books.

And as I re-experienced that moment, every impulse to run to the Registry and retrieve my letter of resignation was paralysed. Not only didn't I deserve a successful academic career, I didn't want one. It had ruined my relationship with Adam. If I hadn't been ambitious, however much by default that was, I wouldn't have lost him. If I relinquished academia altogether, perhaps our relationship might be healed. If I gave up everything for love, maybe somehow I'd get him back. Maybe I'd find love on a human level.

'I've done it now,' I said, shaking my head. 'I can't take it back.'

David Aers' face was flushed. 'Bloody stupid,' he lamented. 'Bloody waste of a good teacher. What do you think you're going to live on?'

I turned to the window. '*Consider the lilies of the field, they toil not, neither do they spin ...*'

'You think you'll be singled out for divine intervention?' David scoffed. 'You think higher powers are going to feed you?'

I couldn't see at the time that this David's anger, like Adam's dad's anger, might have stemmed from hurt and wounded pride. I felt so excluded from the institution, I didn't see I was the one doing the rejecting.

'I'm sure I'll survive,' I said.

Still looking dumbfounded, David shook his head in despair. 'Naïve optimism,' he said. 'It will be your downfall.'

In 1981, it was still possible to migrate between jobs with reasonable confidence. It would take a few more years for the effects of Thatcherism to clamp down on employment flexibility. But this was not a serious part of my thinking. I didn't live in the material world in a way that planned economic strategy. My only calculation, with a sabbatical term due that autumn, was that I could hand in my notice with no-one around to know or react. I would simply fly by night, and by the time everyone returned in the autumn I would have magically vanished. I'd be on full pay until the end of the year, and for someone surviving emotionally from one day to the next, this seemed more than adequate thinking ahead.

What David Aers called my 'naïve optimism' was not totally unrewarded. Within twenty-four hours of my resigning, a friend in London, who also followed Meher Baba, had found me an unfurnished flat to rent in Primrose Hill and a group of students said they'd lease my house on College Road for a year. A post-graduate offered to store my chaise longue and better pieces of furniture (I never saw them again) and by mid-August I'd moved to London NW3.

No one in Norwich said goodbye, but they weren't given much opportunity. Don Ranvaud inherited my room with a view, and reported that at the first board meeting that autumn term Howard Temperley, in the same breath that he announced I'd left, mentioned the exact sum of money this would save the department. There was no soul-searching as to what my leaving might mean. No one phoned or got in touch. The only person to write to say how sorry he was I'd left was Malcolm Bradbury. He sent me an extremely kind letter, offering his support, if ever I should need it, in the shape of a reference. How ironic, I thought, that a man from whom I least expected compassion should show some, while the rest of the faculty – people with whom I'd shared teaching, dinners, drinks, even beds – showed no concern at all.

I still agonise about this decision. Was it, as some have said, 'crazy', one of the stupidest things I've ever done, career suicide? Or, propelling me as it did onto the road less travelled, one of the wisest? I don't know. Heart and mind give different answers. The mind says: Yes, it was madness. You lost your footing on the career ladder. You made yourself vulnerable financially. You erased in one move the efforts you'd made for so long. You slid down the snake back to a blank space. You threw away all your hard-won achievements. You were irresponsible. But the heart, with its creative and spiritual values, responds with different questions: What of trusting to a different order of things? What of the wisdom possible only to those heedless of worldly vanity? What of surrender to the cloud of unknowing? What of learning lessons unimaginable to people who live in boxes? What of the experience you've had of grace?

Since then, over the years, needing to survive, and not knowing how else to generate enough income, I've had other teaching jobs in various institutions of higher education: North-East London Polytechnic, Bristol Polytechnic/University of West of England, Nottingham Trent University. All of them, like UEA, offered me employment on perfectly decent terms and many apparently sane people, some of them women, have stayed working in them (often, it should be said, with the aid of large amounts of alcohol). Why is it that in each one I've felt trapped and unhappy?

Was I just in the wrong job at the wrong time, resentful of a theory factory where I felt I had to churn out ever more complex ideas, when what I wanted to do was live and breathe literature? Or was the problem my gender and class, feeling at odds within predominantly male establishments, the majority of my colleagues ex-public schoolboys, or people hankering after privilege? Why could I not find a more sensible way, as David Aers did, of battling for the values I believed in *within* the system?

Perhaps it was because I was alone, with no partner or child living with me, that I longed for a surrogate family at work, making me want too much of institutions and colleagues, only to find disappointment. Perhaps, still looking for a 'good mother' everywhere, I expected too much of the workplace; perhaps this made me unrealistic, yearning for connection and nurture from people whose priorities were entirely different. Or perhaps I was just experiencing in a more acute way what many women go through in our culture, working harder than men to 'prove' themselves, as if they have to win access to something that the men of the tribe inherit automatically, especially those with social privilege in their blood. Maybe this was my own version of the so-called 'fraudulent syndrome', which many high-achieving women have confessed they experience, unable to internalise their accomplishments, or celebrate the success they've achieved; women hitting a glass ceiling that then seems to be entirely of their own making.

Most likely it was some mixture of all of these. I was certainly burnt out from pushing myself too hard for too long, on a treadmill of one apparently meaningless achievement after another – degree, doctorate, university lectureship, publications – with no reprieve, no day-to-day relaxation or joy.

But another way I also read it now is that I was subject to what Jung calls a 'negative mother archetype'. In *Aspects of the Feminine*, Jung argues that women with a negative experience of being mothered often have difficulty working within organisations such as schools, universities, banks, or any large institutions. As 'holding' places, these become symbolically linked with the negative mother. They're experienced as hostile and rejecting, and so in turn are repudiated and left behind.

Of course it was inevitable that, as a woman, I would feel the conflicts of working in a patriarchal institution more acutely than a man did. But is it a sign of sanity or madness that it is women, not men, who are more ready and liable to leave? A post-script to these questions came a few years later when I was in Bristol, teaching again at university level, encountering the self-same dilemmas. Once more I was struggling with insomnia and depression, and a friend recommended I try acupuncture.

'I know a good acupuncturist, called Deirdre Burton. She travels down from Birmingham one day a week to do her treatments at the Lam Rim Buddhist centre. You'll like her. She's very well read. She's into literature and all the things you are.'

I did indeed like Deirdre. She was a similar age, sensitive, professional, warm and funny. At the second session, I asked if she'd always done acupuncture.

'No. I used to teach English. But I just couldn't take it any more. It was too stressful. Not creative enough.'

I assumed she was a school teacher. 'What age group?'

'Undergraduates. I taught at the University of East Anglia.'

'No! Not in the School of English and American Studies?'

'EAS. That's right.'

'When did you leave?'

'1976.'

'Bloody hell!' I was so startled, I dislodged one of the acupuncture needles. 'That was your job I got, wasn't it? That's the year I started.'

'No!'

'Yes! Bloody hell! What a coincidence.'

Deirdre smiled. 'There's no such thing.'

'You know what?' I said. 'No one ever mentioned your name. Not once. I didn't even know you existed. I thought it was a new post they'd made. That's how it is, then. Women just disappear. The red sea closes over us, and we're gone. Never referred to again.'

We were not the only women to resign from prestigious posts at UEA. In the next thirty-plus years, several names, big and small, disappeared.

The verdict of male colleagues was, I knew, the one I heard from Eric Homberger, one of UEA's American literature lecturers. A few months after I'd left Norwich, I bumped into Eric one day on London's South Bank. He must have asked how I was and I must have said I'd got no work.

'Well,' he said, 'you can't blame anyone but yourself, can you? You really shot yourself in the foot there.'

If I'd been thinking faster, I might have pointed out that in times of war you don't believe in, the practice of shooting yourself in the foot is one way to ensure you stay alive.

19

Persisting in Folly

I know the wayes of Learning; both the head
And pipes that feed the presse, and make it runne...
I know the wayes of Pleasure, the sweet strains,
The lullings and the relishes of it...
I know all these, and have them in my hand:
Therefore not sealèd, but with open eyes
I flie to thee, and fully understand
Both the main sale, and the commodities,
And at what rate and price I have thy love...

George Herbert, 'The Pearl'

F REE FROM MODERN campus life at last, I felt I'd escaped prison and must make the most of my new found freedom. It was at once terrifying, exhilarating and slightly insane. My flat in London was a minute's walk from Primrose Hill, with its panoramic view of the Post Office tower and the city spread beneath. Regents Park was ten minutes away, Camden Lock and Hampstead Heath half an hour. Day after day I just walked, enjoying the metropolitan mix of faces and races. I explored Chalk Farm, Hampstead, Soho, Westminster. I walked by the Thames where Ken Livingstone, newly appointed leader of the Greater London Council, exposed the effects of Thatcher's policies by draping banners over the GLC buildings with tallies of the latest unemployment figures. I gorged myself on art at the National Gallery and the Tate, on the Islamic collection at the British Museum, films in Leicester Square and Camden.

I'd found my flat through Michael Morice, another follower of Meher Baba, who was training as a child psychoanalyst at London's Tavistock Clinic. He was one of a diverse group in London who discovered Baba in the late 60s and 70s, along with Pete Townshend of *The Who*, Billy Nichols,

Mike McInnerney, and Ronnie Lane of *The Small Faces*. They gathered round Delia de Leon, one of Baba's earliest UK followers, who lived in Kew. It was after Pete Townshend discovered Baba in 1967 that he wrote the 1969 rock opera *Tommy*, which was dedicated to Baba. I went to Baba meetings in London and pursued every lead I had for social contacts.

Claire Pajackowska, whom I'd met when she came to UEA with her film *Freud's Dora*, lived near Alexandra Palace and through her I met Chris Berg (soon to marry Peter Porter) and film theorist Claire Johnston. We went together to talks on psychoanalysis and feminism by Jacqueline Rose and Juliet Mitchell. I met up with playwright Michelene Wandor and did some stage management for Julia Pascale, who directed plays at The Angel and other pub venues in North London. I went to see Irina Tweedie, author of the wonderful Sufi memoir, *The Chasm of Fire*. I wrote unpaid book reviews for *City Limits*, the listings magazine that competed with *Time Out*, and they published my first political poem, a protest against Chile's military dictator Augusto Pinochet.

It was easier now to fetch Adam by train from Birmingham, and I was excited about exploring London with him. These days he always wore maroon and blue Aston Villa sweat shirts and scarves. We went swimming, or shopping on Camden market, where a travelling salesman persuaded us that a goldfish was exactly what we needed to turn my one-bedroom flat into a home. Adam carefully transported the fish in its plastic bag back to Ainger Road and we bought the largest glass bowl in the nearest kitchen shop, but, after Adam had left, whether from zealous over-feeding, or the toxic state of London tap-water, the goldfish turned white and died. I wrapped the slippery corpse in an old *City Limits*, wondering if the demise of goldfish left every mother feeling so inadequate and pained.

Philip Larkin once wrote that 'to start at a new place is always to feel incompetent & unwanted.' And as the weeks went by and I thought of term beginning again back at Norwich, the initial euphoria I'd felt at being in London wore off. Why had I exiled myself from what little security and familiarity I'd known in the world? I'd wanted a new life, but hadn't anticipated the loneliness. Some days that autumn held such acute inner pain, I feared it would engulf me.

One afternoon, walking in Hampstead, I bought a string of purple onions from a beret-wearing Frenchman on a bike, took them back to the flat and hung them on a hook by the kitchen window. From my first floor, the view was over the backs of tall Georgian houses with narrow gardens, and as I looked at my string of onions and the world beyond the window, I burst into tears. The onions, the only sign of life in an empty, Spartan kitchen, seemed to embody a terrible poignancy. Filling my days with overwork was one thing, but without any work at all, what was I to do?

Dreaming I might find a different career altogether, I applied for a job at Faber & Faber, who were advertising for a new editor. Doubtless on the strength of Malcolm Bradbury's generous reference, I was invited for interview at their prestigious Georgian offices in Russell Square where T.S. Eliot had been a literary advisor. Photos of Ted Hughes, Sylvia Plath, William Golding, Auden, Spender, Joyce and Sassoon stared down from the walls. I was interviewed by Faber's managing director Matthew Evans, ten years my senior, but decades older in terms of public confidence and privilege. (He was later made a Baron). I even made it through to a second interview, but the editorship wasn't on the literary side, it was in politics and required using one's personal contacts to interview politicians and people in current affairs. It didn't need much scratching of the surface to discover I had none.

Already missing students and teaching, and thinking work in non-vocational education with mature students might be more congenial, I applied for a post in adult education at the University of Kent. But the all-male panel closed ranks with the colleagues I'd rejected and made it clear I'd blown my chances.

'What makes you think it will be any different here?' one asked. 'We're an institution like UEA, we have the same standards and values.' I remembered Germaine Greer's lectures, the way she rejected the historical view of successful women as 'flying pigs'. But now I was one, with my wings clipped. Why had they bothered to invite me to interview?

Unsure of my next move, I contacted Linda Gillman. She, after all, had been one of the main catalysts for this change and I hoped she might explore options with me. We met one evening in a pub off Wardour Street. Through her bio-energetic connections, Linda had landed a lucrative short-term job with a London film production company and with her high heels, smart clothes, make-up, and general sense of bling, I hardly recognised her. She glanced at my unfashionable jeans and jacket as if she was embarrassed to know me. Had she forgotten our confidences and the conversations in which she'd urged me to leave?

'I thought we could do something one night,' I said. 'Have a meal? Go to a film?'

Giving her bangles a shake, Linda sipped her tomato juice. 'We're shooting every day,' she said. 'Then at weekends there's this bio-energetics community we're setting up...'

I felt lost when we parted. Linda knew all that had happened to me at UEA, she was my only continuity from the drama with Allon and how that had pushed me to Meher Baba. But she was no longer interested. After wandering for hours round the maze of streets at the top of Oxford Street, not caring where I was going, I decided India was the only answer. It had comforted me the previous year; now I could go for a longer stay. I bought Adam his Christmas presents in advance and sub-let Ainger Road.

Linda, when she heard, did not approve. She dropped into the flat a couple of days before I left. My large suitcase was in the corner.

'How will going to India help you get your life together?'

'I like it there. It's bliss, being in the *Samadhi*.'

'Heaven is not the only alternative to hell,' Linda said. 'There is such a thing as ordinary life in the middle.'

'Why does my following Meher Baba offend you so?'

'Because you use it as an excuse not to face reality.'

I looked at her expensive clothes, her jam-packed timetable, her new leather briefcase, her exercise regime. Was this the reality I was failing to embrace?

'I can't sustain a friendship with someone who has their head in the sand,' she said. Once more I saw Allon, naked on the bed, delivering his ultimatum. 'I need to be with realists, who engage fully with their human destiny.'

And as she picked up her case, we both knew our former closeness was irretrievably gone.

I spent three months in India, all at Meherabad except for one week in Goa with an American pilgrim from California. She wanted me as a spiritual alibi to hide the fact she intended to find a bloke for a few days. She succeeded, and I was left roaming the beach with the wild pigs, smelling the joints of old hippies. But other than day trips to Ajanta and Ellora to see the caves of Buddhist, Jain and Hindu carvings, in all my fifteen trips to India over the next thirty years, I never felt drawn to go further afield than the area around Meherabad and Meherazad.

To me, the power-house of the *Samadhi* and the beauty residing at Baba's home left me wanting nothing more. They carried a presence and quality hard to put into words, a balm I never found elsewhere. It was as if a magnet drew me to them. I felt I belonged there; they were my home more than anywhere in the West.

On an external level, it was always challenging. India doesn't do subtle or quiet. Despite Baba's vow of silence, Meherabad was impossibly noisy, intersected by a railway track and main road full of trucks. Trains thundered by day and night, tearing through the little village of Arangaon, their high-pitched whistles lasting for several minutes to warn people off the rails (sometimes, with desperate locals, in vain). Wild dogs barked through the night, loudspeakers from Arangaon blared out raucous music at all hours, a constant clatter of metal dishes came from the Pilgrim Centre kitchen, gongs marked prayer time, from everywhere sounded strident Indian voices. The dormitories were noisy places too, with the Eastern women's glass bangles rattling as they swished mosquito curtains on their metal hooks, or narrated to each other the latest episodes of family soap operas. I could never sleep. The climate was fiercely hot. Mosquitoes, bugs and dysentery worked their way through the pilgrims, and there was nowhere to exercise or swim. Though delicious, the food was unvarying, often deep fried, and with no TV or newspapers, contact with world events or culture was negligible. The only films were of Baba.

I made friends with some of the Western residents who were helping run the Trust and met interesting people from around the globe. A tall literature professor from Arizona, Nancy Wall, directed some of the impromptu theatre productions and I worked as stage manager, rushing into Ahmednagar bazaar to hunt down fabric and ribbons. But many of the pilgrims, even some of the residents, seemed especially selected to stretch tolerance. What would Adam make of it all, I wondered? Would he ever come out here with me?

Baba predicted that one day Meherabad would become a city, another Jerusalem, and already the process had started. Where India was once subject to the Raj, now American wealth was taking over the local economy. Over the next thirty years, much of the area adjacent to the *Samadhi* was transformed into building plots. Some were bought by wealthy Indians, but most were acquired by Americans or Australians for second homes, their Indian servants sleeping in small stone huts, working as cleaners, cooks, night watchmen. Nearby were the tiny shacks of Arangaon, which had no water, sanitation nor electricity, only dust for floors and cow dung for fires. Yet pilgrims reacted with astonishment and outrage at occasional thefts. A woman from New York was indignant when her bras disappeared from the communal washing line.

'They were the latest design. They cost eighty dollars each.'

I couldn't sympathise. The current rate for cleaners in the centre was less than half a dollar a day.

One of the few Western children to live there was Rachel Brown, the daughter of a couple of American residents, who spent her childhood in Ahmednagar from the age of seven onwards. Rachel cast a cynical eye over the eccentricities of Baba's followers and, like Adam, considered her mother's devotion to Baba quite batty. She subsequently wrote a brilliantly acerbic memoir, *All The Fishes Come Home to Roost* (2005), and whilst many devotees of Baba were outraged by the book's satire, I enjoyed its witty (often recognisable) portraits of many of the figures living there in the 1980s, and the way it cleverly sent up the worst aspects of slavish belief. But the devil always has the best tunes, and writing that attacks faith is always more popular and easier to write than a measured defence.

I often found it strange, as I climbed Seclusion Hill at the back of Meherazad, or stood watching one of the swift Technicolor sunsets, to think that at the same time, back in Norwich, the usual fights were taking place over critical interpretations of poetry, the usual incomprehensible articles about post-modernism being written. There had been many times in my latter months at UEA, sitting in my office studying post-modern theory, when I'd thought to myself, 'This is the end of Western thought. This is as far as it can go. It has overreached itself.' It was like running into a buffer, the end of the line for the human intellect.

But now, in the *Samadhi*, I felt I'd found a place the mind could go when it had exhausted its own cleverness. Here, the mind could finally admit defeat, lay down its arrogance and be taken into something larger than itself. This was not anti-intellectualism, but using the mind to a different end. As Rumi puts it, *Tie together all human intellects. They won't stretch to here... Language cannot touch that presence.*

I never tired of witnessing the stream of humanity flowing into the tomb building and out again. Dozens of stick-thin school kids, barefoot, the girls with royal blue dresses and plaits pinched into red ribbons; men in frayed white pyjama suits, making the most of a break from a day of pick-axes and stone-carrying, to come and bow down; sari-wrapped women of all ages and sizes, their fabrics a shifting parade of orange, lime green, mustard yellow, fuschia pink; westerners with floppy tied trousers and cushions to sit on; old men on walking sticks; others with missing limbs; newly married couples, the woman's sari glittering with gold thread; families with a new-born baby to be 'bowed' to Baba so its head touched the cloth.

Every time I entered the *Samadhi* and knelt down, my head had to go lower than my heart to touch the ground, a literal and symbolic surrender. And as I knelt quietly in Meher Baba's presence, what happened felt like a spiritual transfusion, waves of love pulsing out of his tomb and passing into me, as tangible as the sea flowing in a slow but unstoppable tide. I was empty but the tomb was full, able to transfer some its abundance of love to me, without in any way being depleted, no matter how many others also came to receive.

I use the word love, but this was way beyond romantic or human love and is near impossible to convey in words. Back in the UK it was bleak mid-winter, but here I was in the dry Indian heat, tasting a divine love which was infinite and timeless. Hard to believe that so recently I'd been reading about the semi-colon in Keats; consuming Lacan's definition of love as always and only nothing but projection, and Freud's dismissal of the divine itself as a fraud. What could be further from intellectual masters who revered words than an Indian master who honoured silence? If the mantra at UEA was Angela Carter's *Nothing Sacred*, in this poor rural area of Maharashtra I'd entered a Blakean realm where *Everything that lives is holy*. It was hard to believe we were covered by the same sky.

Cattle were deemed holy too. During Divali, the Hindu festival of lights, the villagers in Arangaon painted their cows, the bony bodies and humps covered with swirling patterns, their horns brightly coloured, their necks draped with beads, braided ribbon, brass bells and marigolds. For Hindus the cow was a symbol of life and could therefore not be killed; a symbol too of the mother and of the earth, giving so much and asking for so little in return.

When the new Pilgrim Centre was full, I stayed for a few weeks in Ahmednagar at Villoo Villa, a low guest-house with a well-tended garden, run by an Indian family long devoted to Baba. Also staying there were

Tom and Dorothy Hopkinson, with two wealthy women from Italy, Lyndall Passerini and Valeria Violati, on their first trip to Meherabad. Lyndall, Tom Hopkinson's daughter from his first marriage to Antonia White (author of *Frost in May*, which had been newly republished by Virago), had married an Italian count, Lorenzo Passerini, and settled in Tuscany in the Palazzone he inherited in Cortona. Having rejected her mother's Catholicism, Lyndall, recently widowed, was now exploring her father's devotion to Baba. Both she and Valeria were deeply impressed by what they saw, and spontaneously offered to fund the building of a hospital at Meherabad, honouring Baba's directive that free medical care be offered to the Indian community.

One evening at Villoo Villa, I knew the world had turned upside down. A group of elegant and rather aloof American Sufis, dressed all in white, arrived with a massive refrigerated truck in which they'd stashed every conceivable gourmet food for a party for Baba's close women *mandali*. Because I was staying there, they had to include me, and I joined in the feast of smoked salmon, giant prawns, cool drinks, ice cream, fruits and cheese. After dinner, the Sufis rigged up a screen in the garden where I sat in the Indian twilight just behind the women *mandali*, watching, of all things, *The Sound of Music*. Even at a distance of more than four thousand miles, I sensed Don Ranvaud and Ben Stevens once more looking on dumbfounded – how much further could one get from the world of avant-garde film? – and my poor beleaguered ego sweated with the contrast as much as the heat.

At first I felt shy and clumsy around the women *mandali*. Baba's closest female disciple, Mehera, though now in her early seventies, still embodied extraordinary grace and beauty. Her mother had brought her whole family to live in Baba's ashrams when Mehera was a young girl, and she had served Baba ever since; she had also been injured in Baba's 1952 car accident in Prague, Oklahoma. Baba's relations with Mehera and all women were always strictly Platonic, and he insisted on the highest moral standards. His only sister, Mani, was Chairman of the Trust and an indefatigable worker. Dr Goher had been Baba's physician and worked in a free dispensary for the villagers. Mehera's niece Mehru, along with Goher's sister Katy, and an American called Rano, would all sit with us on the porch at Meherazad, sharing the ego-grinding experiences of following Baba, as well as the indescribable joy of his company. They told stories of how Baba preferred jokes and games to long spiritual discourses (he loved playing cricket), and how, even in the midst of intense physical suffering, he never lost his wonderful sense of humour.

Arnavaz, another extraordinary beauty, was Baba's only close female disciple to have married. She'd lived in Bombay with her late husband, businessman Nariman Dadachanji, and it was their money which had purchased the Meherazad property. Because of her greater worldly experience, it was to Arnavaz we Western women turned with our confidences. I told her about Adam and the immense pain and guilt of not being with him. I shared how foolish I felt, leaving my job at UEA without knowing what to do next. The unconditional acceptance and love coming back were always unstinting.

'Suffering can't be escaped,' Arnavaz said. 'But you have this time here now, that's the important thing. Make the most of it. Drink deep. If you were teaching, you wouldn't have this opportunity.'

I had little contact with anyone back in England. This was the time before personal computers. There were no public phones. I couldn't send Adam anything in the post because the loss rate of parcels travelling in India was 100%. My brother wrote a couple of times and my mother sent one letter, full of dismay. 'I never thought a daughter of *mine*,' read her large looped handwriting, 'would be wandering around India like a pauper.'

I loved India so much, felt so at home at Meherabad and Meherazad, I wanted to stay there forever. I may not have spoken Hindi or Marathi, but I shared the same spiritual language as the *mandali* and residents. I felt I'd been allowed a precious glimpse of Meher Baba's reality and presence, still so fragrant only thirteen years after his passing, and my roots, like the long strands of the banyan tree, longed to settle near him in Indian soil. Living was a dozen times cheaper than the West, I could easily survive on the rent coming in from the house in Norwich. But I was on a tourist visa, and Adam thousands of miles away. Mani and the Trust insisted that Adam was too young for me to be so distant and I must return to live in the UK. My 'honeymoon' period with Baba was over.

Meher Baba never advocated leaving worldly life behind. First and foremost amongst his orders was the admonition not to 'shirk responsibilities'. He echoed the Sufi maxim to be 'in the world, but not of it,' urging detachment whilst in the midst of life, and selfless service. 'Real happiness,' he said, 'lies in making others happy.' His template for the wearing away of the ego was a phase of his work from the 1940s and 50s known as the 'New Life', when his closest followers had to renounce every material attachment. They travelled with Baba on foot around India with no security but reliance on God, begging for food and shelter. This was not to advocate irresponsibility, but to model complete inner surrender. And I couldn't help wondering if the way I'd been inwardly ripped away from my security at UEA was my own version of the New Life. If I'd stayed caught up in the mesh of complacency and ego-worship that life-long tenure and material security so often induce, how could I have learned to rely on something larger than myself, something more numinous?

Ever since that night I'd first seen Baba's moving image in the *Parvardigar* film, and, back at home, briefly tasted the ecstasy of union, I'd been trying to recapture that original sense of bliss. But in vain. I knew now, from my time with the *mandali*, that following Meher Baba would not lift me out of the world, nor would it deliver me to a permanent high. As Pete Townshend put it after many years with Baba: 'No all-pervading joy creeps into life.' Difficulties aren't removed. Misery isn't suddenly magicked into bliss. There would be no miracle cure to my depression nor to my suffering over Adam. This was a demanding and uncompromising path of love, and had little to do with ease or sentiment. 'Love is no game,' Baba said, 'for the weak and faint hearted. It is born of strength and understanding.'

Faith in Baba certainly didn't fit neatly into a chest of drawers or altar piece. Opting for the spiritual over the academic life hadn't replaced one set of definites for another. On the contrary, I was learning that this new life was in many ways a kind of riddle, best captured only in poetry and metaphor.

Meher Baba had 'reoriented' Sufism in the States and the essence of his teachings was identical to the Sufi message: that at the heart of all true faiths lies the mystery of a readily accessible, embodied divine love, which religious rituals and dogma all too often conceal. His three favourite poets were the Sufi masters Hafiz, Rumi and Kabir, with their images of intoxication and dissolution of the self. Daniel Ladinsky, a young American living at Meherabad in the early 1980s, started working on his own versions of Hafiz, not literal translations, but renderings of ancient Sufi wisdom into a lively contemporary idiom. Later collected into three volumes: *I Heard God Laughing*, *The Subject Tonight is Love* and *The Gift*, the poems were published in the West to great success.

Before I left India, I had my first experience of *Amartithi*, the celebration held at Meherabad each year to honour the anniversary of Meher Baba's passing on January 31st 1969. For weeks beforehand, scrub was cleared by hand, stones bordering the paths were newly whitewashed, and *pandals* (temporary structures) were erected near the *Samadhi* holding brightly coloured awnings which would shelter the fifteen thousand or more pilgrims who travelled from all over India to descend on the small hill at Meherabad. For three days and nights, Baba's lovers sang, danced and prayed, and at mid-day on the 31st January the whole hillside remained totally silent for fifteen minutes to commemorate the exact moment of Meher Baba's death.

I volunteered at the entrance to the women's makeshift sleeping quarters checking tickets, then, after midnight, had a turn helping to usher the long crowd through the *Samadhi*.

The tomb slab was now buried beneath flowers heaped four feet high, as people left garlands, roses, coconuts (symbols of the self), or hibiscus flowers newly plucked from the hillside. I stood on one side of the marble and Robert Dreyfuss, a Californian who'd met Baba in person in 1968, stood on the other, taking the garlands and making sure the line of people kept moving. Men, women, children, all ages, mostly very poor, had come from Hyderabad, Dehra Dun, Madras, dozens of places Baba visited in his various tours of India. Many of them saved all year to cover the train fare to come for *Amartithi*, regarding it as their annual privilege and treat. The crowd was so pressing, they had but one chance to go into the *Samadhi*, and little more than three seconds to kneel down, yet it remained the highpoint of their year, a small taste of eternal reality in the midst of infinite change.

Robert and I emerged after our stint into the cold of the small hours. With no electricity on the hill then, there was no light pollution. The sky was stallion black and the stars seemed to stretch into infinite space. We walked through the crowds to where Eruch was sitting on a ledge at the back of the tin hut Baba had used for seclusion. Eruch never slept through all the three days and nights of *Amartithi*.

'We have all eternity to sleep,' he said.

I sat next to him, wrapping my embroidered woollen shawl closer around me. It was 3 a.m. Nearby, Indians were playing sitar and tabla, while women sang Baba's favourite ragas. It seemed the veils between the worlds had thinned into nothing. We'd entered the mystery.

20

I Climb Down a Thousand Ladders

What is the difference
Between your experience of Existence
And that of a saint?

The saint knows
That the spiritual path
Is a sublime chess game with God

And that the Beloved
Has just made such a Fantastic Move

That the saint is now continually
Tripping over Joy
And bursting out in Laughter
And saying, 'I surrender!'

Whereas, my dear,
I am afraid you still think

You have a thousand serious moves.

Daniel Ladinsky, *I Heard God Laughing: Renderings of Hafiz*

No SOONER WAS I in London again than I was thrown back into teaching, this time at North East London Polytechnic. I didn't apply for the job. I bumped into the course leader at a lecture and suddenly had a half-time post. I needed the money and should have been grateful for the work, but I wasn't. What I really wanted to do was train in Jungian psychotherapy. Although I'd abandoned Jung at Linda Gillman's behest and turned to Freud instead, Jung had remained a secret love. In India I'd learned that Meher Baba particularly valued Jung and had written to him directly, saying he appreciated his work. Michael, in the flat upstairs, introduced me to Craig san Roque, a therapist who'd trained with the

Jungian Institute in London, and I knew immediately I also wanted to train there. But Craig told me that even in the world of Jungian therapy, Baba did not always go down well. His first psychoanalyst had given him an ultimatum.

'I was talking about Baba, as I often did, and my analyst suddenly burst out and said that unless I gave up this infantile fantasy, he wouldn't work with me any more. It was 'getting in the way of the transference.' So I changed analysts.'

I shared with Craig how one of the most positive dreams I'd ever had, at one of the darkest moments at UEA, had featured Jung. In the dream, I'm emerging from a walk through dense woods towards a clearing. It's a fresh summer day and as I come out from the canopy of trees into the sunlight, I walk close to a man who's sitting on a chair where the clearing starts. It's Carl Jung, in his 80s, as he is in the photo on the front of his memoir. We look at each other without speaking. Jung has a wonderful benign expression as he smiles and nods at me, his face and eyes full of infinite patience and understanding. He's the embodiment of wisdom and compassion and although he doesn't utter a word, I know he's saying he can wait, he has all the time in the world. I can walk through millions of woods, get lost in a thousand thickets, but still he will be here, waiting for me.

'Jung's wise old man archetype,' Craig said. 'With Jung himself as that archetype. That's quite something.'

He gave me details of the London training, which I looked at long-ingly, but the fees were prohibitive. I'd used up my savings in India, and even if I sold the house in Norwich, I couldn't cover the lengthy training. Perhaps I also held back because I'd long since stopped believing I could have what I most wanted.

It took only a few weeks of teaching at North East London Poly to bring me to the same pitch of misery as five years at UEA. I was also running evening classes on women's writing at London's City Literary Institute, alongside Michèle Roberts and Sarah Le Fanu. I loved teaching literature, but at the Poly I was meant to teach Cultural Studies – more theory and politics – in a converted factory in Stratford East, near the site of what would be the 2012 Olympics. I took long tube journeys out to Stratford, got lost on vast grey shop floors with miles of piping, and was expected to spout the same theoretical discourse as at UEA but with none of the perks.

No sabbaticals here, no luxurious research budgets. There must have been a library, but I don't remember one. Everything felt raw and gritty. Students and staff seemed hardened by the metropolis. One colleague turned up at my flat one rainy Saturday morning, put his feet up on my kitchen table and delivered a two-hour monologue on feminism – what he thought I should have said in my lecture the previous week – then departed to meet his wife, leaving behind his (easy to interpret) retractable black umbrella. And without the sugared pill of literature or the watery beauty of Norfolk, I found myself looking back in nostalgia, imbuing Norwich with the colours of romance and my colleagues at UEA with avatar-like qualities.

By the early summer, I was once more desperate to leave. A therapist I'd started seeing, a transactional analyst on Harley Street, tried to persuade me, from his new swivel leather chair, that I should keep the job so I could enjoy the stuff of life. But I was lost and confused. Money was the last thing on my mind. Another Baba follower said he believed I was meant to move to Bristol, where he lived and, without a competent or reliable compass of my own, I let myself be carried like a straw in the wind, surrendering to the south-westerly breeze. Susannah Radstone, an outstanding student at the Poly (she later became a lecturer at Keele University and Guardian journalist) came for a farewell drink and arranged for some friends to come and help me pack up the flat. Then, less than a year after I'd arrived in Primrose Hill, I departed.

When I announced I was leaving, a couple of male lecturers at the Poly, also teaching Cultural Studies, showed themselves rather more sensitive than my colleagues at UEA and started soul searching.

'I'm sorry,' I said. 'I'm just not able to do it. I know it sounds pathetic, but I can't. I don't know why. I suppose there's just something lacking in me, that I can't stay.'

One of the men looked at me sympathetically. 'What if that's not the right question,' he said. 'What if the rest of us should be asking what's lacking in us, that allows us to stay?'

Before I left London, I visited Gay Clifford. We'd only seen each other a handful of times while I was at UEA. I'd borrowed her flat when I went to do research at the British Museum and we'd had supper with Germaine Greer. One night, when Gay and I got absurdly drunk, we'd ended up in bed together, but we never referred to it again. A couple of years later,

Gay invited me for dinner with her current boyfriend and I realised with shock, as sounds came from the bathroom afterwards, that she was bulimic. When she married an American academic, I went to her wedding party but, like most of the guests, I was more interested in Germaine Greer than the groom and failed to remember his name.

Gay meantime had been promoted from Warwick to a post at University College London, but despite her success, she too found academia uncongenial. Not that she struggled intellectually, that was the least of her difficulties, but her relentless perfectionism and hard driving of herself left her no rest. In one of her hand-written letters, she'd described Warwick University as a 'nauseous institution' and when I resigned from UEA, Gay wrote with characteristic support to say how brave I'd been to leave a job that was killing me, and that anything I wrote in the future would be much wiser for being done 'out of, away from, a University':

'Don't imagine that you are seen by me as 'unsettled and soft-headed' – my persistent, persisting connection with academe is not a sign of moral commitment or maintained values, but rather of cowardice and lack of energy. I greatly admire you for having sloughed it off, admire you even more for going to India, for taking the space to feel and be what you want... I now find myself squinnying down a chasm of future life with an awful kind of weary vertigo.... I have somehow allowed my life to seep into trivial (and ultimately egotistical) barrenness. You, with greater prescience, are trying to avert that. You have all my blessings and hope.'

By this time her marriage was over. I'd caught sight of her in London only once, when I was waiting outside a cinema in Leicester Square and glimpsed Gay and a new man trying to jump the queue. Her hair was shorter, curlier and she looked different, impatient, as if trying to escape something drawing closer behind her. Now, as I visited to tell her I was leaving for Bristol, Gay seemed surprised.

'But you've only just come here. You've invested so much energy into making a new start.'

'I know,' I said. 'But I'm restless.'

What I hoped for was a dialogue about our mutual battles with patriarchy, or one of the intriguing discussions of literature we used to have. Failing that, perhaps we could talk more personally, about children – we'd talked before about her ambivalence towards them – or I could tell her about Adam, but Gay seemed to have forgotten he existed. In fact, she said she was ill and remained in bed throughout my visit, though what was wrong with her was unclear. Finding her kitchen and fridge totally bare, I went out and stocked up on groceries, cooked fresh soup, eggs and veg. Not that Gay would eat anything in front of me. She seemed to want to do nothing but stay in bed and watch TV. Was this the same beautiful vibrant woman I'd once so idolised? I had no idea then what a complicated slide into illness had begun for her.

This proved to be the last time I saw Gay in *compos mentis*. When we next met, in 1986, in her parents' flat in Victoria, Gay shuffled to greet me at the door, her feet in carpet slippers, her straggling hair pinned back with Kirby grips. After a long series of illnesses including Crohn's disease and heavy drinking, a massive brain haemorrhage had felled her, leaving her little more than the ghost of the woman she had been, with no short term memory,

Later still, I visited Gay in the home she came to share with her parents near Minchinhampton in Gloucestershire. I sat with her in her room, where the familiar furnishings and art evoked the same beauty she'd once created in her cottage at Kenilworth. A larger than life black and white photograph of E.P. Thompson hung on the wall above her desk, his handsome intelligence looking over us, and I remembered the operatic pair the two of them had made in the student protests at Warwick nearly twenty years before. Now Gay 'read' as avariciously as ever, but no sooner had she turned the page than the words on it melted away from her memory like snowflakes on a warm screen. Her mother brought in tea and cakes and Gay ate a plate of iced buns with no awareness of how many she'd consumed.

I walked to the window thinking of Chief Bromden in *One Flew Over the Cuckoo's Nest* when he saw the lobotomized McMurphy. I wanted to howl, to keen. I got it now, the love that wanted to put an end to a life that had become such a travesty of itself.

When I finally learned of Gay's death through a newspaper obituary in 1998 – I discovered her original name was also Rose – she'd only reached her mid fifties, and her life had delivered none of the ripeness or joy that her rare intelligence, generosity, love and beauty deserved. Germaine Greer, who was the staunchest friend to Gay throughout her illnesses, dedicated her book on *Shakespeare* to her, and put together a collection of her poems. 'Gay,' wrote Greer, 'tore herself to pieces trying to say something truer than fact... She was aiming for the top of the glass mountain in the full knowledge of the terrible consequences if she fell.' Gay remained a haunting figure in my inner world, but her meaning had now shifted significantly, from the woman I wanted to be, to the woman whose tragic fate I somehow, by various leaps of miraculous faith and fortune, managed to avoid.

Within days of arriving in Bristol, I knew it was another grave mistake. Washed there on a tide of false expectations, caught up briefly in an unlikely relationship with a follower of Meher Baba with whom I had nothing in common, I stupidly supposed that our mutual love for Baba might erase or transcend all our glaringly obvious incompatibilities. It didn't. We made treks on his motorbike up and down the M4 each Thursday evening to visit Fred Marks, an octogenarian who'd met Baba and held meetings in his little council bed-sit in Putney. But other than clinging on tight as we sped down the motorway in the dark and cold, my arms wrapped around his waterproof jacket, cowering against oncoming wind and rain, there was little closeness. I was too exhausted to move again. I rented a room in the tall terraced house of one of his neighbours in Cliftonwood, then, panicking how I would survive, started hunting for work.

The UEA credentials were still surprisingly hot currency, for soon I'd landed a job at the Arnolfini Gallery. Once a tea warehouse, this imposing Byzantine building on the side of Bristol's floating harbour had been a contemporary art gallery since 1975. They needed a librarian for their recently opened video library, one of the first in the country to show artists' film and video, and I bluffed my way through an interview with the Arnolfini's founder, Jeremy Rees, though I knew nothing about video technology and could barely turn on the monitor.

When I first arrived, the Arnolfini was hosting an exhibition by Richard Long: a circle of stones on the gallery floor. I assumed building work was underway. Much of the experimental conceptual art, with the exception of Helen Chadwick's, which I loved, I found overly cerebral. My reaction was to select videos for the library with a subversive down-to-earth edge. One, perhaps honouring my maternal grandmother's legacy as a housemaid, was a feminist film of lines of washing blowing in the breeze. Rees was not impressed. I knew my days there were numbered and when a lecturing job was advertised at Bristol Polytechnic, with a mixture of relief and dismay, I fell back onto the road much travelled.

Housed in the College of St Matthias in Fishponds, a Bristol backwater behind the M32, the English department had emerged from a college of education and was staffed mostly by ex-school teachers. Bristol had the Old Vic, the Watershed and Arnolfini, the Downs, but it also had the history of the Quaker slave trade – Whiteladies Road, Blackboy Hill – and the black population was now largely confined to the ghetto of St Paul's. When I arrived in the early 80s, Bristol was rapidly expanding its financial services industry, and I found it a harsh, mercantile city. None of East Anglia's beauty here, nor the magic of the fens. None of UEA's gold dust. My office on a down-at-heel campus looked over brick halls of residence and Nissan huts.

I was to stay for six years, mostly going through my teaching by rote. UEA was a hard act to follow, and I knew now I'd been spoilt with stimulating colleagues. Bristol Poly, by contrast, was dull and pedantic, locked in old-fashioned pedagogy and values. I fought a losing battle to get women onto the poetry syllabus. And I wondered what I was doing back in a profession I'd abandoned, under working conditions a hundred times worse.

Rosie Bailey, U.A. Fanthorpe's partner, was a kind and benign presence in the department. The only other colleague to show any friendship (or ambition) was Helen Taylor. Her partner lent me his flat and they were welcoming and supportive. Eventually Helen and I taught women's studies courses together, her stronger political leanings nicely balancing my interest in psychoanalysis and the unconscious. We invited women writers to speak – Margaret Atwood, Helen Dunmore, Michèle Roberts, Nicole-Ward Jouve, Penny Florence, Jill Miller – and Helen organised a conference for a nation-wide network of literature teachers working in higher education, called LTP – Literature Teaching Politics. Once again, literature was seen first and foremost as a vehicle for ideology, and the task for the reader was to unearth the political sub-text.

All went well until the day Helen and I were teaching together some black slave narratives from the American South, one of her specialisms. In the coffee break, I made the mistake of musing out loud about the inconceivable injustice of slavery, wondering if slave owners maybe had to reincarnate as slaves and *vice versa*. Helen and I were standing in a tiny cubby hole which housed the English sector's kettle – no senior common rooms here – and when the word 'reincarnate' escaped from my lips, her protest took me aback.

'Please don't suggest ideas like this to me again. Reincarnation! You know it's a discourse I don't understand!'

I never did mention it again. But how was it that free speech was something to be defended to the death only if it was deemed politically correct? Why was I the one who had to be silenced? Why couldn't I be as voluble about my beliefs as Helen and others were about theirs? According to Meher Baba's account of evolution, not only do we reincarnate more than once, but precisely 8,400,000 times. Who was to say he was wrong and the secular 'you only live once' hedonists were right? Yet again, I was made to feel I was the one who didn't belong and therefore must leave, pushing my own beliefs into a tiny mouse-hole and scurrying after them. When we first met in 1982, Helen and I were on much the same level. But while her ambition and thinking took her to the top of the career ladder – a senior lectureship then readership at the University of Warwick, a Chair in Literature at the University of Exeter – I slithered down further and further till I hit the bottom, unemployed and unemployable.

Spiritual matters, I realised, were as inadmissible at Bristol as they had been at UEA and I once more parroted ideas in which I strongly disbelieved. I even returned to Norwich to give a lecture along lines I borrowed from Helen, that Mills and Boon and other romantic fantasies were valid women's reading, when actually I thought they distracted women from really changing their lives. I took the opportunity because it was an excuse to go back to UEA and be reminded what I'd lost, but it was a masochistic mistake. I felt deep grief, and was relieved only two former colleagues turned up for the lecture.

Throughout my six years teaching at Bristol, I played much the same role I had done at Norwich, pretending, even trying, to succumb to the Literature Teaching Politics version of events, just as I had tried to take on the left-wing ideology of the Marxist group at UEA, and cloned Allon's ideas in my book on *Fantasy*. But it was intellectual hypocrisy.

To start with, I functioned adequately enough, if rather automatically, pulling some magic out of the hat for teaching. Many of the students I liked enormously. One, Sophie Edwards, was the daughter of Tory Cabinet Minister Nick Edwards, then Secretary of State for Wales, subsequently Baron Crickhowell. Sophie had to withstand considerable pillorying from left-wing students for her father's Thatcherite credentials, let alone for knowing Thatcher herself, and her brightness and good humour turned her into a lifelong friend. She travelled to India with me in 2000 and also became devoted to Meher Baba. In 2015, after defying a 'terminal' cancer diagnosis, Sophie – now married to John Sabbage and the mother of their five-year old daughter Gabriella – asked me to help edit her wonderful book, *The Cancer Whisperer*; when this was published by Hodder and Stoughton early in 2016, it shot straight into the best-seller list.

By now I'd sold the house in Norwich to Walter Bachan, and bought a top floor flat on Bristol's Royal York Crescent. The flat was directly above neuro-psychologist Richard Gregory, author of *Eye and Brain*, who had recently founded Bristol's first applied science centre, The Exploratory. His father was an astronomer and Richard had several impressive telescopes in his lounge, which he invited Adam to use.

Of all my homes, Adam loved this sky-high flat most, with its views over Bristol and the Cumberland basin. We would watch hot air balloons sail over from Ashton Court and traffic snaking round the harbour. I discovered Bristol Cancer Help Centre a few minutes' walk away, met its founders, Penny Brohn and Pat Pilkington, and started going there for workshops and peace. It modelled what I believed about physical health being inseparable from spiritual and emotional well-being, and I found it the best foil to my over-intellectual days. My spare time, far from following through on the theoretical research for which I'd largely been appointed, was spent listening to talks by Penny Brohn on the importance of creativity to health, or going to meditation sessions.

Occasionally, I dropped in for a coffee at a whole-food café attached to the Steiner school in Clifton. One morning, at one of the small round tables, there sat Geoffrey Summerfield, looking exactly as he had at York, the same long Ginsberg beard, glasses and hair. We stared at each other in shock. We'd not met since I left York for UEA.

Geoffrey greeted me warmly, 'Where have you been all my life? One of my favourite women!' Then he introduced the American at his side: his new partner Judith. They'd met at a summer school and now were living together in New York, they were simply visiting England. But what about beautiful Catherine, I wanted to say. What's happened to her?

I soon wrote to Catherine and invited her to stay, when she reflected on the break-up with irony. 'It was Geoffrey who wanted the country idyll. I'm a city girl. But now I'm stuck with the cottage and dovecote while he's in the heart of New York.'

A little later, in 1987, Geoffrey was made a Professor of Creative Writing at New York University. He married Judith. But in February 1991 he died, aged only fifty-nine. His precious book collection had long since been disbanded.

If that wasn't enough loss of idealised parent figures, I was also contacted out of the blue by Faith Broadbent. She was seeing a friend in Bristol, could she visit? I was shocked when I opened the door to a thin, frail woman I hardly recognised. John, newly retired from his professorial role at UEA, had left their marriage for Caroline, the wife of M, my ex-counsellor. M seemed cushioned by his faith in Meher Baba, but for all her own belief, Faith was visibly broken. She and John had been together twenty-five years and had four children together. She could barely talk. I persuaded her to see a friend of mine for acupuncture and healing. 'I don't know if she'll make it,' Ben said. 'It's touch and go.' She did make it, but never remarried. She became a Buddhist nun in North Norfolk. John and Caroline married and lived in a converted windmill, painting, until John's death in 2012.

I was deeply affected by these marital break-ups. Both Catherine and Faith were women I admired hugely, and I'd envied what I now see were romantic images of their marriages and happiness. In 1987 too came news of the suicide of Claire Johnston, the feminist film theorist I'd known in London. And I learnt again, as I did with Gay, that even, perhaps especially, the most intelligent women cannot be shielded from misfortune.

All mothers have to experience their children growing away, but because Adam and I hadn't gone through the usual togetherness during his younger years, the reality of his moving into adolescence and adulthood felt all the more painful, the time we'd lost more irretrievable than ever. As Adam entered his early teens, I realised the service David had done us, ferrying Adam to me for so many years, insisting he honour commitments, for now he was old enough to travel down alone on the coach from Birmingham, Adam often chose not to do so. I tried to accept that he needed to spend time with his peers, playing football, going to matches and parties, but still it hurt. When he did come, things were more awkward between us. My limited, mostly meat-free, menus didn't satisfy – 'Not risotto again!'

– and we talked less. I sensed I was losing him and the huge heaviness that hung around me grew ever stronger, as if I was carting around a dead body.

Not that I ever really knew how 'mad' I was. Depression had been so constant in my life, I thought it was part of the human condition. Following Meher Baba hadn't changed that. The man for whom I'd moved to Bristol soon disappeared to London and there were no other followers in the area. Being with Baba simply intensified my sense of difference, and made my spiritual life ever more secretive.

Again, over the years, I turned many times more to G.P.'s begging for help. I tried every possible anti-depressant, but the side-effects – nausea, dizziness, stupor – made me worse, and I would fall downstairs, or sit all day in my pyjamas staring into space as another tricyclic stunned me into nothingness. On a few occasions, I was referred to consultant psychiatrists. The first put me into the hands of his social worker, a girl I recognised as a fellow post-graduate from York. Proud of her new role, her long red hair artfully permed, she informed me my trouble was 'unfinished business,' but offered no clues for completion. The second smoked two cigarettes in our meeting and at the end of the hour she still didn't know my name. The third, years later, offered me medication so strong, he warned that an overdose of one tablet would be instantly fatal – a bizarre prescription, I thought, for someone craving oblivion.

On the one occasion I was so fearful of my safety I asked to be admitted to a psychiatric unit overnight, it was a dark farce. Patients wandered through the rooms with dazed faces like swarms of bees whose nests have been sprayed with poison, no longer able to find home. An elderly chap came up to me and asked, 'Are you a doctor?', his puzzlement compounded when I answered, 'I am *a* doctor, but I'm not *the* doctor.' Nurses came round with trolleys of drugs, knocking patients into pharmaceutical oblivion so they could sit in the TV room silently smoking. 'I don't want drugs,' I said. 'I want some therapy.' One young male patient talked at me in a stream of language – English, but devoid of meaning – and I nodded, as if once more listening to academic discourse I didn't understand. In the morning, after a sleepless night in a nursery full of toddlers' soft toys, the only room available, with the door left open and a nurse on vigil to make sure I stayed alive, I discharged myself. The NHS, I concluded, may be brilliant for physical ailments, but it is hopeless for metaphysical ones, and I stopped trying to find there any lasting help.

I turned instead to private psychotherapy. After the Rogerian Counselling in Norwich, which I'd found too bland, and London's Transactional Analysis, which I found unempathic, in Bristol, I now tried gestalt therapy with a woman my own age. Armed with her old tennis racket, in an hour I could demolish several telephone directories and grow hoarse. It was a great way to expend energy. But expelling long pent-up rage didn't introduce much light into the dark night of the soul, and I started looking elsewhere. I helped run a conference in Klagenfort, Austria on 'The Feminine in Higher Education,' and through its other facilitator, Colin Evans from Cardiff University, I came to meet one of the therapists running the Bath Centre for Psychotherapy and Counselling, BCPC. When I told her about my dream of Jungian training, she encouraged me to enrol on the BCPC training programme, which required me to enter long-term therapy myself. And I started at last on the long process of turning into a human being.

I first met N in an attic space opposite the Theatre Royal in Bath. It was a shabby room under the rafters, with no furniture, where N sat on the floor waiting for me. Dark haired, attractive in a brotherly way, he was marginally younger than me, though he seemed about the same age. I recognised him at once as the one who would help me through, and for the following five years, first at Bath then in his new psychotherapy practice in Taunton, I saw N once or twice weekly. Even after that, with gaps of months or sometimes years, I contacted him whenever the black dog got hold of my heels again, grateful for his constancy that let me re-animate the link when needed.

Shedding, or coming to terms with, a difficult past is a gradual, complicated process. Stories of childhood do not emerge logically or chronologically in therapy; they tumble out tangled together with other narratives and struggles, and meantime your present day self continues to act out unwittingly some of the dramas scripted in said childhood. One thing I found thwarting about my labyrinthine descent into the world of psychotherapy was that it offered no immediate immunity from exactly the same mistakes I'd repeatedly made. N practised 'psychodynamic psychotherapy', which, like psychoanalysis, engaged simultaneously with past, present and the 'presenting past' in the therapy room. He strictly observed the rules of never offering advice, which, with my habits of indecision and wrong decision, I found very frustrating. The result was that even as I was trying to disentangle my history, I still managed to get knotted up in compulsive, quasi-abusive relationships.

One of these was my next marriage. When I'd been in India, a newly-wed American friend, knowing how I longed for a partner, goaded me to ask Mehera, Baba's chief woman disciple, to pray for a husband for me. Mehera had touched me gently in the middle of the forehead, the same place where on her own forehead she still carried a scar from the 1952 car accident, and said quietly, 'Your destiny is written here.' But she had agreed to pray, and the general opinion was that, as she was Baba's favourite, such requests were unlikely to be refused.

Tony was lean and hungry looking, with a shaved head, dark baggy clothes, soft black espadrilles. A jobbing actor, he was part of an actors' co-operative, his CV boasting a couple of minor TV appearances in villainous roles. One friend, Malcolm Parlett, a gestalt therapist, said he thought Tony 'looked like a sociopath.' But we met on a psychodrama workshop, a place full of illusions, and I was gratified when we got together, proud to defy bourgeois assumptions by accepting Tony's unusual living situation (my mother would surely disapprove of this one). He lived still with his ex-wife in a small terraced house in Bedminster, along with three teenage daughters, two of them twins, and his ex-wife's new lover.

Anyone with a shred of sanity would have known this was a crazy situation. The seven of us, plus rescue-home mongrel, sat in their cramped lounge in front of a small TV, and while they competed with each other to shout out identities of actors before the credits rolled, I fondled the dog and tried to read my latest thick tome on psychotherapy. I suppose I hoped that by arming myself with theory – Melanie Klein's *Love, Guilt and Reparation* – I would somehow be kept immune from the collective madness. My credo was that every experience was good for me, the more extreme and distant from my Puritanical background, the better.

Mere weeks after we'd met, Tony asked me to marry him. I took this as an answer to Mehera's prayer, not questioning Tony's desire to keep it secret from the rest of the family. When he gave me his birth certificate for the marriage formalities, I was taken aback.

'Wait a minute,' I said, 'This isn't your surname.'

'It is,' Tony said. 'The one I told you is what I use for acting.'

'This can't be your name,' I said. 'It's too much of a coincidence.'

'Why?'

'Because this is my name too. My maiden name. I use Jackson because it's Adam's name. It makes me feel I'm linked with him. But this is my family name. This is really uncanny.'

The 'coincidence' felt strangely incestuous – I hope N made something of this at the time – but I didn't heed the warning of the obvious symbolism, that I was marrying part of myself. We had the ceremony in Bristol Register office, with gold rings I'd bought and witnesses grabbed from the wet street. I don't remember what I wore. No one took any photos. By this time my brunette-red hair had been sacrificed for Monroe blonde and Tony was too cool to let me wear a dress or suit. He preferred mini-skirts and leggings. Harder to forget was the theatrically earnest way Tony declaimed his wedding vows; even the Registrar commented on his impressive delivery.

Tony hadn't told his family about the ceremony, nor had I told any of mine. When Adam and his girlfriend had stayed with me in Bristol, we'd gone for a picnic with Tony, but I didn't tell Adam we were getting married, which was just as well, because as soon as we re-emerged into the rainy city centre, the wedding ring was removed from Tony's finger.

'Here,' he said, as he thrust the new gold band into my hand. 'You'd better look after this. I don't want anyone seeing.'

I stared at him for a moment in confusion, then put the ring on my own finger, the second sign (in case I'd missed the first) that I was marrying myself, and off we drove to Bath for a celebratory lunch. We were entering a small restaurant when Tony gasped in horror and grasped my arm.

'Oh my God! I've just remembered.'

'What?'

'The girls' dinner. I promised I'd do it.' (Wife number one kept a rigid eye on his parental duties.)

'Tony! You've just got *married*. We're having a wedding lunch.'

'No. I put some chick peas on to cook for them.' (His daughters were staunch vegetarians.) 'Oh my God, the house might have burnt down.' (They did have a gas cooker). ' I'll have to go back and check. Give me the car keys and I'll drive over.' (He didn't have a car of his own.)

'I'll come with you.'

'No, no, you stay here. I'll be back soon.' (Would he? Was the whole charade a ruse to get hold of my car and cash?)

The waiter was showing us to a little table in the window and I was trying to explain that maybe we didn't need it after all, when Tony legged it towards the door and disappeared in a sprint to Charlotte Street car park.

The rain had ceased as I walked out into the Regency beauty of Bath, dilute sunshine taunting me as I wandered aimlessly past the Pump Rooms towards Milsom Street. Too numb to think clearly, I fell back on my habitual solace from an impossible reality: to bury myself in a book. My feet propelled me over the threshold of the nearest independent bookstore (long since gone). I climbed blindly to the first floor, found myself in a spiritual section and picked out at random a volume I still have, called *Tales of the Sufis*. This told me, with apt timing, that life is an illusion, happiness does not endure, attachment leads to pain and only God exists. *'La ilaha ill-allah.'*

The solicitor I consulted a few months later, her smart office overlooking Bristol's Cabot Tower, was unperturbed by my story.

'You'd only known him a few weeks when you married?' she asked.

'About a month.'

'And he was still living with his first wife?'

'And her boyfriend. He still is.'

'He never moved in with you? You never lived together?'

'No.' (Does a week in a tent count? A smart maroon tent which Tony persuaded me to buy, with all the trimmings, though I hate camping.)

'But the marriage was consummated?'

'I'm afraid so.' (Let's not elaborate on sado-masochistic details.)

'You say he does drugs. Marijuana?'

'He's stoned all the time. It's impossible to have an adult conversation with him.' (Let's ascribe it to the drugs.)

'He's not trying to get money out of you?'

'No, thank God. It was all such a big mistake, you know? I'm supposed to be a professional woman.' (I'm in therapy too, that's the joke). 'What the hell was I doing?'

Suddenly the impeccable trouser suit leaned towards me, her long ear-rings dangling onto the desktop. She flashed me a conspiratorial smile and in a confidential, almost confessional tone, said *sotto voce*, 'We all have these youthful aberrations.' Then she sat upright again and glanced down at her papers, her voice back to its normal briskness. 'Divorce on the grounds of unreasonable behaviour. Uncontested. Perfectly straightforward. You'll soon be single again.' Happily, if briefly, I was.

21

The Glass Mother

... long is the way
And hard, that out of Hell leads up to light...
Milton, *Paradise Lost*, Bk II, 433-4

IN HER BOOKS *Banished Knowledge: Facing Childhood Injuries*, and *The Drama of Being a Child*, Alice Miller points out how we live in a culture which tends to make light of, or even laugh at, the sufferings we endured as children, especially the invisible, mental ones. We are expected to be 'proud' of a 'lack of sensitivity' towards our own fate and above all toward our own childhood. But now, little by little, session by session and week by week, often going in circles rather than neat forward lines, N took seriously and helped me unearth and understand the various strands and causes of my long-term wretchedness. I ticked many boxes.

Research shows a far higher incidence of depression and mental illness in the adult lives of people born significantly prematurely. I was very premature, nearly two months early, a jaundiced baby induced then delivered by forceps at Leeds Infirmary. My mother always boasted I didn't weigh as much as a bag of Tate and Lyle sugar. Being so fragile, with a weak neck that could barely sustain my head, I wasn't latched onto mother's breast, but thrust into an incubator, which in 1951 would have been a crude and noisy affair.

N always highlighted this fact of my incubation: how it had shaped my early experience of being mothered and therefore my whole identity, both literally and metaphorically. Instead of a warm, loving female body to hold me, I was put into a transparent box with artificial feeding tubes. I was mothered by a machine: I literally had a glass mother. In the 1950s, N pointed out, little research had yet been done into the psychological effects of being in an incubator for the earliest days of life, and there was little understanding of what is known now about the importance of parents staying close; how even for an incubated baby, parental thought and love can have a beneficial effect. This was 1951: I would simply have been plugged in and left in my primitive box in the hospital nursery, unable to understand what was happening to me, my body a flood of adrenaline as electrical wires and tubes tried to force life into me. For days it was touch and go whether I would survive.

Being premature and incubated might have been countered by careful physical and emotional nurture once I got out, but this didn't happen for me, either as a baby or a child. Everyone needs to understand how they became who they are, and I say all this in the spirit of detective work, unearthing the facts, not as complaint or reproach against my mother. Indeed, when N made explicit what an unusually loveless childhood I'd had, I was shocked and ready to leap to my parents' defence. At the time, I was berating myself for not moving on faster, for still being stuck, useless, a failure as an adult, unable to function like Helen Taylor or other colleagues, and I kept asking *why* I couldn't grow up, *what* was wrong with me. Suddenly N interrupted me in a voice louder than he'd ever used.

'You had fucking awful parenting.'

We looked at each other in silence. In all our years of working together, it was the only time N ever swore. I'd been brought up on the Ten Commandments: 'Honour thy father and thy mother: that thy days may be long upon the land which the Lord thy God giveth thee.' The order to respect parents even took precedence over the injunction not to kill. And now N had broken the tablet of the law. He'd sworn because he wanted me to get it. The tactic worked.

This was the moment when I finally saw that my dark moods and death wishes, my so called 'failures' socially, career wise, were not to do with intrinsic flaws in my nature, but came entirely from the way I had been responded to, or more accurately, the way I had not been responded to, as a baby and child. I had my minimal physical needs met, I was kept alive, but emotionally I was totally ignored. No wonder this had repercussions for my own attempts at mothering. Again, in *Banished Knowledge*, Alice Miller stresses that if in childhood 'the innate ability to feel cannot blossom,' a person is then incapable in later life of providing his or her own child with the protection and love which that child in turn also needs. Parents, Miller claims, who have never known love are in their turn also unable to bestow love – an inevitable broken chain, since they have no inner idea of what love is and can be. The lack of love, an inability to give or indeed receive love, is like a virus passed on from parent to child. And now I was trying change the pattern.

This was also when I started to recognise that I'd reproduced my own sense of abandonment by constantly abandoning myself and others, not least Adam. Jobs, places, partners, friends, who and what had I not left? But my parents were not bad people; they did their best. How, then, had this 'fucking awful parenting' happened?

Both my parents came from Nottinghamshire. Born in Tuxford in 1917, the youngest of four children, Dad had not known his own father, a railway worker, who died in World War I. Dad was the baby of the family, protected by two elder brothers and cosseted by his lace-making mother and elder sister. This made him the gentlest, least macho man imaginable. He never looked at home in the blood-spattered aprons he wore for his work inspecting meat in abattoirs. He was sensitive, kind, wrote poetry and had not an ounce of aggression in him. But he was also weak and spineless.

Symbolically enough, in his early thirties, when I was barely one, he contracted TB of the spine. For the next two years he lay flat on his back at Pinderfields Hospital in Wakefield, which specialised in spinal troubles. He came out of hospital when I was three, bringing with him the plaster cast in which he'd been encased. This heavy pink memento travelled with us wherever we moved, a monstrous strait-jacket with buckles on the side, falling out of the fitted wardrobe like a dead body whenever I opened the door. For Dad, it was a symbolic reminder of God's mercy. He'd received some faith healing at Pinderfields and made a bargain with God that, if he recovered, he'd attend church every week for the rest of his life. He honoured the deal. But from then on, Dad was always weak and sickly, under par, slow in movement, never loud, never a sportsman – the most he managed were games of French cricket and table tennis. Quietly depressive too, sad and insomniac, aware of his failings, always the first to go downstairs in the morning and rake the ashes in the grate, make the fire, take my mother a cup of tea in bed.

His self-esteem, never high, took repeated blows from my mother's cold treatment. Perhaps because he was always a kind of invalid, he was in-valid in my mother's eyes as a result. I've mentioned before how, in my teens, I heard through the bedroom walls (council house walls, cardboard thin) the sound of my father sobbing.

'I'm sorry,' he kept saying. 'I'm so sorry. I know I'm not good enough for you.'

Not that my mother gave him vocal reproach any more than she gave him reassurance, just the silence that was her mode of operation within the family. By then Dad was already taking heavy medication for high blood pressure and a series of mini strokes eventually gathered momentum until the final cerebral haemorrhage which killed him when he was fifty-six.

Dad's religious impulse was that of a child trusting in a good father. He attended church, cleaned the car at weekends, did the worldly things expected of him, worked conscientiously as a Public Health Inspector, which included rat catching and regular visits to local slaughterhouses to check carcases for dangerous bacteria. He was proud to be an expert on the four stomachs of a cow. But it was all in an acquiescent, passive spirit. He couldn't change plugs or put up shelves. He didn't dig the garden. He was terrified of authority or breaking the law.

Both my parents seemed to be secretly waiting for another parent to look after them. Dad's version was the fairy godfather who read the football results on the wireless on a Saturday afternoon. Everything else had to go quiet when the results were on – 'Hush. Can we have a bit of hush?' – so Dad could check the scores against the neat crosses and zeros he'd marked on his pools. 'Wolverhampton Wanderers 1, Blackburn Rovers 1. Manchester United 2, Aston Villa 0.' The serious tone of the male presenter and the devout attention my Dad gave to the results produced a nervous atmosphere and I'd try to lighten the tone. 'You know, Dad, the Church doesn't approve of gambling.' But I was shushed to quiet. 'Can we have a bit of hush?' He never won more than a few quid. The tension held all the suspense of a household waiting to be miraculously transformed, if only those noughts and crosses would land in the right place.

Mum was more complicated. I always thought she was the eldest of three children, but at the end of her life I discovered there were four. Her father, too, died young and her mother, Nanna Barks, had worked as a cleaner to support the family. Mum hated their poverty and lack of culture. As a child, she'd had holidays with cousins near Leicester who were wealthier and better educated; she never lost a sense of envy of their privilege, and resentment at being forced to leave school at fourteen to work in a stocking factory. She felt cheated and carried a certain grudge all her life towards those who were financially or socially better off. She was bright, a bookworm, and wanted the grammar school place her mother couldn't afford. My brother and I were the ones meant to bring her vicarious success. I've often thought my career was never really chosen but taken up as a default position, acting out Mum's unfulfilled schoolteacher ambitions. Playing school, the one game we played together, was the only thing I could imagine doing as an adult. And when I did stop teaching, I realised I was at a loss, unable to imagine what else to do.

Mum was doing office work when she met and married my father in Mansfield Woodhouse, where they both lived, during the Second World War, with a week's honeymoon in Matlock Bath. They made a handsome couple. My father tall and slim in his army uniform, with a high forehead and dark hair swept back from strong features. I can see his likeness in photos of Adam at a similar age. My mother, very pretty, with wavy brunette hair and a soft mouth, always well dressed, in exquisite cardigans she'd knitted, or dresses she'd sewn, their full skirts flattering her small waist. One of her favourite stories was of neighbours pooling their ration coupons to make her wedding cake, and how her younger brother gave her away. He died soon afterwards from lung poisoning, after being stationed in Pompeii, and Mum never recovered from his loss. Counselling help was unheard of; all bereavements were meant to be endured with a stiff upper lip. She behaved as if this brother had been the love of her life, and named my brother after him.

I don't doubt she loved my father in her own way, though I never witnessed any physical evidence of it. I saw no gesture of affection. They never kissed or touched. I could discern no *joy* in their relationship, no laughter or passion. And after Dad was ill, Mum seemed frustrated by his lack of vitality. When he was in Pinderfields, she was alone with two children under five and no transport. I don't know what we lived on. She told me she'd had to fight to stop us being taken into care. Somehow she managed, but with a grim endurance that left a residue of resentment towards my father for not being the strong, sexy Clark Gable figure that she, along with many women of her generation, longed for in her fantasy life. I never saw her in trousers, only skirts (home-made in Viyella or Crimplene), though by default she was the one who effectively wore the trousers in our family. But, like Dad, Mum too was always waiting for the mysterious parent, who never quite appeared, to take charge.

Mum was thirty-five when I was born. She'd had two other children: my brother, three years my senior, and before him her first baby, a still-born girl. She never openly grieved this lost daughter, but went inwards into a kind of suspended world, a death-in-life landscape where wandered the ghosts of her child, and all her other lost loves, the primary one her adored brother.

Whether my mother's lack of emotional affect preceded these losses is hard to say, but I've never known anyone respond so little. I can count on two fingers the times I saw her laugh or cry in all her ninety-five years. She never got angry or raised her voice. It was like living with a literal 'mummy', this Mummy who wasn't one, who seemed more dead than alive.

Donald Winnicott, the child psychoanalyst, famously said, 'There is no such thing as a baby – there is only a baby and a mother.' Everything stems from that original relationship. It determines our feelings of safety in the world, our identity, our emotional and mental well-being. Yet inwardly I had no real relation with my mother. She was another version of the cold incubator: from one glass mother to another. She kept me alive, but even when she was physically present, she was emotionally absent.

Not once in her life did she initiate a conversation to ask how or who I was. She never really asked me anything; she was utterly uncurious about my life or experience. In one of our family photos, taken at a picnic on Ilkley Moor after Dad came out of hospital when I was about three, my face has a puzzled and depressed look, as if I can't work out what I'm doing wrong, that life should already feel so unbearable. I spent much of my childhood in my bedroom, escaping into the pretend worlds of books, and crying. I'd weep in public too, sitting on the back steps of our council house, watching crowds of tiny red ants crawl over the concrete, trying to see them as company but sobbing my heart out because I felt so alone. Mum would walk by with the washing as if I was invisible. She said and did nothing, never asked me what was wrong, just watched me cry with absolutely no response. She could have been looking at the sky and seeing the rain fall. Raining was what the sky did. Crying, it seemed, was what I did. There was no attempt to stop either.

Until I was eight, we lived in Leeds, first in a small flat, then a mid-terrace in Headingley, made from black slabs of dour Yorkshire stone. With no bathroom or indoor loo, we 'topped and tailed' ourselves at the kitchen sink, washed in a tin bath in front of the fire once a week and dashed out to the cobwebbed privy in the back yard. Yet the years in Headingley were more idyllic than anything that followed. Behind our house in Claremont Road lay a collective lawn, with well-tended allotments where I could wander freely. From the midst of our patch of grass rose a mature crab apple tree, its pink-white froth of blossom creating a Samuel Palmer miracle each spring, with a feast of crimson haws in autumn. Mum seemed relatively content in Leeds. She liked its concert halls, parks and museums, the nearby moors of Otley and Ilkley with their vast expanse of sky and stone and bracken. Once a year we'd go to the seaside and visit the cliffs of Whitby or Robin Hood's Bay.

Leaving Yorkshire for the Midlands when I was eight, to be nearer my parents' families in Mansfield Woodhouse, was a huge mistake. Dad's new job was in Shirebrook, one of many grim towns dominated by pit wheel and slag heap on the Nottinghamshire-Derbyshire border, the heart of D.H. Lawrence country. Shirebrook was just twenty miles from Lawrence's native Eastwood, close enough for him to have cycled there. Indeed, this was the town's only claim to literary fame, that on 19 August 1911, Lawrence biked from Eastwood to Shirebrook to visit Alice and Henry Dax, and sent a postcard from there to Louie Burrows, his fiancée in Derby. Like Lawrence's mother, mine too loathed living in a mining town, hated the bingo halls and shabby shops watched over by the pit wheel, and despised the neighbours – 'not our sort'. Whatever joy in life she had found in Leeds vanished overnight.

Our newly-built council house in Shirebrook was designed by a fool. We had an indoor toilet at last but it was just inside the front door, barely hidden from the small lounge, and the other rooms were hardly large enough for Borrowers. From the moment we moved, Mum became more and more inaccessible. She never shared how she felt, she was terrified of displays of emotion or distress. When my much-loved feral black cat died, Mum refused to let me have another pet. 'You were too fond of him. You were too upset.'

She was happiest treating me like a doll. The most animated I ever saw her was when we got Rebecca, the beautiful doll she won for me in a church fête by guessing the doll's name. How excited she was as she handed Rebecca to me, each curl of black hair individually stitched in, moving limbs and eyelids, sweeping lashes. Mum was an excellent seamstress, she'd always knitted and sewed my clothes and now she dressed me and

Rebecca in identical garments. She took me to ballet classes to try (unsuccessfully) to correct my floppy neck and bad posture. Well into my fifties, birthday cards from my mother were more suitable for a little girl. But the real me was more unmanageable for her and, like Frankenstein's monster, I came to sense my ordinary needs were excessive and monstrous.

After a year or so in the red-brick house in Shirebrook, we migrated a couple of miles to the adjoining town of Langwith Junction, which had no pit of its own but was impossible to reach without passing several others in all directions – Shirebrook, Langwith, Bolsover, Creswell, Mansfield, Kirkby, Sutton-in-Ashfield. Here, I became as feral as the cat, sneaking through the scruffy garages to climb down into disused railway lines and walk for miles along old cinder tracks fringed by dog roses, brambles, rosebay willow herbs. I would wander alone for hours, finding pockets of wilderness: caves in sandy railway banks, streams that wound through farmland to boggy woods, fields of ragged robin, poppies, 'egg and bacon' vetch, purple clover. I took library books and bags of apples and sat consuming both, hidden behind the trunk of an old oak deep in woodland.

My brother and I scrapped a lot as kids. It took me years to forgive him for stealing one of my chocolate Easter eggs. We'd both been given one, but where I immediately cracked mine open, he saved his for months, but stole half of mine. When I challenged him, he said, 'Don't tell the parents. They won't believe you anyway.' He was right, they didn't. He was the white sheep and I the black. But I suppose he never forgave me for being born. We fought because there wasn't enough love to go round and we resented each other for taking what little there was. He was always my mum's favourite and I was my dad's, but Mum had the power, so I felt I'd drawn the short straw. But I secretly loved him and was proud of my brainy big brother. He wasn't physically robust and when I found him being bullied in town, I'd turn on his aggressors, ready to defend him to the death. They laughed at my raised fists and angry words, but they still moved away. Only since Mum's death have we become closer and mutually supportive.

Mum often put me down in public, not only comparing me unfavourably with my brother, but with the stillborn baby girl she'd had before him. Whenever I was less than perfect, I would hear, 'your elder sister wouldn't have done that'. This may have been another source of my interest in the double, this dead sister who was my Gothic alter-ego, reproaching me with the ideal self I had failed to become.

From an early age, I fantasised I was secretly adopted and that one day my real birth mother would appear to claim me. Not that Mum was anything like the vicious adoptive mother Jeanette Winterson evokes in her wonderful memoir, *Why Be Happy when You Could be Normal?* Mum wasn't actively sadistic. She just wasn't there, sometimes not physically present, always inwardly absent. When I walked home from junior school crying because of bullying or friends falling out, and entered the living room where Mum was ironing, I would hope against hope she might ask me what was wrong, wipe my tears, talk to me, listen at least. But as soon as she saw me coming she put down the iron, turned her back and walked away upstairs to her bedroom. I waited for her, but she didn't return.

How could I know such behaviour was unusual? How could I not believe something was wrong with me that accounted for ordinary human contact being so unattainable? Later, as I entered adolescence, Mum walked upstairs before I even got into the house, or made herself invisible by being elsewhere. I never understood where she went, she had no job outside the home, but often the house was empty. If, as a teenager, I turned joyfully to homework assignments, four or five hours of solid study each night, creating a slight curvature in my spine from seven years of hunching over a drawing board on my single bed, it was because there was no one to talk to and nothing else to do.

We lived on the edge of town in Langwith Junction, and most of the kids at Brookfield Junior school came from mining families in Shirebrook. Mum disapproved if I chose friends from amongst them. 'They're not good enough for you. Why do you always go for the underdogs?' So I made a best friend she could not look down on: the daughter of one of our junior school teachers. Jane was loyal, round-faced and plump, but what I really loved about her was her mother. Mrs. Edworthy was the most perfect mother imaginable: attractive, interesting, affectionate, witty, who laughed a lot and spoke her mind in a voice husky from smoking. When I stayed over in the detached house they owned in Bolsover, I felt I was in Buckingham Palace, with the fridge well-stocked, piles of soft freshly laundered towels, pale pink carpets and feather eiderdowns. They had a swing in the garden, bikes (I didn't have my first bike until I was twenty-two), ball games, several cats.

Best of all was Friday evening, wrapped in a warm borrowed dressing-gown, after a hot bath with bubbles, when I sat on Mrs. Edworthy's knee in front of a modern open fire (we still had a black range), with a whole packet of crisps to myself, crushing them into minute shards to protract the pleasure, sprinkling them with salt from the blue twist of paper. Mrs. Edworthy murmured to me the things I imagined mothers should say, about how lovely I was, and all night, lying next to Jane as she slept under the plush eiderdown, I plotted a way to move in.

Returning from this luxury to the cold council house next day was like being exiled from Eden. Mum would be in bed with a migraine. Dad would sit forlornly with a tray on his knee. The kitchen was piled with pots and the whole house smelt of sickness.

'Why can't you do something?' I'd ask Dad or my brother, as I ran around washing up. 'You've got hands, haven't you?'

But Dad sat in a helpless way with his cup of tea and said, 'You'll make someone a lovely wife one day.' He often spoke in clichés, uttering his maxims with total lack of irony. In my keepsake book with its rainbow coloured pages, he wrote in his elegant copperplate: 'Be good, sweet maid, and let who will be clever.' But being clever was my escape route. Who cared about being good?

When Jane stayed over with me, she whispered in my ear as soon as tea was over, 'Could we go to your room? It's more homely up there.' And so we left the cramped living room, with its table, sideboard, two small armchairs by the old-fashioned range, and fled to my room, making up stories and vows of eternal friendship.

In reality, our lives separated as soon as we passed the eleven-plus and went to rival grammar schools in Mansfield: Jane in her bottle green uniform to the mixed Brunts, me in my navy one to the single sex Queen Elizabeth's for Girls, on opposite sides of the street. Jane became a school teacher like her mother, working back in the grounds of our old junior school, teaching children with special needs. She would die in her forties, surviving her mother by only a few months. Mum, always vague about medical facts, couldn't tell me the exact cause of death, but made a gesture that suggested a bottle. Rumour had it that Jane made a disastrous, abusive marriage and started drinking. My theory was that, once her adorable mother had gone, Jane simply drank and drank until she could float herself across the Styx to join her.

I used to wonder if my own mother was depressed, if it had been her depression which caused my own. And I became more and more extreme in my attempts to win her back from what I thought were low moods so she might give me the mothering I craved. I saved up pocket money to buy bunches of flowers on the weekend market. I cleaned the bathroom to cut down her chores. I dug and weeded the garden. I gave her mothers' day cards with the requisite 'to the best mother in the world' carefully written inside, hoping she might get the hint. When she had her monthly migraines, I was the one who nursed her, fetched her Lucozade, supplied her with fresh damp flannels.

If I excelled at school, always top of the class, with perfect results at O and A levels, it wasn't because Mum pressured me to do this, it was simply the unspoken and unconscious assumption my brother and I fulfilled, as if we knew this was the only way Mum would get reparation for her own lack of education and truncated ambition; she'd longed to be a school teacher. Her frustrated ambition was in our DNA – we knew without being told we were meant to excel. I read the Bible, went to church two or three times every Sunday, memorised the prayer book, sewed tapestries of country cottages with hollyhocks outside the door, didn't let butter melt in my mouth when relatives visited.

When such goody-two-shoes behaviour didn't elicit any response, I swung to the opposite. When I was very young, I would keep silent for days at a time. After I'd read Enid Blyton, I begged to go to boarding school. Later came teenage rebellion, angry ripostes, wildness, courting the most uncouth and unsuitable boys Mum would disapprove of, then the ultimate black sheep act of getting pregnant. All were part of an unconscious melodrama trying to draw her out, force a response, smash the glass passivity and push her into the role of a mother. But everything failed. She remained impassive, frozen, sitting at meal times grim lipped, staring out of the window, not eating, barely pretending to pick at things, as if she longed to be anywhere but with us, in this compromise of a life and family.

Things became more sinister as I entered adolescence. I suppose Mum was jealous of my teenage prettiness and cleverness, the way I had every opportunity she'd been denied. One Christmas, she gave me a shoe box filled with make-up, cheap cosmetics wrapped in newspaper. I threw them all away. I resented the way Mum encouraged a family friend from church, Mr Jarvis, a lay preacher and Latin teacher, to come visiting. Jarvis had a crush on me and would sneakily hold my hand under a travel rug in the car, or find excuses to be alone. 'Do come round anytime Bob,' Mum told him. 'I know how found you are of our Rosemary.' I felt like a trade-off and wanted to vomit. I found him repulsive. I started to get paranoid, peering out of the bedroom windows at night to make sure Bob Jarvis wasn't outside, stalking. It reminded me of the way Mum had let the vicar, Timothy Marshall, bring up a glass of water for me and sit on the bed, saying prayers together. Had I trusted my mother, these might have been innocent episodes. But I didn't. I felt more and more wary.

Her unspoken hostility increased as I got older and I began to think she was trying to poison me. This was, I'm sure, part of my anorexia, unable to eat food she'd cooked. I had dreams where she fed me dishes of dead birds, their feathers unplucked, or she was in the kitchen with a long sharp knife, about to cut off my left hand. I didn't feel safe in the house. When I had a bath, I'd hunt for a clean towel at the bottom of the airing cupboard, fearing that the one she'd put out for me might be poisoned. Linda Gillman, after meeting my mother a few times, repeated her negative judgement that night she thought my mother was a narcissist, completely self-centred, and that I'd do better to shed all contact with her.

But, while it was true that Mum lived in her own world and couldn't engage with others profoundly, I don't think this was crude narcissism; her ego wasn't strong enough for that. She had no belief she was worthy of love and admitted to me once, towards the end, that she 'never felt she deserved' a daughter 'as lovely' as me. Nor was she particularly selfish, she would give anything away to anyone. But she had never grown up. Emotionally, she remained a child. She could do sentiment, she never forgot birthdays or anniversaries, and on her own birthday she would boast about the dozens of cards she received, from acquaintances she'd done some kindness for. She joined the local W.I. and became its president for many years. But like Mrs Jellyby in *Bleak House*, with her support of the natives of Borrioboola-Gha, my mother was better able to relate to distant strangers than to family. Ignorant of the needs of her own daughter, or grandchild, she was keen to work for charities abroad. In her later years she spent all her spare time sitting at her fancy new computerised sewing machine, constructing elaborate patchwork quilts to send to orphans in Africa.

It was only after I'd been in therapy for years, and learned more about child development and human personality, that I was able to reflect more objectively on my upbringing. And I saw then how all my relationships, especially that with my son, had been affected by this 'glass mother', whose emotional systems were completely closed down. Slowly, the pieces of the jigsaw started to fit together.

Eventually, thinking of Mum as clinically as if she were a client in therapy, I listed her symptoms.

This was a woman:

who never made direct eye contact

who could not put herself in the place of others

who had no empathy

who withdrew from any display of feeling

who didn't cry, even when her husband died

who rarely laughed

who substituted sentiment for deep feeling

who didn't think for herself, but fell back on received opinion

who showed no real interest in others

who could manifest total indifference to suffering

who didn't grasp another person's emotions in a conversation

who didn't understand dialogue was a two-way, give-and-take affair

who often talked too loudly to others, unaware she was doing so

or who froze and sat in silence, giving nothing away

who was oblivious to the effect of her behaviour on others

who was overwhelmed by life and found it hard to handle practicalities

who often withdrew, preferring solitude to people

who expressed no needs, asked for nothing

who didn't live fully in her body

who didn't know basic facts about the body

who had an incredible ability to focus on detail

who could spend hours concentrating on difficult sewing or knitting

who mastered complex patterns with ease

and who, in her eighties, taught herself the mysteries of a computer-
    ised sewing machine.

With the list in front of me, the penny finally dropped. This, surely, was the profile of a woman with Asperger's.

It all seems so obvious to me now, that Mum was somewhere on the autistic spectrum, with many features of Asperger's syndrome, but had I not done my therapy training, or not kept reading widely around mental illness, I would not have recognised the clues. How many other people, I wondered, live with parents whose undiagnosed mental health issues have blighted their lives, leading them to blame themselves for their supposed inadequacies? How can a child know that a mother's lack of response is nothing to do with them? How can a child with such a mother know he or she is OK and loveable?

But now my life started to make sense. There was an explanation for everything. I could now understand and bear to replay the sad scenes from my childhood: my constant sense of being alone, in relationship with nothing but an absence, as if the incubator in which I'd started life had come with me as a kind of glass wall, an invisible bell jar standing between me and the world.

I believe now that Mum didn't intend to deprive me, or hurt me, any more than I meant to deprive or hurt Adam. She was simply unable to do more, completely out of her depth. She gave what she could: knitted me jumpers, sewed me clothes, dressed my doll, made curtains and cushions. She helped with my doctoral thesis, doing the notes. She was just oblivious to what I needed on an emotional level, thought that when I appealed for help, it would work to give me a jar of home-made chutney. Many times I got angry with her, unfairly I see now, raged at her for not being the mother I needed, especially for not giving me the implicit skills to mother Adam, not intervening in Leeds when I was about to lose him. But she was terrified of anger. She'd look frightened and say in a mousey voice, 'I don't know what you want of me.' She was telling the truth. She didn't.

But though I eventually came to this understanding of some level of Asperger's in my mother, understood where my difficulties began, this didn't magically solve my problems. Mental and emotional health are not crossword puzzles, they can't be solved intellectually. A diagnosis is only the beginning. I remember the epiphany when N said to me, 'You can learn how to love.' But I still had to heal the fall-out of my formative years of not being met, still had to practise relating to others in a way that transcended the damaged template forged in childhood. In *Why Love Matters: How Affection Shapes a Baby's Brain*, Sue Gerhardt points out the long-term psychological wounds carried by children who have not been loved. My battle with recurrent depression and the consequences of badly chosen relationships have persisted throughout my life. As has the lingering grief over separation from Adam, and the struggle to undo the damage which I, in my turn, inflicted on him.

Not until the very end, a few weeks before my mother died, did her emotional incapacities finally fall away. She was ninety-five; I had just turned sixty. She'd had a fall in her sheltered accommodation and was hospitalised. As I sat with her behind the screens, waiting for nurses to examine her, she took my hand.

'You don't know how proud I am of you,' she said. 'I love you. I've always loved you so much. My beautiful little girl with the curly blonde hair.'

I stared at her in disbelief. Why, I thought, has it taken you six decades to say this? Do you have any idea how different my life might have been? Why does it take death to start creeping over the horizon before your worldly persona can fall away and the cold symptoms of Asperger's can retreat? Why wait until the end to say, for the first time in your life, that you love me?

I leaned over and kissed her on the forehead. 'Thank you,' I said. 'I love you too.'

After that, as if her work was done, she stopped eating or drinking. She never left hospital and within forty days she was gone. She'd been insistent she didn't want to go back 'up north' where my father was buried in a grave near his family in Mansfield Woodhouse. So I hid some of her ashes in my suitcase and took them to India, to the holiest place I know, buried them secretly one quiet afternoon under a tree on the hill at Meherabad. The remaining ashes my brother and I scattered at Stourhead, a beautiful National Trust property in Wiltshire, not far from where I live. Mum loved it there.

I often go and sit near her on a lichened stone bench, watching swans and Canada geese on the lake as the seasons change. First the January snowdrops, spring's magnolia and daffodils, June's rhododendrons and azalea, then the maples once more reddening into winter. And I feel we are at peace.

22

Grief in Reverse

See how the fig leaves disappear, the awkwardness lost,
the kisses honey-filled once more, the me-you and you-me
translated back into a love before sorrow or war.

Rosie Jackson, 'Love Letters'

THROUGHOUT MY TIME at Bristol, I was still unaccountably obsessed with Mary Shelley and *Frankenstein*. Virago gave me a contract to write a book on her. I planned an anthology of essays on Mary Shelley and Romanticism. I took part in a BBC TV Everyman programme on *Frankenstein* and got pilloried in a cartoon in *Punch* for my pains, the re-assembled monster looking puzzled as he listened to my feminist account. Only when I made a lecture trip to the States in February 1988, virtually the last act in my affair with academic life, did the obsession with Mary Shelley start to make sense. The University of West of England (recently upgraded from Bristol Poly) set up a teaching visit for me at Hartford University, and thanks to Allon White's contacts (he still had four months to live), en route to Connecticut I also gave lectures on Mary Shelley at Stony Brook New York, through Ann Kaplan, and at Princeton, where Elaine Showalter, who'd visited UEA when I taught there, was now professor.

What better place, in fact, for my academic swan song, than Princeton, one of the pinnacles of the Ivy League Universities? In the teaching room, fruit and cake were served on silver platters. Afterwards I stayed in the guest house, a white mansion, luxuriously appointed, my double bedroom packed with antiques. The 'butler' who showed me to my room was the only black person I saw on a campus of well-heeled whites.

Elaine Showalter proved extraordinarily supportive, and cast some welcome light onto my obsession with Mary Shelley. She said she used my book on *Fantasy* for teaching, and that I was right to have claimed it as a subversive genre – its questioning of the 'symbolic' social order could itself, she thought, be seen as a feminist enterprise, almost regardless of theme. But she argued that when women write female Gothic, it's not about confronting the father, but the mother – an expression of ambivalence towards her. The lost mother haunted Mary Shelley too, she wrote her own drama about the Demeter Persephone myth, though she used the Latin name *Proserpine* for the title rather than the Greek. Was this ambivalence towards the mother why I was so obsessed by the legend of Mary Shelley, why I found it so hard to leave her behind? Everything about her haunted me: the death of her mother, Mary Wollstonecraft, in childbirth; her oppressive father William Godwin; her love for Shelley and their belief in sexual and political freedom; their close tie with Byron and the other Romantics; Shelley's drowning and Mary's lifelong bereavement; her devotion to their one surviving son; but most of all the story of *Frankenstein* and the loss of Mary Shelley's baby on which it was based. 'Dream that my dead baby came to life again – that it was not dead, but lived.'

Perhaps it was now time, Showalter suggested, to take Mary Shelley into myself, to come to terms with what she represented and move beyond her, to run her instead of her running me. Her students told me I should read theorist Julia Kristeva (hello again), that Mary Shelley's depression was all to do with 'abjection'. I still didn't understand fully what Mary Shelley did represent to me, but I knew Showalter was right: I was desperate to move beyond *Frankenstein* and all things Gothic.

The following week, in Hartford, home of Wallace Stevens, I remembered the quote of his I'd used as the last lines of my D.Phil. thesis: *Beneath every no lay a passion for yes that had never been broken.* And after another quick visit to the Meher Baba Centre at Myrtle Beach, where I repeated my inner commitment to all things positive and spiritual, I resolved to take action. On my return to the UK, I took every volume of Gothic fiction and criticism on my shelves to second hand bookshops, burnt my reams of notes on the almost completed book on Mary Shelley, cancelled the contract with Virago and gave in my notice at the University of West of England. I didn't understand why, but somehow felt the whole package went together, as if, along with Mary Shelley, academia and the Gothic, I needed to dump 'bad mother' and depression all in one fell swoop.

By now I'd bought a tall terraced house in Cliftonwood, Bristol, almost identical to the one I'd lived in as a child in Leeds, and made a small income from renting out rooms and seeing therapy clients. Wanting to engage and train more with psychoanalysis, I signed up for supervision with a staunch Kleinian. I'd read Melanie Klein (in ex-hubbie Tony's living room), but now I came across a more evangelical approach. When I shared the case of one of my clients, a sexually abused girl, who'd been repeatedly raped by father and brother with broken bottles, the supervisor embarked on a lecture on Klein's ideas of the nipple and breast. I stared at her in disbelief.

'Sorry to interrupt,' I said, 'but this is a political issue, isn't it? I need to know the best way of helping her. What's this got to do with a theory of the breast?'

The supervisor looked out of her casement window at her beautiful garden, with its nearby river, and sighed. This was the trouble with people who'd not done a strict analytic training. They didn't grasp the basics. They wanted to solve everything on the external social level when it was all internal. But I had in front of me my young client, the struggle she had to tell me anything, the way she hated the very chair I sat in because of the pain she shared, her whole body shaking as she remembered her anguish. And at the end of my expensive fifty minutes, I closed the door on the Kleinian's lovely stone house, knowing I wouldn't be back.

But other psychoanalytic trainings were available in the Bristol area and I was soon offered a programme with the Severnside Institute. Their first requirement was Infant Observation, which involved closely observing a woman with a new born baby for several months. The logic behind this was undeniable: to best understand the formation of human identity, you need to study first-hand this primary bond, the dyad of mother and child. Once again, as Winnicott said, there is no such thing as a baby alone, only a baby and its mother.

For weeks I tried to persuade myself I could do this. Of course I could. I wanted to train as an analyst, I'd been offered a place. The trainer called me one day and tried to break through my hesitancy, saying, 'You know, the time comes when we have to make a *conscious* decision.' But all my life had been governed by *unconscious* decisions, and here was another. For when I thought of the reality of sitting with a mother and her baby, hour after hour, for months on end, I knew it was an invitation to hell.

Time after time, I imagined it. The mother's ripe body, soft flesh, the baby at the breast, the nipple in the mouth, the closeness, intimacy, sucking, love, as if they were still one, and I looking on, the perennial outsider, watching a bond I sensed I'd never had, with my cold incubator then a mother with her back turned.

But worse than that, far worse, were the memories of Adam new-born. I remembered laying his naked body on mine in the weeks after his birth, swearing to him that we would never be separated, that no-one would ever come between us. I smelt again his down of hair, recalled the sensation of breast-feeding him in the student union at Warwick, or in the flat above the hairdresser's, with an odour of shampoo and the sound of muzak underfoot. I could feel once more the delicious tangible delight of him, his chubby arms and legs, his cuddly body, holding him close and caressing him in a way that for so many years had happened only at night, and still haunted me, in dreams that took me back to his infancy and left me bereft and anguished in the morning.

Perhaps the trainer would have told me I could work through these painful memories and come out the other side. One of the favourite mythical archetypes for the therapist, after all, is Chiron, the wounded Greek healer. Speared in the leg by Achilles, Chiron spends his life trying to find a cure for his wound, and though he fails to fully heal himself, he learns enough about medicine to give healing to others. Perhaps, with my deep wounds, I too could help others. But I knew this was deluding myself.

To look on, not only at a new-born baby being mothered, but at a new mother nurturing her baby, would have been, for me, double torture. Then, on top of the observation itself, would have come theories about the dire and damaging consequences of breaking such a defining bond. Wasn't I a perfect example of both, on each side? It was all too lethal a mix, emotionally the most painful thing I could imagine. As both infant and mother I would be bereft, left out, lacking and failing. With a history like mine, only a masochist would have said yes to such exquisite agony. The visceral decision once more made itself and, without going into explanations that might be challenged, I declined the training place. Thus another profession was lost to me, one for which my many wounds, my habit of self-scrutiny, and perennial love of the unconscious might otherwise, ironically enough, have made me particularly well-suited.

But the ditching of all things negative seemed to work, for that year my fortunes changed. Soon after the farcical divorce from Tony, at a series of psychoanalytic lectures in Bristol, I met a trainee analyst called Rachel. She'd recently split from her boyfriend and moved to Bath, where she invited me to her housewarming party. When a good-looking dark-haired man entered the crowded room, I recognised him instantly, not from the past but from the future. I knew this would be my third husband. Not that we'd met before, but his face was dearly familiar, as if I'd been trying to find him for centuries. This was Rachel's ex-boyfriend, John. A brief courtship later – walking coastal paths, exploring woodlands, picnics at Stourhead – I'd rented out my Bristol terrace and we were living together in his house in Evercreech, a small village in Somerset, about ten miles east of Glastonbury.

My constant refrain as I reported my new-found life and love to N was that I couldn't believe my luck. 'It's too good to be true. John's just perfect for me.' He was everything I was not: grounded, practical, pragmatic, ingenious in the material world, an utter genius with all things inanimate. A potter by trade, he'd been forced to relinquish his pottery in the Quantocks when he left his first wife (and their two sons) for Rachel (considerably younger). Unable to afford to set up a second pottery, he'd taught himself computing skills and was now working full-time in the computing department at Bath University. Ever resourceful, he'd converted his garage at Evercreech into a small pottery, with a gas-fired kiln and small showroom in the garden, where he worked at evenings and weekends.

John's pots were in a classic Bernard Leach style, substantial but graceful domestic stoneware, hand-thrown and glazed with dark autumnal coloured slips: chestnut brown, deep sage, midnight blue, near black, with streaks of russet, rust and chrome. His brush work and throwing were impeccable, with exquisite Japanese influenced decoration and calligraphy. One of his heroes was Michael Cardew, a studio potter who had worked with Leach and was influenced by the Japanese pottery of Shoji Hamada. Like Cardew, John's ideal was pottery in the 17th century English slipware tradition, to be used daily and not priced beyond the reach of ordinary people. For someone like me, brought up with the cheapest china – white plates with roses that seemed to be stuck on with transfers, so easily did they scratch or peel away, while the best (parents' wedding present) tea service was kept in a glass-fronted china cabinet that was never opened – to use hand-thrown stoneware all the time felt like I'd moved from the servants' quarters into the banqueting hall of a medieval castle. We had ceramic wine goblets, huge bread crocks, water jugs, casserole dishes, massive salad bowls, all works of art in their own right, rich with layers of colour that seemed to have captured and solidified the very flames of the kiln.

John didn't tolerate pretension in art, or in anything else. Like Leach, over 'fine art' pots, he preferred 'ethical' and 'functional', simple utilitarian forms that could be used for cooking on an everyday basis. This made him impatient with trends in ceramics veering more towards experiment and aesthetics than usefulness, and he often dismissed them as 'self-indulgent'. If things weren't useful, they were useless and he had no time for them. (Take note, wife number two).

I felt as if I'd known John forever and found him attractive in every way. The detour with Tony had just been a mistake. *This* was the man who was the answer to my prayers, the man I'd always dreamt of finding. Perhaps this was because he bore a striking resemblance to Meher Baba. I'd put up various of my gold-framed photos of Baba on the walls and one weekend when John's elder son, Jonathan, then in his late teens, was visiting, he stopped suddenly in front of one, contemplating it more closely.

'Dad,' he said, 'when was this picture of you taken? I've not seen it before. Was that in the 60s?'

John raised his eyebrows and left it to me to explain that the black and white photo, from the 1930s, was actually my spiritual teacher from India. The mistake was easy to make. They had the same dark moustache, the same strong bold nose, slightly hooked (in Baba's case from his Persian origins), the same carved cheekbones, darting eyes and long hair tied back in a pony tail. At Meherabad and Myrtle Beach, I'd met many Baba would-be look-alikes, indeed the thick moustache seemed almost mandatory. But John outdid them all. Anyone who'd seen photos of Meher Baba couldn't help remarking on their uncanny facial resemblance.

Retrospectively, I realise this should have rung alarm bells. Did I adore John for his own sake or because he was the spitting image of my other Beloved? Perhaps I was never able to see John clearly, with his human flaws and shortcomings, but projected onto him the perfection I believed Baba embodied. Not that I worried about muddling them up at the time. I simply felt doubly blessed. I had both a spiritual teacher and a partner to adore and love, and if they looked alike, if they merged in my mind and heart, so much the better. Each magnified the love I had for the other. Not having met Baba in the flesh myself (just nine years too late), John was my own version, a special gift to remind me how Baba must have looked in human form, though in reality John was 6' 2" to Baba's 5'5", and probably weighed half as much again as Baba's slight, much fasted figure. John never betrayed much curiosity about Baba, never read books or asked questions, but he seemed happy to tolerate the photos which appeared round the house; perhaps, for him, it was merely like looking in the mirror.

What he didn't tolerate was psychotherapy. He'd been persuaded by Rachel to work with the same Kleinian analyst I'd seen for supervision, and had not been impressed. Several times, in his early morning sessions en route to work, the Kleinian had nodded off to sleep. This left John very dubious about therapy's value, and gave him the perfect excuse to confirm the superiority of his utilitarian outlook on life.

Socrates might have declared the unexamined life not worth living, but for John the unlived life was not worth examining. And though he actively discouraged me from continuing any therapy training, when he discovered how much I wanted to write – my dream since childhood – he offered to support me, including financially. ' I have to pay these household bills anyway,' he said, 'you may as well get the benefit of it.' I returned to Bristol one or two days a week to see clients, but when one by one they moved towards a natural completion, I didn't seek to recruit more. 'I'm so happy,' I told N. 'I don't need to come to therapy any more. John and I are so close on every level. Everything between us is perfect.'

I felt I'd ascended into worldly heaven. This was the kind of love that righted wrongs; what Carol Ann Duffy, in *Rapture*, would call *grief in reverse*. I was living in the country with the man of my dreams, doing what I'd always wanted. I wrote all morning and gardened, walked or explored Somerset in the afternoon: the mythical Camelot at Cadbury Castle, the equally legendary Glastonbury Tor. In the evenings we ate together, then curled up with a book, or John would work in the pottery. He was a Renaissance man. He could do anything. He was still travelling to Bath University (at least an hour each way) five days a week, and he leapt up the promotions ladder several rungs at a time, until, despite no university degree or doctorate, he was Director of Computing Services.

When we married and pooled our money to buy a dilapidated Somerset farmhouse, with two acres of land, five large barns and outbuildings in various states of ruin, John attacked the renovation work at the same full throttle. The day we moved in, he ripped off wooden boards in the living room to expose a vast inglenook; that night in the field we had a huge bonfire for all the old carpets, lino and wood. Soon he had another pottery in one of the barns and one of the pig-sheds had been converted into a small white-washed shop.

Despite my failed attempts thus far, I still felt marriage to be important, not socially, but as an archetype, a symbol of the deep meeting of male and female, inwardly and outwardly, and I wanted to celebrate having found this union at last. We had a midsummer ceremony in a Methodist chapel in Castle Cary. Adam, nineteen now, came down on the train for the wedding, handsome and slim in a smart grey suit, his hair fashionably cut. I was very slim too, no longer comfort eating now I was with John. I wore a bespoke raw silk suit, pale pink, with matching high heels and nails. One friend said I looked 'pearlised'; 'nacreous' was the adjective I later used in a poem. Karen Cohen was the only guest from my UEA days, Sophie Edwards from my Bristol time, along with a few dozen friends and relatives.

As I drove Adam to the B & B where he was staying with my mother, he threw me a seemingly casual question.

'Mum, now you and John are married, are you going to have any babies?'

I turned from the country lanes in full blossom to view Adam's face in profile. He seemed mature, with a quick wit, but I knew that under this adult veneer hid a heartache few could fathom.

'John can't have children,' I said. 'He's had the snip. That's why he and Rachel split up. But even if he could, I wouldn't have any.' I briefly touched his arm. 'There's only room for one child for me, Adam. You are not replaceable. I'm a one-man mother.'

Adam didn't say anything, merely nodded and smiled a little as he looked out at the white cow parsley nodding over hedges and fields. I felt he was reassured and I was pleased he'd asked. But my answer, while true, was not the full truth. The whole experience of having Adam, and even more of being without him, had been too devastating to risk repeating and I'd sworn to myself many times I'd never have another child. Perhaps I'd also chosen John for this reason. He too was adamant he would never parent again.

His younger son Simon came to stay with us every other weekend, and I was keen to be a good step-mother, often driving to collect or return him to his mother in the Quantocks while John carried on potting or building. On Saturday afternoons they flew their model aeroplanes on Creech Hill while I cooked my mother's Yorkshire recipe for ginger parkin and gave thanks for this miraculous reprieve from loneliness. Adam was doing odd jobs for a living, he never went to college or university. So euphoric was I to be married, with a new 'family' of my own, I failed to pick up that Adam's question about children might have indicated a worry that he felt excluded from my new situation, where Simon was just a few years his junior, as well as from the nuclear family David and Jan now had with their two young children. They'd recently moved to Yorkshire and left Adam behind with his job and friends. Where did he feel he belonged?

Jung reputedly said that it doesn't really matter who you marry, because you'll wake up next morning and find they're someone entirely different. This had happened with Tony, and now it happened with John too. We'd gone for our honeymoon to Italy, to a small house perched on top of a Tuscan hillside. Failing to live up its charming description in the *Observer* small ads, the house was actually a hut full of scorpions, a stuck water tap, with neighbours who activated strimmers from dawn to dusk. The ideal husband I thought I'd married would have blown money on a decent *pensione* for a few nights; after all, for our second week away I'd set up a free stay in an apartment in Assisi belonging to Valeria Violati, one of the Italian women I'd met in India. But John sat in the noisy garden smoking his roll ups.

'I think we should just cut our losses and return home,' he said.

'You're joking.' I looked at him in dismay. 'We've had three days solid driving to get here. Anyway what about Assisi? We can't miss seeing all those Giottos in the Basilica. I've spent weeks learning Italian. Why don't we go to Florence for a few days?'

A silent John blew his smoke into spirals that snaked against the vivid blue sky. I'd never heard him argue or lose his temper; he often boasted he never got angry; we'd never had a fight. But by next morning, our suitcases were back in my car and we were returning to England. We spent the remainder of the fortnight in the semi at Evercreech, where John immediately took up his paintbrush.

'Being a tourist is such a waste of time,' he said. 'It's much better to be creative.'

Art was another of his myriad skills. He'd introduced me to oil painting, and I'd produced a few Georgia O'Keefe inspired semi-abstractions. But that week, cheated of a honeymoon for the third time in my life, I was too stunned to paint or write. While John produced several wonderful oil paintings of trees in blossom, Klimt-like in their fairy tale appearance, I delivered cups of tea and thank-you letters for our wedding presents. But I soon recovered. A lost honeymoon wasn't going to spoil my happiness.

John too came from a modest background, and we were both driven by a dream of living in the kind of country property we'd seen as kids on jigsaws and chocolate boxes. We bought an old stone farmhouse, once the village bakery, in East Pennard, and became two grown-up kids playing house, lying in bed devising plans, sketching designs for windows (which John made and installed), bantering over which outbuilding we wanted for our own studio. We weren't bourgeois aspirants like our parents, but bohemian artists who didn't mind mice in the skirting or buckets catching the rain, and we'd live frugally to realise our mutual dream. With no central heating, it was freezing cold in winter and even when wood-burners were installed in the two main rooms downstairs, a bitterly cold edge persisted. The kitchen, bathroom and bedrooms remained arctic. Washing was a matter of a quick bath then racing along the corridor to the bedroom and diving under the duvet in a shivering heap. But this was part of the game.

From our orchard there was a glimpse of Glastonbury Tor on the horizon and we lived within easy walking distance of the Glastonbury festival site at Pilton. My daily tramps often took me over the empty fields where the Pyramid stage suddenly appeared at midsummer. This proximity entitled us, along with all the surrounding villages, to free festival tickets, but we gave ours to Simon; his mates would meet him inside once they'd scaled the high perimeter wall. One year one of these mates took his girlfriend, who dutifully followed him over the top of the fence and dropped down several feet on the other side, only to find that she'd left behind one of her fingers – a metal spike on the fence caught in her ring and, as she fell, her finger was severed.

John never welcomed the festival, he saw it as intrusion into his homeland. We would walk over the fields near the house to look down over the thousands of cars and tents spread out below like a battleground. We often encountered exhausted or drunken festival goers who'd walked the eight miles from Castle Cary station and were trying to find their way to the site. One evening, we came across four Cockney youths facing a herd of cattle, seemingly paralyzed with terror.

'What the fuck are they?' said one.

'I dunno,' said another.

'They're cows you moron. Aren't they?' said a third.

'Shit,' said the first. 'I've never seen a cow before.'

For our first Christmas at the Bakehouse, John gave me a copy of *A Very Close Conspiracy*, about the lives of sisters Virginia Woolf and Vanessa Bell. On Christmas morning, I lay on a mattress on the floor in our still-camping-in-the-ruins bedroom, reading the book and listening to John potter downstairs, making me a cup of tea. In all our time together, he never stayed in bed beyond 6 or 7 a.m., always driving himself relentlessly, compulsively up and doing. But I felt deliriously happy. When had I ever been closer to the ideal Woolf and Bell represented? I too could write and paint, I was married to a loving active man (the complete opposite of my second, often-stoned 'husband') and living in the house of my dreams in beautiful rural Somerset, worlds away from my council estate origins and former loneliness. This was where Adam and his future partner would bring my grandchildren to visit, and John's sons Jonathan and Simon would bring his. We would be the indulgent Granny and Grandpa, and later the many grandchildren would come on their own for holidays, throw pots and play with the clay, or so I dreamt.

Adam did visit occasionally, each time bringing a different girlfriend, though he and John were never close. Socialising was not John's priority; even when his own mother visited, let alone mine, it was left to me to be the host while he escaped to the pottery. His appetite for company was more than satisfied by his daily trips to Bath and he resisted my requests to go out more. East Pennard had neither shop nor pub, but we did have a couple of friends in the village, more potters.

Also nearby were Lindsay and Phoebe Clarke. Lindsay had recently won the 1989 Whitbread Fiction Prize for his novel *The Chymical Wedding*, one of the first to successfully exploit a divided historical narrative. Our lives were strange mirror images. Lindsay too was born in Yorkshire, with a degree in English literature (from Cambridge, where he'd lodged with John and Faith Broadbent) and he'd lived in a reclusive village in

Norfolk. He'd also resigned from the security of a teaching job in Norwich (at the City College) with no notion of what to do next, and had been given some work at UEA by John Broadbent. But he'd felt much as I did about the place, his soul 'chilled by those brutal concrete walkways of the mind.' Lindsay believed the creative imagination was a greater power for healing than the intellect, and his rare vision and warm friendship gave me the inspiration I needed for my own writing. He not only knew George Barker, but had made him the model for his priapic, ageing poet Edward in *The Chymical Wedding*, using his eloquence to voice a sense of the passionate urgency of shifting our world view from an alienating, secular one, to something deeper.

My other soul mate was Diana Taylor, a highly gifted artist I'd met through our mutual connection with Meher Baba. Married to renowned jazz pianist John Taylor, Di lived in Kent, but we had close and frequent contact by phone and letter. One of the happiest days of my life was a summer afternoon a few years after we'd moved to East Pennard, when Di and John Taylor visited us. My John was unusually sociable and the four of us sat on tartan rugs under the old cider apple trees in our orchard, sun glancing through the branches, the ripening fruit only weeks from harvest. We laughed and talked – music, art, politics – drank sparkling wine and ate our picnic of salad, cheese, crusty bread and fruit. I'd never been happier. I'd finally arrived at the place I'd always longed for. I'd tasted spiritual ecstasy in India, felt at home there, but this was a worldly love; I didn't have to deny my human needs to claim it. Looking back, I mark these as some of the best hours I've known. At last, I felt I belonged on this earth. I'd found reciprocal love. I was so proud to have John as my husband and Di and John Taylor as close friends. Even without the wine, we were all rather heady, as Di had just heard she was in remission from her recent breast cancer.

That evening we went to a concert of John Taylor's at the Arnolfini, the art complex on Bristol's waterfront where I'd worked so wretchedly ten years before, but could now revisit with new joy and inner peace. As John Taylor and his musicians received a standing ovation, Di and I exchanged smiles and embraced. Little did we know, as we hugged each other, what shadows were stretching toward us.

23

Esther Rantzen's Scissors

The father's absence from his child is seen here as redeemed,
the mother's absence... unredeemable.

Rebecca Bailin on *Kramer versus Kramer, Jump Cut,* 1980

O NE EVENING IN April 1990, shortly before John and I married, I caught by chance a BBC TV documentary called *How Could She?* telling the poignant stories of several women who, through various circumstances, had felt impelled to leave their children. This was the first time I'd seen my own reality made public and I was riveted and shocked in equal measure. When I wrote to Sylvia Paskin, one of the mothers who collaborated on the programme, I discovered she'd planned a book on the subject, but had felt singed by the media exposure and worried about its negative effect on her relationship with her son. Despite these warnings, I felt inspired to take up the baton, and began research for my book *Mothers Who Leave.*

Through MATCH, a self-help organization for Mothers Apart from Their Children, I discovered my experience was far less singular than I'd supposed. Figures were inexact, but estimates put a hundred thousand women living away from their children in the UK, half a million in the US. Some were famous names: Doris Lessing, Yoko Ono, Joni Mitchell, George Sand, Frieda Lawrence, Margaret Trudeau, Shirley MacLaine, Ingrid Bergman. History, I discovered, had not treated them with compassion. When Bergman left her daughter Pia in the States and moved abroad to live with film director Roberto Rossellini, she was cursed from the heart of the US Congress itself. On the floor of the Senate, 14 March 1950, Senator Edwin C. Johnson accused Bergman of being 'an alien guilty of turpitude', for surely 'her unnatural attitude toward her own little girl indicates a mental abnormality.' Supporting Johnson's verdict that Bergman was therefore 'a powerful influence for evil', the house agreed to banish her: she was forbidden to set her cloven foot on American soil ever again. With such examples before us, no wonder that I, like other mothers who'd left children, often felt isolated and stigmatised, trapped in negative judgements from others which we swallowed and inflicted on ourselves.

A new book appeared in 1990, Helen Franks' *Mummy Doesn't Live Here Any More*, but when I hurried to read it, her implicit assumptions and complacent tone left me enraged. Hers was clearly not first-hand experience and this was not the study we needed. Not that I was yet ready to disclose much personal material myself. What I put together over the next couple of years was a collection of case studies, alongside sociological and psychoanalytic perspectives, with critiques of various demeaning images of mothers who've left in modern literature, film and popular culture.

The earliest novel I could remember reading which featured a mother who left was Warwick Deeping's *Sorrell and Son* (1930). One of Mum's favourites, it sat in our glass-fronted family bookcase, sandwiched between the *Pears Cyclopaedia* and the set of Dickens. It had also recently been turned into a TV adaptation starring Richard Pasco, so it felt particularly pertinent to see how it shaped assumptions.

Sorrell, Captain Stephen Sorrell, is demobbed after World War I, single parent to his only son Kit. A porter in provincial hotels, Sorrell is suddenly spotted by a wealthy Lord Sugar type entrepreneur who recognises his intrinsic worth, employs him, then promotes him to his business partner, with a lucrative antiques business on the side. Kit's mother, Sorrell's ex-wife Dora, makes no appearance until we are well into the novel and our sympathies for the two lone males have been firmly established. Then the mother who has left makes her entry: vampiric, greedy, ruthless, nymphomaniac.

'But the rampant sex of her!... a vampire, a woman who, having had all the satisfactions she desired from men and sex, was seeking others... That red mouth of hers was ready to feed upon the young vitality of her son...'

Sorrell's one passion is to 'keep her and Christopher apart'. He wants the boy to himself, refuses to let Dora offer any financial or emotional support, denies her any contact with her boy. It's a deeply misogynist novel, and any mother who has experienced any form of reluctant separation from her children would recognise all too well its plot, projections, sensational melodrama and blackening of character.

When Sorrell ponders on Dora's reappearance, he wonders, 'Did the mother ever think of the boy? He hoped not.' In fact, Dora has mothered Kit for the first eleven years of his life, staying in her unhappy marriage to the repressed and controlling Sorrell for Kit's sake till she was forty, but now she has broken the rules by leaving, she must be punished. She is not allowed to know where her son lives, not permitted to write letters or send gifts. Kit's last words to her – 'I belong to the pater' – wipe out all her years of mothering, and she is condemned to total exclusion and invisibility.

This was the kind of fable I'd grown up with, part of our family heritage and social mythology. Even though I hadn't, as Dora supposedly had, left my marriage for another man, still I recognised the closing of the ranks between father and son, forbidding the 'bad' mother's re-entry. I knew I couldn't change my own back story, but I could direct my sense of injustice into unpicking some of the stereotypes. Whether in fiction or fact, the hostile depiction of absent mothers such as Dora Sorrell or Ingrid Bergman were damaging caricatures, hard to undo, harder still not to internalise and I was determined to put them under scrutiny.

After *Sorrell and Son*, I turned to Mrs Henry Wood's *East Lynne*, one of the best-selling of the so called Victorian 'sensation novels', first published in 1861; then to *Kramer versus Kramer*, a modern version of the same story, where the mother who leaves must suffer and be punished, while the men left behind become victims and heroes. The mother in *East Lynne* endures the worst penance the moral imagination can devise: she leaves her husband and children, only to be abandoned when pregnant by her lover (who turns out to be a murderer) and seriously disfigured in a railway accident (in which her new baby dies). She returns crippled and unrecognisable as a governess to her own three children to whom she can never reveal her true identity (even when one of them is terminally ill). She has to witness their closeness to their step-mother, the happy and virtuous replacement wife.

The moral punishment is laid on with a thick Victorian trowel, yet this is exactly the same kind of revenge unconsciously inflicted on mothers who leave by late 20th century culture. The film of *Kramer versus Kramer* (1979) starring Meryl Streep, has the mother leaving for work rather than another man, but the same punitive revenge-plot kicks in: the mother is hysterical and can't sustain career and motherhood, though the heroic father – Dustin Hoffman – is miraculously able to be a better mother than he ever was a father. As in *Sorrell and Son*, the father-son bond is deeply romanticised; even male critics identified the subtext of *Kramer* as misogynistic, part of the backlash against feminism that took hold for the next few decades.

Hardly surprisingly then, especially given Sylvia Paskin's warnings about the media, I kept my own story to a minimum in *Mothers Who Leave*. It was easier to hide behind discussions of the ideology of mothering, to paint broad brush strokes of the politics of the situation, than to share my own guilt and heartache. I made it clear I came under the same category, but apart from two pages in the introduction, was almost coy about my history with Adam. Nearly all the many women I interviewed also chose to remain anonymous: they found it too painful to add to the trauma of being wrenched from their child or children the added shame of going public.

I was surprised how many women volunteered to talk to me. Suddenly, friend after friend knew someone round the corner in hiding about the fact that at some time in her life she had left her children, whether short or long term. I was shocked too by the circumstances of many women's lives, far darker and more tragic than my own. One young woman, pregnant again when I met her, kept having child after child only to give them away; it was as if she simply had no maternal glue, compulsively repeating the process in the wild hope this next one might magically stick. One had lost her daughters to their father's religious cult. Another, rather bizarrely, had left her children with their father and moved in with sugar daddy in a Knightsbridge flat – this way her kids got financial treats and outings they would never have had at home.

But I never accepted or argued that leaving was in any way a 'feminist' act, and resisted any such reading. All very well for Germaine Greer to make her provocative polemics in *The Female Eunuch* about rejecting prejudice against women who leave, arguing that if a wife who is leaving can only bring up the children in pauperdom, she 'must make a sensible decision, and reject out of hand the deep prejudice against the runaway wife.' I knew that even without her buoyant income, Germaine had far too generous a heart and belligerent a manner ever to have contemplated such a choice, had she had children.

What couldn't be denied was the replay of history. Every mother I met had a background of some form of broken mothering, whether adoption, abandonment, physical or emotional abuse. Damaged patterns of mothering seemed to be handed down like old clothes from one generation to the next, cloning and reproducing themselves in uncanny fashion. There seems an undeniable sense of inner logic to this. How can we give what we have not been given? How can we pass on innate mothering when it is outside our own experience? As if trapped in a hall of distorting mirrors, mothers often 'left' children at precisely the age they themselves had been left, as if a set of unconscious impressions is passed from one generation to another, repeatedly breaking through and being acted out.

Mum didn't visit often when I was with John, perhaps a couple of times a year; when she did, John described her as 'a rocket in outer space with most of its functions cut off.' I would take her to her much-loved National Trust gardens – Stourhead, Montacute, Lytes Cary – or to the Dorset coast. One afternoon I drove her to Lyme Regis, where we had cream tea in one of the old-fashioned cafés on the high street. Then we sat on the sea front, staring out at the Cobb and the honeycomb cliffs towards Charmouth and Golden Cap.

'I've got a new book coming out soon,' I said. 'It's about women who live apart from their own children.'

Mum said nothing, but sat frozen, her eyes fixed on the watery horizon. I was used to having no response, but on this occasion I thought the subject might just kindle a spark. I never knew whether she'd registered what I'd said, or if she was going through any shade of pride or disgust. My announcement simply drifted away on the sea breeze as gulls screeched overhead and incoming waves battered the walls of the Cobb.

It left me wondering if John Fowles' wife Elizabeth had sat in the same spot when she was missing her daughter, Anna. A friend had taken me to visit John Fowles a few times at Belmont, the 18th century maritime villa at the top of Lyme Regis where Fowles lived. He was encouraging of my writing and proved very helpful over *Mothers Who Leave*, as he was too over the book which quickly followed, on *Frieda Lawrence*. Like Frieda, who left her children to elope with D.H. Lawrence, Elizabeth had left her young daughter Anna so she could be with John Fowles and they'd spent most of their married life in Lyme. Elizabeth was dead now, but when I interviewed Anna for my book, I heard another poignant story of mother and daughter separation and grief, the male writer's needs having seemingly taken priority over the young child's.

Harper Collins bought the book and when their publicity machine was rather ineffective, I took it on myself to launch *Mothers Who Leave*. Susie Orbach kindly gave it a plug in the *Observer* magazine. Rosalind Coward, who'd been to UEA on the lecture series I organised, interviewed me and wrote a large article for the *Observer* news section. But the photographer they sent was still stuck in *East Lynne* melodrama. He placed me against a backdrop of ruins (not hard to find amidst our ramshackle barns), and shot me wretched and unsmiling, my hands clasped together, staring upwards as if in supplication, like something out of *The Nun's Prayer*. Despite my protests, this Gothic image was selected over several perfectly decent photos of me in front of my art work, where I appear sane and smiling. A mother who's left must, it seemed, be depicted as a little unhinged and repentant. The result was to increase my suspicion of journalists and make me scared of publicity. From then on, I was ambivalent, no longer sure whether I wanted to come out of hiding or go back into it, and instead stood with the door half open, a frustration to media people and friends alike.

I had literally dozens of requests for TV appearances. I was invited to go on *This Morning*, then to give an interview with Kirsty Wark, all of them wanting my personal story rather than taking on my ideological analyses of motherhood. Almost every day I was phoning Lindsay Clarke for advice.

'Should I do *This Morning*? Do you think they'd be sensitive?' 'Oh, now London Granada has phoned. What do you think?'

Eventually, Lindsay's patience grew strained. 'Look, you've done something important and you have to see it through. You can't stay in the closet and come out at the same time.'

But I felt paralysed with fear, terrified of public humiliation, even more terrified of making things worse with Adam. Instead of answering phone calls, I dug and re-dug the garden for hours at a time, trying to stem the panic. It was the same with magazines and newspapers. First, editors phoned with assurances of a non-sensational, sympathetic approach, then an interview with some kindly seeming woman would lead to articles bursting with a lexicon of 'abandonment', 'desertion', 'betrayal'. One headline boasted the smug question: 'Your kids might drive you mad, but could you leave them?' I was left feeling angry and vulnerable, knowing now what Sylvia Paskin had meant about being singed.

When an invitation came to appear on Esther Rantzen's *That's Life*,

I accompanied another woman from MATCH to London to meet the researcher. Immediately I mistrusted the programme's approach, which was far less sympathetic to the mother's perspective than had been promised, and I requested a meeting with Esther Rantzen herself. We were led to her office. She was far more beautiful than on screen: striking, charming, charismatic and vibrant, talking with a quick polish and slightly husky panache. Remembering I was speaking on behalf of many other women, I shared my misgivings about the way the programme was slanted.

'I'm not sure I like the way this is being constructed,' I said.

'*Constructed?*' Esther Rantzen, perched on the edge of a table, shifted impatiently. 'I don't think anything's being *constructed* at all,' she said. 'This is not a building site.'

Suitably put down, I returned to Castle Cary on the train, arguing with myself. I had to stop being such a baby. I had to stand up and be counted. What was the point of writing a book, if I wasn't prepared to deliver it properly to the world? Other writers would kill for this kind of exposure. A prime time TV appearance! What better publicity could there be? But still I couldn't decide. That night, curled against John's sleeping body, I prayed for a dream for guidance. My journal entry next morning reads:

'Dream. I'm in London to record the Esther Rantzen programme. My hair is a huge thick leonine mane of curls. I'm sitting waiting for Esther to come and talk to me on camera. But when she comes in, she's carrying a giant pair of silver scissors held at an angle towards me. The scissors are almost as tall as she is. She's coming towards me with a disarming smile, and then I realise she's going to chop off all my hair. I have to will myself to wake before she starts cutting.'

I had wild curly hair at the time and, remembering Samson and Delilah, heeded the warning. Not only did I decline *That's Life*, but all subsequent TV requests. I phoned the other MATCH mother to share my misgivings, but she chose to go ahead, only to call me after the show's transmission.

'Did you watch it?' she asked.

'No. I couldn't bear to.'

'Very wise. Esther was completely on the side of the children. She didn't keep any of her promises. I feel dreadful. I cried all the way home. She completely humiliated me.'

The one exception to this hypocritical media circus was *Woman's Hour*. Sara Davies, one of their presenters, whose impeccable reputation in Bristol I already knew, came to East Pennard to do an interview, and produced a sensitive, well-edited feature. Years later, during the early days of writing this memoir, BBC Radio 4 interviewed me again for a series called *Coming Out*, discussions with people whose lives have been changed by traumas where stigma makes public openness difficult. Thanks to Christine Hall's sensitive production, this too undid many of the usual preconceptions about absent mothers and helped me feel I was contributing to a gradual removal of hysteria from the public debate. My inbox was flooded with grateful emails from other women.

But most coverage reproduced exactly the preconceptions and projections I exposed in my book, as if a mother's very character, her status as a woman, are in question if she has 'failed' her children.

Small wonder that most of the mothers I met often dissimulated, as I did, by not admitting they had any children. By now, I could be around older children fairly comfortably, but still found it difficult to be with very young kids and avoided babies wherever possible. I didn't talk much with anyone about what had happened with Adam. It was too painful to be reminded of what had been lost, too shameful to be reminded of what I had not been able to be.

The double standards surrounding all this – the heroics attaching to Adam's father and the villainy attaching to me – never ceased to sting. John's friends who saw the newspaper coverage of my book were shocked: they didn't know I had a child, let alone that I'd 'left' him. How very 'strange'. My brother's first wife heard the *Woman's Hour* programme and dubbed me a 'weird woman'. But John had left his first wife and their boys; why was his action deemed normal and mine so bizarre? He didn't trail grief or guilt behind him; his friends weren't shocked by his story, indeed many of them shared a similar one.

'Don't you feel bad at not being with your boys full-time?' I would ask him.

'Sometimes,' he shrugged. 'You just have to get on with it.'

I'd told John from the start that living with me would not always be easy.

'I don't find it easy living with myself,' I joked, 'so why would anyone else?'

My bouts of depression were less now, but they still happened from time to time, and made it hard to predict how I would be from one day to the next. I knew I wasn't bi-polar, for I never had manic highs, but I couldn't quite define what I was.

'I'm not used to being loved,' I explained to John. 'You'll need to be very patient with me. It will take time for me to learn to fully trust. Babies who've not been loved often push people away at first when they try to love them.'

But I gradually discovered I was not the only one in our marriage who found it hard to let love in. I was so euphoric in the early years, so grateful and happy to have what I'd always craved, I would write little cards to John, saying how lucky I was, how I loved and adored him. Before he left for work, he'd leave loving notes for me on the kitchen worktops, and I'd write back in kind. But he seemed unable to receive my praise or appreciation. When I bought him little gifts, he'd invariably try to give them back to me, or get me something bigger in return. He told me that because his father had never honoured him, indeed had often put him down, he didn't believe anyone's approbation. Perhaps this was the cause of his relentless over-achieving and compulsive overdoing; I don't think he ever actually took in my love, or believed it. He later complained to people that I hadn't appreciated him, which I found bizarre. I spent a lot of time praising him, amazed at his many skills, sincerely grateful.

Our first three or four years together were blissful. John was kind and solicitous. He made canvases for my paintings, taught me computing, mended my car, mended my friends' cars when they visited, cooked vegetarian meals, built wardrobes, replaced ceiling beams, sent Adam money. I was utterly spoilt. For the first time in my life, I started to sleep naturally, my head resting on John's chest, feeling utterly safe and content.

But once we'd moved and were wrestling with our cold, insatiable ruined property, with huge tasks always asking to be done, the romance started to fall away. I was out of my comfort zone, being a builder's navvy, and couldn't keep up with John's relentless pace. I felt I was trying to be a female version of John, doing what I was not best fitted for. I knocked down lath and plaster walls, rotated compost heaps, stacked tons of logs, shooed away cattle who'd wandered into the garden from the dairy farm next door, hand-stripped paint from doors, put paint on walls, dug and planted a neglected garden, weeded the woods, sold pots, lived in a vacuum and generally endeavoured to be a good wife with no needs or money of her own. We lived miles from any cultural centre, and I probably should have made more effort to seek out activities that would feed me, but this was unknown territory. John was at work all day and wanted solitude at home. I was alone all day writing or working on the property and craved more dialogue with him and more connection together with the world; but the more I said so, the more John closed down, as if he experienced this hunger as attack.

I'd always needed words, they were part of my life breath, but John didn't talk much. In fact, I soon realised he had this in common with my mother, never initiating conversation or asking how my day had been. When I said I needed more connection with him, he complained I was harassing him.

One day, a few years into our marriage, I also realised with a shock as I turned to him in the car, that John had the exact profile of my dad. Why hadn't I seen this before? I'd married my father! What skill in my unconscious, to marry both parents rolled into one! Jung was right, then, I thought. It doesn't really matter who you marry, because not only are they not who you thought they were, but you will eventually find they are your father or your mother, or the two inexplicably and magically rolled together.

Little by little, we fell into a classic Mars-Venus antithesis, where the man *does* and resents being asked to *feel*, while the woman *feels* and is out of her depth being asked to *do*. The depression I still carried from childhood, compounded by losing Adam, started to creep back. And the more I took a leaf from John's book, trying to bully my depression and grief out of existence by staying busy, forcing myself to be ever more active or creative, the worse it got. Perhaps, in this, a craftsman, with his focus on *production*, has different expectations of himself. John was happiest when the pottery shelves were filled with hundreds of mugs or jugs waiting to be glazed. I was more interested in *process*, in the inner workings of creativity and the unconscious. But, feeling guilty now that John was supporting me financially, I took on his intolerance for fallowness, and stepped onto a conveyor belt which was always moving and expected delivery. I wrote for several hours each day, and when I wasn't writing I was gardening or decorating. The enemy was stillness or rest. Sex, sadly, counted as another time-waster. When I pointed out our relationship might improve with a little more love-making, John walked out of the room.

'The important thing,' he declared over his shoulder, 'is to create. Anyone can fuck.'

When I first moved in with John, I'd made the most of my newly liberated time to start writing short stories and, with fabled beginner's luck, the Women's Press took my first collection, *The Eye of the Buddha*. I'd never attended a writing class in my life, knew only by osmosis from many years of reading the basics of dialogue, character and plot, and was still to discover Hemingway's famous maxim of 'show don't tell.' Stories about psychotherapy, *The Eye of the Buddha* is rather too full of telling, voicing conflicts between psychoanalysis and softer-bellied new age therapies, like the ones I saw advertised on Glastonbury High Street. But the final story, 'The Last Session', worked better: a fantasy of Sigmund Freud arriving in the afterlife and discovering that there is, after all, something beyond the human: the deity he has always derided turns into his own analyst.

Another of the stories, 'Hideous Progeny', was a much compressed version of the book I'd been writing on Mary Shelley, so greatly crunched it was mostly beyond comprehension, though Sarah Le Fanu, then editor at the Women's Press, was undeterred. 'It's good for the reader to have a challenge. I loved it.' When she sent a copy of the book to Michèle Roberts, her verdict was that it was an 'angry' collection. But I didn't know it was angry, didn't even realise that my black and white photo on the back of the cover, which I thought was rather beautiful, also looked pretty pissed off. I was just delighted I had my first book out, and John, to whom it was dedicated, was equally thrilled. He came with me to readings in Exeter and at Bristol's Watershed, pride visible on his face as he sat tall at the back of the crowd, smiling me on to victory.

Over the next couple of years, I wrote *Mothers Who Leave*, then *Frieda Lawrence*, a study of D.H. Lawrence's wife, who had left her three children in Nottingham to elope with Lawrence. Both these books had only tiny advances which barely covered my research expenses – I had to go to Italy to interview Frieda Lawrence's daughter, Barbara Barr, in Tuscany – and neither of them earned anything over their advance. But part of the patriarchal nature of our marriage was that money was never discussed. We didn't have a joint bank account nor did we share debit or credit cards, and though John paid the house bills and mortgage (I'd paid for half the property), and he wanted me to stay at home and write full-time, we never discussed where my own personal expenses were meant to come from. So I started running creative writing workshops at local colleges in Street and Yeovil, then in Bristol and from home.

At last, I felt I'd found work which suited me, bringing together the best of my skills from teaching, writing and counselling. I was fortunate to work with several writers who went on to publishing success, including Maria McCann (*As Meat Loves Salt, The Wilding*), and Deborah Gregory (*The Cornflake House*), who'd studied at Bath Spa, and gave me a brilliant plug: 'Rosie's workshops did more for me than the entire M.A. course'. I was always struck by the alchemy that happened in these groups, far more than any conventional teaching situation, as if we were all sitting in a pool of light.

Inspired by this, and needing money, I applied for lectureships in creative writing. I think I fantasised I could redress the error of leaving UEA by re-inserting myself on the academic ladder in a more creative way. The novel based on Allon White and the Faust myth was by now complete, in with the same agent who represented John Fowles, and I'd started another. After an unsuccessful interview at Liverpool John Moores University (an absurd distance from Somerset), I then landed a half-time post in creative writing at Nottingham Trent University (slightly less absurd, but still a hundred and sixty-seven miles from home and at least four hours of commuting). Di Taylor begged me not to take it.

'John will think you're leaving him. Anyway, it's too far.'

What I couldn't see was that the relationship with John was already dying, and that my attempts to inject new energy into our lives with work I loved and some income of my own, were doomed before they began. John had by now realised that, far from being a female version of himself, I was as much practical use as a lace tea cosy, and he couldn't help betraying his contempt for my ineptitude. If I read his efficiency as insensitive, he read my introversion as self-indulgent, and he withdrew from me more and more. I'd find him hiding behind the garden wall with his pellet gun, knowing he wasn't just wanting to cock it at the unwary rabbits. Needing a miracle, I tried to persuade him to come to India with me for a visit to Meherabad, but he angrily refused. If Italy was too foreign, India was definitely so.

Now, in the evenings after work, he'd retreat to his large barn with the door shut, throwing his pots on the wheel and playing music at maximum volume – Mary Black, Peter Gabriel, the LadySmith Black Mambazo Simon had given him. John had once been lead guitarist in a band and loved folk music. If I ventured into the barn with a cup of tea, I was a visible nuisance.

'Can we talk?' I'd say. 'I want to make this relationship work.'

'I need my space,' John replied. 'I've been at work all day.'

'But – '

'This is emotional harassment.'

After the interview at Nottingham and an overnight stay with my mother, I drove back to Bath with the unexpected news of my success, wanting to tell John in person. I was feeling excited. I'd narrowly beaten Kathryn Hughes to the creative writing post (her prize-winning biography of George Eliot had yet to appear) and was to share the job with Graham Joyce, a prolific novelist. Up Brassknocker Hill to the university campus, round to the back of the Computing Services building, where John was standing outside, smoking a roll-up. He was leaning against the wall, and watched as I approached, still in the tailored grey suit I'd worn for the interview.

'Isn't it great?' I said. 'I'll only have to be there a couple of days a week, and the rest of the time I can be at home. It means when a job comes up closer, say at Bath Spa, I'll be perfectly placed.'

John drew silently on his fag. Where had I seen those eyes before? Oh yes, the day I got my degree result and David had met my success with the same coldness. And now my body caved into a familiar hollow space. Rebuff. Disappointment: not being met.

'Aren't you pleased?' I persisted. 'Aren't you going to congratulate me?'

John stubbed out his cigarette on the step. 'Congratulations,' he said, then turned to go back inside. It sounded like a death warrant.

24

The Bed is Split

Past cure I am, now reason is past care,
And frantic mad with evermore unrest,
My thoughts and my discourse as mad men's are,
At random from the truth vainly express'd.

Shakespeare, 'Sonnet 147'

M Y MOTHER STILL lived in Mansfield Woodhouse, only fourteen miles from Nottingham. One weekend, after the work at Trent had started, I took her for an afternoon's shopping, then to a multiplex in Mansfield to see *Titanic*. We sat together, watching the ship's huge hull smash into the iceberg. The Dolby system made it sound as if the cinema itself was collapsing, and I felt a sense of dread I couldn't explain, even from the events on screen. It seemed my whole universe was dying. When we got to Mum's, I phoned John, but there was no reply. I lay awake all night in the spare room, in the same single bed I'd occupied as a teenager, listening to a gurgling bathroom tank. When I did eventually fall asleep, I dreamt I was drowning, trapped underwater with a sheet of ice on the surface that stopped me coming up for air.

It would be nine months before I discovered (through covertly reading his diary) that was the night John had his first dinner date with his new girlfriend, Mary. Perhaps the moment of impact of the Titanic was their first kiss, or more. Mary was a print-maker in a collective of artisans where John too sold his work, but he didn't confess their affair until the autumn, when a friend who knew threatened to John that she'd tell me if he didn't. But by that time, naively believing John's repeated protestations that he 'just wanted to be alone', I'd agreed to a shabby buy-out, leaving me displaced while John stayed in the property and paid no maintenance even of an interim kind. I was so depressed by the break-up, once more not wanting to live, why would I bother fighting for money?

Christmas and New Year following my success in getting the Nottingham job had been hell. John hid himself in the pottery and refused to talk. On Valentine's Day, I made an earnest prayer for the marriage to change or end. With unusual alacrity, the prayer was answered: in less than two weeks the marriage was over.

John informed me of his decision in a letter. I was staying over for my teaching one or two nights a week in West Bridgeford with Liz Yorke, a lecturer turned counsellor whom I'd met at literature conferences years before. I was about to leave her house for the new semester when she handed me an envelope that had just arrived. My heart sank when I saw John's handwriting, though the letter inside was typed.

The first lines – 'I know this will not be what you want to read' – led into a formal notice of our impending divorce and a financial breakdown, carefully argued sums and columns, which explained why he wasn't giving me x and y (deducting rent and expenses for the years I'd lived with him), but was keeping the property to himself for his pottery and would buy me out at no more than half the lowest market value. If I didn't agree to these figures, he would sell it cheaply and make sure I got less. There would be no alimony.

I sat back on the sofa and handed Liz the letter. 'I was only with him this weekend,' I said. 'He never told me then. But he was plotting this all the time. He must have written it while I was there! Why couldn't he talk about it?' I was too shocked to move. 'My first day of teaching too. Talk about shooting me in the back.'

'A coward's way,' Liz agreed. 'You never know who someone is until you split up.'

Liz, a renowned scholar on the poetry of Adrienne Rich, was by now senior counsellor at Nottingham Trent. Divorced, with grown-up children, she'd recently taken the same path as Rich and turned to a woman for the enduring love that had eluded her with a man. Every night, she had long transatlantic calls with her new partner in the States. Now, Liz said she'd support me, we'd talk it through later, she knew a good solicitor.

I wasn't sure I'd get through the day. I didn't want to appear a drama queen with new colleagues, spilling a sudden divorce or tears all over them, but I felt winded. I drove to campus mouth clamped tight, raging inwardly at Meher Baba with his cold comfort promises. 'All your problems will be dissolved in the Ocean of My Love.' I remembered the prayer

I'd made on Valentine's Day. How many days had it taken to answer it? And as I calculated the exact number, eleven, I realised with shock the current date: February 25th, Meher Baba's birthday, the equivalent in the Baba calendar to Christmas. Was this 'coincidence' meant to reassure me that Baba's hand was behind it all? That this was less human accident than divine will? I didn't know. I felt I was splintering into pieces. My marriage was breaking up. I was breaking up. Happy Christmas!

Liz's terraced house was a short walk from the River Trent and city football ground. I returned there the following week after several days in Somerset, trying in vain to persuade John to change his mind about separating.

'I'll give the job up,' I said. 'I didn't know you were going to react like this.'

John shook his head and refused to talk. He didn't look so much like Meher Baba these days. His hair was shorter and greyer, his body stooped. He seemed more ordinary. A man who claimed he never got angry, now cashing in every Green Shield Stamp of unexpressed rage. I reminded him that he was a potter, that cracks could be mended, but he shook his head, told me he threw away any pot with a flaw. No Kintsukuroi for him.

'Why didn't you tell me you weren't happy with me going to Nottingham?' I persisted. 'If you don't tell me things, how am I meant to know?'

With his words ringing in my ears that I should find a house to rent in Nottingham, I drove the four hours back to Liz's. I was determined not to collapse, though fear and nausea ferreted away. In the motorway services, a cold remedy advert on the back of the loo door seemed to have been posted there by my mother or John or both. 'Stop snivelling and get back to work!'

I tried to calm my nerves by running each day along the river bank near Trent football ground, repeating to myself for moral support words that Lindsay Clarke had said to me. 'Find the vertical place in yourself. You must move into self-possession.' One morning, out jogging for an hour before I went to teach, I dodged the traffic and headed under a bridge onto a muddy track alongside the Trent. I'd run a few hundred yards when, on the opposite side of the river, concealed by shrubs from boathouses and moorings, a man waved and gestured. He was naked, flashing his prick in the morning sun.

'Fuck off!' I shouted. 'Just 'cause this is Lawrence country. Who do you think you are, bloody Mellors?'

I remembered the time I'd been flashed in Fiesole, when I was staying with Frieda Lawrence's granddaughter Ursula, en route to see her mother, Barbara Barr. To get back to Ursula's house one evening, I had to walk through a graveyard, and out of the dense yew tree shadows crept a rain-coated man, opening the front of his mac to wave his prick.

Now I ran my circuit by the Trent faster than usual, but on the way back there he was again, the same naked male body, a little nearer the water now, thrusting his pelvis in my direction. Rage spurred me to race on, head down, splashing through mud and puddles.

Trent football ground was undergoing major renovation, and con-struction workers were hanging on scaffolding, shouting their usual morning chorus. Still I kept my head down. I'd had quite enough male libido for the day. When one particular cry was repeated and got ever louder, I did eventually look up, but it was too late. One of the builders had lost his grip on the Heras fencing he was erecting, and all ten feet of the metal, with protruding spikes, fell towards me. I tried to sprint out of the angle of the fall, but the fence caught me before I could escape, and toppled me to the ground. The spikes tore into my left thigh. I lay there in mud and blood, watching white clouds smear a suddenly turquoise sky. So much for finding the vertical place. Was this what Job felt like? Emotional torment not enough? Let's try some physical blows.

Yet as I reflected on this accident over the next few days, immobile but with no bones broken, I wasn't at all angry with the tubby youth who'd dropped the fence. He was new to the job and full of sincere apology. His team had berated him for his carelessness, called a doctor, carried me back to Liz's and promised compensation. I knew the youth hadn't dropped the fence wilfully; he simply wasn't in control of what he was doing. I was hurt as a kind of side-effect. And I knew this was the narrative I should be telling myself about John. He surely hadn't intended to hurt me so badly, it was simply his emotional clumsiness. He didn't know how to separate in any other way. Months later, John admitted he spent a long time in those early weeks, wondering if he was making a mistake. I felt he was. I often still feel that. Even as we were separating, he still bought me presents as he'd used to – a stunning retrospective cata-logue of Paula Rego's paintings, a mobile phone – as if his heart wanted to act one way, his mind another, but his pride wouldn't let him back down.

The solicitor I consulted in Nottingham for compensation for the damage to my leg had a waiting room from Monty Python: people of all ages and shapes wanting to cash in their bandages, plaster casts, patched eyes. There was no predicting how lasting the damage to my thigh would be, but I accepted a one-off payment of £2,000. At the time it seemed generous enough, twice as much as any of my book advances. As it was, I only limped for a few weeks, though from then on the scar tissue has periodically inflamed with pain. It felt like my body's metaphor for less visible wounds.

In the midst of our early happiness, John and I had solemnly promised each other that if we did ever split up – which we knew, of course, we never would – we would remain firm friends and support each other. I was determined to keep my word. I didn't pursue meetings with the high-powered female divorce solicitor Liz recommended in Nottingham, but went to a cheap, incompetent law firm in Somerset. I didn't at that stage care about the money. Without John, life felt meaningless, and I didn't foresee any future. Anyway, surely fighting was not a spiritual thing to do? So, believing John's protestations that he was a born bachelor and needed the pottery for his work – as he said, I could never manage such an estate alone – I acquiesced to everything he wanted. I wasn't a material girl. I could think small and let myself be truly thankful for whatever I was about to receive. Amen.

Whenever I returned to the farmhouse to collect things that summer, John disappeared into one of the barns as soon as he saw me coming. It reminded me of the times I would come back from school to a mother who turned her back and walked away. But my mother had never been there for me. John had. He had been my first and only haven. And now the light in which we had stood had disappeared. I felt the whole world had gone awry. There was no mutual mourning, no expression of sympathy or regret. I had become a dead fuse, and whatever connection linked me to his heart, John had simply switched off.

'We're going through a major ending,' I said. 'Can't you at least honour what we had? Do you have no sense of... of ritual?'

'Ritual, astrology...' John said, turning to the cement mixer. 'Don't give me this new age crap.'

I would look round at the beautiful garden he'd designed and I'd planted, feeling I was standing on the wrong side of the gates of Eden. All I wanted was to be allowed back in, but John was the angel with the flaming brand. Couldn't we talk about it? Couldn't he explain? He wasn't quite yet my no-longer husband. Couldn't we stand together and watch the sea go out? But for reasons I didn't then understand – reasons any more worldly-wise wife would have grasped in another-woman instant – John was impatient for the ending to be come and gone, as if with my unhappiness he could also shed all of his own.

'This is so painful,' I said. 'I don't think you have any idea. This is the only real home I've ever had.'

'Well, it's not your home now,' he said, disappearing with his wheelbarrow. 'So don't eat any more of my nuts in the kitchen.'

In my hurt, I told him he was an emotional cripple, and in return he told me I was a practical one. One day, my rage could no longer be suppressed. John and a male friend had removed a huge terracotta chimney from one of the outbuildings – heavy, it had taken two of them to carry it – and now it stood in one of the flower beds, planted with trailing honeysuckle. My anger lifted the chimney pot, complete with soil, and hurled it across the lawn with a loud yell of protest. Futile as the action was, I felt proud of it. Germaine Greer had been right after all, in *The Female Eunuch*: 'Women have very little idea of how much men hate them.'

When I did discover, a few months later, after all the legal shortfall, that another woman, Mary, was involved, had been involved since that evening the Titanic collided with the iceberg, I was too shocked to be angry.

'But you said you wanted to be on your own,' I said.

'I'm happy with Mary,' John insisted. 'She's a happy soul.'

We were standing in the kitchen, by a drawer where I'd puzzled over a stray packet of dog biscuits earlier in the year. Suddenly the penny dropped.

'Does Mary have a dog?'

'Yes. Rackett, who makes a racket.'

'You always said you didn't like dogs. You wouldn't let me have one.'

'I don't like him. I hate him.'

In fact, John constructed in the yard an elaborate Heath Robinson contraption, so whenever Mary left Rackett with him for the day, he needn't waste time taking the dog for a walk. It reminded me of the many weekends I'd tried to persuade John to come for a walk with me and he'd declined. The dog lead slid along a horizontal metal wire suspended above the yard, and here Rackett raced hopefully the full length of the car park, first one way, then the other, never quite understanding the trick, that liberation was beyond him. What a perfect analogy, I thought. I'd deceived myself I was going somewhere with John, and all the time I'd been a dog on a wire, being teased back and forth.

John expected me to relocate in Nottingham but I never felt at home there and would wake at night not knowing whose house I was in. Nottingham was where we'd gone shopping at weekends when I was a teenager and Mum would treat us to Battenburg cake in Lyons Corner House. It was where Adam was conceived, in the Ashley's flat in Mapperley Park. Bob Ashley still taught at Nottingham Trent, and I reintroduced myself over the photocopier, asked if he knew anywhere to rent long term, but he gave an indifferent shrug. I tried to throw myself into work. I helped Graham Joyce organise a series of talks by novelists: Jim Crace, Louis de Bernières, Nicole Ward-Jouve, Lindsay Clarke, Barry Hines whose *Kes* had long since been a favourite. 'Better write and fail,' Hines advised, 'than not write at all.' Wonderful M.A. students supported me quite as much as I them, and we had humorous discussions about their novel writing efforts. ('What doth it profit a man to have a perfect opening, if it can't go on?')

But I had no inner resilience. I felt in exile, not only from my home, but from myself. I didn't know who I was. I couldn't eat or sleep. I was back on the aptly named Zopiclone and lived in a permanent fog. I was falling into tiny pieces and constantly phoned N for therapy.

'Dislocation creates a sense of emergency and dependency,' N said. 'You have lost all that is familiar. Anger is vital. Anything that stops you being passive.'

Di Taylor and Liz Yorke (busy organising her green card so she could emigrate to the States) were unflagging in their support. But most people, I discovered, shy away from depression and grief, as if it's infectious. They handed out truisms like loose change: 'Remember, this too will pass.' 'By the yard it's hard, but by the inch it's a cinch.' I found psychobabble a poor substitute for compassion. 'You must find the positive in this. It's part of your spiritual training.' 'You and John must have had all this in your soul's contract. He's only doing what you both agreed on before you came in.'

One weekend in Somerset, I hurried to a psychic in Glastonbury.

'You and John have served Islam in a previous life,' she said. 'But now he's one man and three demons. Does that make sense?'

'As much as anything,' I replied.

When I consulted Charles Harvey in Frome, a brilliant astrologer and head of the British Astrological Society, he pointed to some complicated geometry in John's birth chart. 'This configuration here,' he said, 'which governs relationships, is exactly the same configuration you find with Goebbels. You can imagine what that does to intimacy.'

One Saturday morning, I called my brother. 'I need help. I'm cracking up. I can't cope.'

'You've got to,' came the reply, and the receiver was replaced.

I felt that if I'd lost John to death, I might have encountered more kindness, but bereavement by divorce was seen as a lesser thing, though to me it was worse than a mortal blow. Maybe it was some kind of retribution, I thought, a karmic balancing for my leaving Adam. Maybe that curse David's father had made all those years ago, just before he died, was still active. I'd gone to York for my D.Phil. and lost Adam. Now I'd gone to Nottingham for academic success, and lost John. Love was forbidden me. I was doomed, like Faust, my aspirations cursed, every victory carrying a cost and demons laughing behind my back. I should have stayed at home and been the good wife and mother Jean reproached me for not being. Once more, I should have cooked my husband's meals and darned his socks. This was all my punishment for putting worldly ambition before love, and now happiness would be denied me.

In my Bristol days, while I was training in psychotherapy, I'd occasionally visited Runnings Park, a large healing centre at the foot of the Malvern Hills. I'd stayed in touch with Diane Furlong, one of their founders and healers, also training in therapy in Bath, and when I told her about this crisis, explaining I now needed to find a more secure source of income than the temporary post at Trent University, Runnings Park invited me to be their deputy manager, organising retreats and creative courses. Divine intervention, I thought: a part-time job on a much larger salary than Nottingham, in a beautiful location where I would meet kindred spirits. I found for rent a delightful timber-framed cottage nestling in the Malvern hills, with streams and fairies in the garden, gave my notice at Nottingham, once more loaded my car with my survival kit of books, clothes and computer, and at the beginning of July set off for my new life in the Malverns.

After a few days settling in to the cottage, I turned up at Runnings Park for my first morning's work. Andy, the young manager, greeted me with an embarrassed smile.

'Rosie. How nice to see you.' He looked awkward. 'The thing is... I'm really sorry to say this, but we've made a big mistake. We have no work for you after all. We can't afford to pay you.'

There were so many ankhs and crystals radiating rainbows in the room, and Andy emanated such sweetness and light, I didn't at first register what he was saying.

'But... I gave my notice at Nottingham.'

'Oh, you're so well qualified, you'll find something else in no time. I'm sure the universe will take care of you.'

White-light angry, I marched over to see Diane. The huge window in her lounge overlooked lake, valley and lush farmland.

'Did you know about this?' I asked.

Diane nodded. 'Andy made a mistake with his calculations. I'm sorry.'

'A *mistake*? He's got to be answerable to someone. Because you were friends, I trusted you. I haven't even got a contract.'

'I'm sorry,' Diane repeated. 'If you need a free healing anytime...'

I drove back to the pixie cottage wanting to shoot someone. I phoned Nottingham Trent, but Kathryn Hughes had already stepped into the post. In fury, I drove off to Worcester, wandered round the dead cathedral, indulged in a bottle of scarlet nail varnish meant to lift my mood, but back home, I found the bottle had smashed and coated the entire contents of my shoulder bag with red gloss.

That evening, in desperation, I phoned Lindsay Clarke. After a long talk and careful listening, he suggested throwing the I *Ching* for another angle on what was happening. It gave me Hexagram 23.

'Po. Splitting Apart. It does not further one to go anywhere. The leg of the bed is split. Those who persevere are destroyed. The bed is split up to the skin. Misfortune has reached its peak. It can no longer be warded off.'

My journals from that summer are filled with heartache.

'11 Aug. Felt utterly black all day except in the theatre at Malvern with people around. Saw Diana Rigg in Racine's *Phèdre* – a new version by

Ted Hughes – utterly brilliant. *When passion boils, reason evaporates...* Got back to the cottage to a phone call from John. He was more civilised. Has agreed to pay solicitor's fees and offered to repair my coffee table for me. (Though what use is a coffee table with no home to put it in?) He's converted the top barn (the one which was to be my studio) into a showroom and said the garden is 'looking wonderful'. The compassion rose and yellow clematis are out. I couldn't believe he said that. The garden was my baby. I planted the whole damn thing.

14 Aug. Phoned Lindsay to wish him happy birthday. He and Phoebe had bumped into John and had a run-in. John said what a fool I was to have given up the Notts job and to be thinking of returning to India, at which point Lindsay defended me against his 'Olympian judgements' and told John he couldn't dismiss as romantic idealism everything that didn't fit into his own bourgeois scheme. He said I must stop idealising John and dreaming of going back. 'He definitely wants you out of his life.' Fire went through my heart.

15 Aug. Last night the physical pain in my chest was so intense, I thought I was having a heart attack. I feel like that card in the Tarot pack, where a woman's lying on her back, her body thick with swords.

16 Aug. Leo Tolstoy: 'Marriage is a perilous delusion.'

17 Aug. Pauline Stainer: 'Make an art of bearing pain.'

20 Aug. Walked along the ridge of the Malverns playing Elgar on my Walkman. Somewhere beneath lay the field where the medieval writer of *Piers Plowman* had his dream vision which I so loved in Gay Clifford's course on allegory. *Meatless and moneyless on Malvern Hills...*

26 Aug. Email from Graham Joyce: 'Well, that Malverns fiasco just about puts the lid on your year, doesn't it? I won't say the only way is up 'cos the way your luck is panning out, I could be wrong. When going to India, avoid travelling by sea.'

28 Aug. Dream Di and John Taylor come to visit me and John at The Bakehouse. I sit coughing blood into a handkerchief, but no one takes any notice.'

The only blessing that summer was renewed contact with Adam. Through the eight years of marriage with John, our connection had been intermittent. We could go for long months at a time with very little contact. Trying to bridge the gap was often awkward and painful.

When *Mothers Who Leave* was published in 1994, I'd driven up through a blizzard to Yorkshire (John refused to come with me) to give Adam his own copy of the book. He was living near his dad, and I made my usual attempt to talk, to convey to him my love and regret for our fractured history. Adam listened, nodded, placed the book on his shelf, then went out partying with his current girlfriend, leaving me to shiver in his rented room and eat the remains of a box of soggy cornflakes. Since then he'd visited once or twice with girlfriends, but there was still a rift between us, as if we were merely going through the motions of being mother and son, and the basic fault line could not be repaired.

Now, at the end of August, before I left the Malverns, Adam came on his own to the fairy cottage for a long weekend. At twenty-seven, he was lean and handsome, with a Gemini charm and quick humour. Seeing the state I was in, he took over the shopping and cooking, prepared a chicken curry, poured generous amounts of alcohol. We walked up Worcester Beacon, the highest of the Malvern Hills, where a photo at the trig point shows us windswept, smiling, though my face is strained, my eyes sad.

Adam was sympathetic, but also anxious for me to bounce back from the blow John had dealt. He gave me a pep talk about letting John go, remembering how 'heavy' John had been.

'You're still young and attractive,' he said. 'In fact you never seem to age. I don't know what John's up to. Has he met someone else?'

I shook my head. 'He just wants to be on his own. He said he should never have got married, he's too selfish. He's right about that anyway. He chucked me out of the house like a sack of potatoes.'

'I'm really surprised,' Adam said. 'Not that I ever found him easy to talk to, but I wouldn't have expected him to be like this.'

'His Mum died in June,' I said. 'But John wouldn't let me go to the funeral. He claimed I didn't know her. Didn't know her! Every time she visited, I was the one who looked after her while John escaped to the barn to do his pots.'

'I'll go and see him if you like,' said Adam.

'I don't think so, darling. I don't want you getting into trouble.'

'You'll be alright, Mum.'

'I don't know...'

'You will. The thing is,' Adam went on, 'you keep choosing the wrong men.' He looked at me directly over his glass of beer. 'You keep going for men who are weak but think they're strong. Whereas you're strong, but you think you're weak.'

I stared at him, astonished at his astuteness. Where did he get such emotional intelligence? Perhaps this was one advantage of our unconventional connection: that we saw each other less as 'mother' and 'son', and more as people we had to assess anew every time we met. He had not a scrap of self-pity. He didn't take himself too seriously, and had a brilliant sense of humour. I could see why he had such ease attracting women.

'I'm going back to India,' I said. 'Try and recover. Start again.'

Adam shook his head. 'Honestly, Mum, I don't know why you bother. All that Meher Baba stuff. I'd give up on him if I were you. I mean, you've been following him for years now, and he hasn't exactly made you happy, has he?'

'You're right,' I conceded. 'He hasn't. But you don't give up on someone you love just because the going gets tough, do you? Where would you and I be, if we'd done that?'

'Fair enough.'

'Baba says it's like digging for water. You don't keep moving the site just because you haven't got there yet.'

That Sunday Adam and I drove to the Black Mountains. We parked at Llanthony and walked above Offa's Dyke, racing wild in the wind and sun. Up on the hills, breathless from running, we lay side by side in long golden grass, staring up at the scudding clouds.

'It's so beautiful up here,' I said. 'It's magical. Let's make a wish. No, three wishes each.'

'I wish,' Adam said, 'for a relationship that works, that lasts. And for work that works and pays. Telephone sales are not what I want to be doing for the rest of my life.'

'Me too,' I said. 'Ditto on both counts. Enduring love. And meaningful purpose.' I pulled on a tall grass stalk and chewed the end, leaning on my elbows to look at Adam. 'What about your third wish? I know what mine is.'

'What is it?'

'Pipe dream, probably. I want one of my books to do really well. I want to see people reading it on the train. To have it stashed in piles in Waterstones.'

'Oh, if we can have pipe dreams,' Adam said, 'I've got one.'

'Go on.' I waited for an apocalyptic revelation.

Adam smiled roguishly. 'To have Aston Villa win the premier league!'

And we both rolled down the hill, unable to stop laughing.

While I was in India that winter, I took into the *Samadhi* a photograph of a man on Death Row in Florida. A Quaker I'd met in England ran a support network for prisoners in the States on Death Row. This took the form of organising letters between people in the UK (mostly white women) and inmates (mostly black men). I didn't want to join the network, but did agree to correspond briefly with Mike, thirty-eight, who'd been inside since he was twenty-three for a murder he claimed he didn't commit. Now he was close to his execution date. The Quaker friend forwarded me one of Mike's handwritten letters and asked me to pray for him in India.

'Ask Meher Baba to do something,' he pleaded. 'Mike's been totally framed.'

In the *Samadhi*, Baba's tomb is a marble slab raised a little from the ground. People take *darshan* by bowing their heads to the slab, often leaving garlands of jasmine and roses and sometimes placing onto the slab a photo of a new child, or someone ill or dying, to ask for blessing. I put Mike's letter and photo there and made an earnest prayer. An hour later I retrieved the papers from a growing mound of flowers, and walked back to the villa where I was staying.

A couple of weeks later, my Quaker friend phoned me, unable to contain his excitement. 'You won't believe this, Rosie. I don't believe it. In all my years of working with Death Row, it's unheard of. Mike's been reprieved.'

'Reprieved? You mean he's free?'

'Well, not free as such. But his death sentence has been transmuted to a life sentence.'

From where I was standing in the cool villa, I could see the top of the neem trees that masked the path to the *Samadhi*. I thought of Mike's laboured handwriting, the son whose childhood he'd missed.

'It's incredible,' my friend continued. 'First, one of the witnesses suddenly withdrew their evidence. Then – and this is totally unprecedented – the judge on the case was declared incompetent.'

'Good Lord. Thank you, Baba.'

'What?'

'I left Mike's photo on Baba's tomb. It must have worked.'

Suddenly the voice on the phone was coy. 'That's just coincidence.'

'Jung says there are no such things as coincidences.'

More silence. Catch 22, I thought. If nothing had happened, he would have said it was proof Baba was a charlatan. But now something had happened, it was a happy 'coincidence.' If even Quakers doubt the power of prayer, what chance with the world's doubting Thomases?

When I flew back from Mumbai (Bombay had become Mumbai in 1995), I was squashed into my window seat by a burly young Englishman. I spent most of the long flight staring at his bald head, which was inscribed with a blue tattoo of the globe complete with oceans and land mass. Was this another symbol, I wondered – a sign that we carry our whole world with us on our heads, wherever we go?

25.

A Feast of Losses

I have walked through many lives,
some of them my own,
and I am not who I was,
though some principle of being
abides, from which I struggle
not to stray...
Oh, I have made myself a tribe
out of my true affections,
and my tribe is scattered!
How shall the heart be reconciled
to its feast of losses?

Stanley Kunitz, 'The Layers'

IT TOOK MORE than a decade to recover from this latest round of traumas. Indeed, as in a battleship game where targets are repeatedly hit till they sink, all my past losses seemed to accumulate to knock me out and stall my movement back to life. In the year immediately following the separation from John, I moved a total of forty-six times. From room to room and friend to friend, a few days in one place were all I could tolerate before the fantasy of moving on and leaving the pain behind once more took hold. India and back twice, Devon, the Malverns, Cambridge, Somerset, Wiltshire, Hampshire, London, Wales, then back again in a different order. People I've met in similar distress call it 'doing a geographical.' I'd always been restless, moving from place to place, but now it was ever more frantic, the endless dislocation exacerbating my sense of belonging nowhere and having no-one. I had no idea what to do next. I suspected that the Nottingham fiasco, on top of my previous track record, made it unlikely I'd be offered any more academic posts; I was right. The few applications I made subsequently led nowhere.

It was hard, then, to suddenly become aware of the incredible success of so many people I'd known over the years. From my time at Warwick, Gay Clifford was gone, but her death was marked by a scholarship set up in her name at UCL and Germaine Greer edited and published Gay's poems. As for Germaine herself, constantly in the public eye, what better template of female achievement was there, to confirm what a eunuch I'd become?

Nicole Ward-Jouve, my supervisor at York, was now a professor, and had a long string of publications to her name: fiction – *Le Spectre du Gris* (*Shades of Grey*, the original), critical studies including *Baudelaire* and *Colette*, and a disturbing account of Sutcliffe, the Yorkshire Ripper – *The Street-cleaner*. I discovered on Google that, of my fellow post-grads at York, Penny Florence had moved on from lecturing in art history at Falmouth to become Emeritus Professor in Fine Art at the Slade; Susan O'Brien, now married with two daughters, was a leading Scottish barrister; and Elizabeth Wallace's husband, the trumpeter John Wallace, had been the soloist at Charles and Di's wedding in 1981 to a live TV audience of 750 million; later he was Principal of the Royal Conservatoire of Scotland. Clive Bell, I thought. Surely there will be nothing on Clive Bell, the flautist at York who'd said he wouldn't touch the UEA job with a bargepole. But yes, he too jumped up on Google: world-renowned, playing on the *Harry Potter* soundtracks.

This practice soon developed into a new form of self-torture: sitting in libraries, Googling names of past friends and colleagues to see how many I could find, so my ego could rub its nose in the lingering smell of envy, nostalgia and regret.

UEA, of course, had a whole crowd of names to torment me. My lodger, Donald Ranvaud, had produced films in America and China – *Farewell My Concubine*, *The Constant Gardener* and *City of God* – and went on to promote Latin American cinema in Bolivia and Brazil. Ben Gibson was head of the London Film school. Thomas Elsässer was Chair of Film Studies at the University of Amsterdam. I turned on the radio one night, and there on *Front Row* was Ginette Vincendeau, a French assistante in the days when Allon White was at UEA, now professor of Film Studies at Warwick. The friend for whom I'd become an accessory after the fact by storing his stolen books (he never did reclaim them) was a professor. David Punter had made a career out of the literature of terror and was a professor at Bristol. The list went on and on. Chris Bigsby, still at UEA, was professor of American Studies. His novel, *Hester*, won the

McKitterick Prize, and he had a long chain of awards. Malcolm Bradbury was knighted in 2000, just before he died. When Guido Almansi died in 2001, he left behind him forty-one books.

This was when I discovered Lorna Sage's memoir *Bad Blood*, which won the Whitbread Biography Award in January 2001, a week before she died, though she'd been a professor at UEA since 1994. We'd met again at a conference on feminism when I was teaching at Bristol and Lorna had reproached me for not telling her I was struggling to stay afloat at UEA. 'We'd have found a way', she said. And I thought back to the day I'd stood outside her office door, too ashamed to ask for help. Thought back to the night she too, like Gay Clifford, had invited me for dinner and we'd got drunk and ended up in bed together, but never repeated it, or even mentioned it again. So many silences in a place so full of words.

I felt even more inadequate when I learned that Patricia Hollis, the labour historian who'd taught with Lorna at UEA, had become a life peer as Baroness Hollis of Heigham and was Parliamentary Under-Secretary of State at the Department for Work and Pensions. She it was who carried through the Lords proposals which later became law, for an equal sharing of pensions on divorce. And I hadn't even managed to fight for my own small claim against John.

David Aers was now Professsor of English too, at Duke University in North Carolina. But the internet told me what I hadn't known when our desks were only inches away – that David was a Christian: 'When I think about ethics, I can't help but think about politics. When I think about my Christianity, I'm also thinking about social justice.' Like Lorna Sage with her secrets, he'd kept that well hidden. Or perhaps I'd not asked the right questions.

Ann Thwaite's literary biographies had done well, her life of A.A. Milne won the Whitbread Biography of the Year in 1990; Anthony Thwaite had received an OBE after editing Philip Larkin's *Letters*. And all this without the big names that came out of the MA creative writing programme at UEA, from McEwan to Ishiguro and Chevalier. Then Michèle Roberts was Professor of Creative Writing at UEA. Everywhere I looked I seemed to see a name I knew. Even when I turned on a friend's TV, trying to escape, I'd see Philip Bird in an ad, and remember playing in *Woyzeck*, when I was Marie.

On one of my stays in London, I wandered into Camden Arts Centre and found they were showing a documentary made in 2000 by Claudia von Alemann, the film director I could have worked with on the Mary Shelley project. *Shadows of Memory* described Hitler's rise and fall from the perspective of Alemann's eighty-four-year old mother, once a Nazi supporter. On my next Google assault, I found Alemann was now married to Cuban director Fernando Pérez. When I was with John, I'd buffered myself from a sense of failure by persuading myself the world was well lost for the sake of love and gardening. But now love had proved illusory and my little garden of Eden was irretrievably gone, I could find little compensation. How had I garnered such absences?

At Nottingham Trent, Graham Joyce went on to produce a novel a year; *Requiem, The Tooth Fairy, Indigo* and *The Facts of Life* were all British Fantasy Award winners; though during the writing of this memoir, in 2014, Graham sadly died of leukaemia. Kathyrn Hughes, who had taken the job I left at Nottingham, followed her phenomenally successful biography of *George Eliot* with a study of *Mrs Beeton*, and later became Professor of Life Writing – at the University of East Anglia. Where else?

Even writing students from my days with John had overtaken me. Deborah Gregory published *The Cornflake House*, and in 2001 Maria MacCann's first novel, *As Meat Loves Salt,* became a bestseller through the Richard and Judy bookclub. Nor could I simply blame my background for my obscurity. My brother had risen to the top of the Civil Service and was serving as a diplomat in Brussels.

From my newfound 'homelessness', limping from friend to friend, too broken to care about a proper roof over my head, I found it hard to view these catalogues of success with equanimity. A feast of losses, indeed. If I'd stayed at UEA, I told myself, I too would have been a professor by now, with *Fantasy* and other publications to my name. But not only was my study of Mary Shelley literal ash; every attempt I'd made at human happiness had collapsed. Was this Ernie's curse still? Or was John right, and I did have a worldly function missing? Perhaps I would have done better to care less about the condition of my soul than the buoyancy of my bank balance. Taking the road less travelled, it seemed, had done me little good. Not that I ever completely lost faith in Meher Baba. I have never doubted that what he offers is unfathomable grace and love unlimited. But what use was that to me, if I didn't have the right internal apparatus to hold love? It was like trying to capture water in a sieve.

For more than a decade after the break-up with John, my nights became nights at the opera. Anywhere I stayed looked in the morning as if it had been visited by the Valkyries: a Wagnerian battleground of warring bedding, beaten pillows, knotted clothes, open books, unfinished drinks, CDs, lavender bags, bottles of pills, herbal and medicinal remedies. I'd never slept well, but now I was permanently on high alert.

Clutching at straws, I phoned my mother, who'd recently moved in with my brother and his second wife.

'I'm not well,' I said. 'I'm cracking up.'

'Oh yes,' Mum replied, in a blithe definitive tone. 'Everyone here thinks you're having a breakdown.' Then she changed the subject, once more talking about her trips with the W.I.

Most of my friends' patience had worn thin. Di Taylor's cancer had recurred, this time in the bone and, knowing she was leaving her life, she severed all her friendships one by one. Adam was going through his own struggles with relationships and work, and we were distant again. Anyway, I couldn't put my burdens on my own son. I was left in the night with long calls to the Samaritans and, in the day, from wherever I was in the country, with long calls to N, who effectively kept me alive. Many mornings, after only a couple of hours of sleeping-tablet coma, I took a few more pills to sedate me through the day. N and I were both fearful that one night, I would simply take a whole bottle of pills and have done with it.

When the anniversary of the break-up with John came and went and my wandering still showed no sign of exhausting itself, an exasperated female friend insisted I put some stones around me.

'You're racing round the country like a headless chicken,' she said. 'You'll get put away if you don't find a home soon. It doesn't matter where.'

Somerset was the most obvious and loved choice. I explored Glastonbury, but it was too near to John. I couldn't afford the beautiful Georgian city of Bath. So I plumped for Frome (pronounced Froom), 'the poor man's Bath', bought the first house I saw with no survey (who cared if it fell down?) and once more started a new life in a place where I knew no one. It was the best move I ever made.

Frome, a market town built on the wool trade, had a non-conformist history and was the funkiest, liveliest place I could have hoped for. Half-way between Bath and Glastonbury, it had much of Bath's culture without its cost and a touch of Glastonbury's spirituality without its shadows. I found the community vibrant and supportive, with a higher percentage of talented artists, musicians, writers and artisans than anywhere outside London, along with eco-poets, eco-warriors, alternative health practitioners, sustainable energy aficionados. I was able to buy outright a terraced house, once an old weaver's cottage, and kept back a little to live on. I never thought of claiming benefits, I didn't know how. Eventually I received some very welcome help from the Royal Literary Fund. But I was used to living frugally. I didn't switch on the heating. I ate little. I bought my clothes from charity shops. I joined a system called Lets, which collectively bartered services and was a way of making friends; in exchange for many hours of babysitting, I had help painting my lounge and kitchen. But I was still battling profound depression, struggling to find meaning that might make sense of my ragged past and give purpose to my shapeless future. With nothing to fall back on but my own imaginative resources, I once more started to write.

When I was with John, I'd begun a novel based on the Cosmati Pavement, the exquisite medieval floor in front of the high altar in Westminster Abbey. The writing had been abandoned during my wild wandering, but now I rediscovered my notes and tried to stitch them together. The novel was first triggered by one of my writing students, Nick Durnan, a stonemason and conservationist, who'd helped restore Salisbury cathedral to its glory, and who was working on the Cosmati floor. When I went up to London to see it, I fell in love at once with the magnificence of the cut stonework – *opus sectile* – set in a design of spheres and stars, as if the very heavens had landed on the floor. Purbeck marble, green and purple porphyry, serpentine, limestone, alabaster, *cipollino*, all patterned into an esoteric symbolism representing man's progression from earthly to celestial time. The walk from the perimeter to the centre signifies the movement from here to eternity; the huge disc of red onyx at its heart, traditionally the site for the coronation, the place where man loses his human identity and becomes divine.

Will Furlong, the main character in my novel, restoring the Cosmati pavement from the outside in, finds that as he works ever nearer to the centre, his life disintegrates. His marriage collapses, he loses his home and experiences total breakdown. In this fragmented state, he encounters a host of previous selves who have also been linked with the floor. The first is Richard Blake, a Roundhead billeted in the Abbey in the Civil War, party to the partial vandalism of the stones. Another is Petrus Oderisius, the pavement's actual medieval architect. Different strands of narrative, 13th, 17th and 21st century, follow various winding roads and romantic episodes until eventually they converge. Will pursues Petrus to his origins in Italy, and there, beneath the hilltop town of Anagni, he witnesses Petrus drown himself. Will becomes convinced he is Petrus' reincarnation, and realizes his own life will only move forwards when he comes to terms with and forgives himself for this previous self-slaughter.

The more I wrote, the more an uncanny sense grew that these characters were all aspects of my own psyche, as though from a dream. This wasn't just a fictional plot, I was sure, but the hidden story of my inner life. What if I, too, had once committed suicide? Could that be the reason for my endless battles against a death wish? Was I simply encountering, again and again, my unresolved despair from a previous life? I later discovered Tolstoy had the same idea. 'How interesting it would be,' he noted, 'to write the story of the experiences in this life of a man who killed himself in his previous life; how he stumbles against the very demands which had offered themselves before, until he arrives at the realization that he must fulfil those demands. The deeds of the preceding life give direction to the present life.'

Soon after I'd met John, to his dismay and raised eyebrows, I'd taken a course with Roger Woolger, author of *Other Lives, Other Selves*. Woolger was one of the first to use the idea of reincarnation as a therapeutic tool. He led guided regressions to apparent past lives, where people often found events that related uncannily to traumas in this one. Unresolved issues from previous lives, Woolger argued, were carried over like residues from one life to another. I briefly regressed to a Russian life which had left me 'owing' a baby to David, Adam's father. But the most recent life I unearthed was in Germany, as a young Jewish girl. When I was eight, hiding, Nazis captured the rest of my family and shipped them to a concentration camp. Left behind, overwhelmed by terror and grief, I drowned myself in a river. This fitted perfectly with the scenario my psychic friend in London had described after my frightening sense of déjà vu in East Berlin: it was all down to the negative legacy from my last life in Germany.

Faced with John's scepticism, I didn't do much at the time with my experiences at Woolger's workshop, though they seemed to me as viable an explanation as anything else for my lifelong sense of residual grief. Even if John was right that such ideas were new age claptrap and past lives were not factually true, surely they were still useful as metaphors. Perhaps my unconscious also identified with this narrative of regression because it mirrored so well what had happened this lifetime. From the time we moved from Leeds to the Midlands when I was eight, and my mother had withdrawn more and more, I'd felt I'd lost my 'good' family and couldn't find them anywhere. From then on, I'd wanted to die. Through my teens, I kept reciting *Hamlet* to myself. *O, that this too too solid flesh would melt, / Thaw, and resolve itself into a dew, / Or that the Everlasting had not fixed / His canon 'gainst self-slaughter.* I'd promised myself I'd try to stay alive until I was thirty, but if nothing improved by then, I'd allow myself to go. Then, aged twenty-eight, I'd discovered Meher Baba, who repeated the Everlasting's *canon 'gainst self-slaughter*. The soul of the suicide, he explained, got 'stuck' and was hard to retrieve. 'Neither seek death,' Baba cautioned, 'nor fear it.'

Reincarnation was central to Baba's philosophy, as to most of the world's major religions, including Christianity until its teaching was banned by the Church in a synod in Constantinople in 543 A.D.. Baba explained that in each incarnation, all our experiences, thought, felt and acted, leave impressions, or *sanskaras*. The subsequent life is then determined by the accumulation of *sanskaras* from the most previous incarnation, demanding to be 'spent'. These are the main determining factors in a person's life, and will affect the soul's choice of family, place, work, health, wealth, and so on. Thus, if someone commits suicide, the *sanskaras* of that act, and all that led to it, will be carried over into the next life and work towards expression again. If indeed it was true that in my most previous life I committed suicide, I would have entered this life with the same unresolved despair inside me. The repeated losses and traumas I encountered were, in that case, neither bad luck nor accident, but my self-destructive *sanskaras* trying once more to push towards resolution.

Once I was with Baba and took seriously his injunctions against suicide, my primary aim in life became to arrive at a natural death. (It still is my aim, though, thankfully, not now my only one). If I could endure life until it was taken away, not ended by my own hand, I would have vanquished the suicide *sanskaras* once and for all. I would have won. And in the chaotic months and years following the break-up with John, unable to heal, I clung to these theories, true or not, as to a life raft.

When *The Cosmati Pavement* was complete, I placed it with a top literary agent. She'd tried unsuccessfully to sell my previous novel based on the story with Allon White, though her enthusiasm for that had been lukewarm. This time, by contrast, she announced she was 'jumping up and down,' and drove to Salisbury to meet me and collect several copies of the manuscript. But when it failed to sell to major publishers, ('too like Kate Mosse, we don't want to offend her', 'I love the writing and will go to Anagni to see the Cosmati floor there, but it's not for us'), the agent lost interest.

I went to London to ask her what to do next. 'Should I rewrite?' She interrupted our talk to take a call from Melvyn Bragg, then turned back to me. 'If you were thirty years younger,' she said, 'even twenty, I could have sold this novel yesterday. As it is, you'd better write something more in keeping with your age. Try copying Joanna Trollope.'

I was shocked. I'd been convinced it would sell, but once again that must have been what David Aers called my 'naïve optimism' surfacing. I'd just turned fifty. Was I really too old to publish a first novel? After three years writing this and four on the previous one, it seemed futile now to start anything new; seven years on two unpublished novels. I tutored a little for the Open College of the Arts and ran a few workshops. For three summers I ran courses for the Writers' Lab on Skyros, wrote a few stories for journals and women's magazines. But none of this brought in real money.

Meantime, still unable to discern healthy relationships from abusive ones, I'd fallen into another emotional pot-hole in the form of a transatlantic romance with an American businessman I'd met in India. Once more deluded by the belief that someone who followed Meher Baba must inevitably be a loving partner, I travelled back and forth across the pond for several years, often at his expense, sometimes at my own, and threw myself into the excitement of the States: New York, Washington D.C., New Orleans, California. Ignoring the warnings of worried friends who met him that this was a cat and mouse game, and despite N's concern that I was once again throwing myself around the world in the hope someone might catch me – in love with yet another version of my self-pre-occupied mother, one more encounter with narcissism - I sold the terraced house in Frome, gave away my possessions and books, and moved to the States. When the man finally proposed, I returned to the UK and arranged my papers and medical examinations so we could marry. More naïve optimism. At the eleventh hour, with no explanation, he bluntly by email withdrew his proposal – 'no discussion' – and returned my clothes and pictures through the post in a disintegrating cardboard box. My friends shook their heads. Hadn't they warned me the cat would win? One of them, an extremely generous woman, picked up the pieces and took me in. And another new chapter of recovery haltingly began.

Happily, one gift that had emerged in this transatlantic leapfrogging proved more enduring than any relationship or marriage. I became involved with a Sufi school in the States – not connected to Meher Baba – and trained for three years in Sufi spiritual teaching and healing. I was quickly disillusioned by the school's material bias (charging $150-300 for an hour's healing), which was a huge contrast with Meher Baba's refusal to ask for money. But as I immersed myself in the essence of Sufism, I found it complemented perfectly all I'd learned with Baba, taking me deeper into practices which healed and nurtured my heart.

Sufism, a mystical path of love which seeks the ecstasy of union with the divine, explained and answered the homesickness I'd always felt in the world. The soul remembers its separation from God and longs to return home. And when I was given my Sufi name, meant to mirror the soul, I felt an immediate sense of recognition: Rabia, after the Sufi mystic Rābiah al-Barī.

Born around 717 A.D. to impoverished parents in Mesopotamia, Rabia became homeless, probably after her parents' death, and was sold into slavery. Legend had it that her great beauty took her to a famous brothel where she was forced to work for many years until, when she was about fifty, a rich patron bought her freedom. The rest of her life was devoted to meditation, prayer and healing, and she became the first female Muslim saint as well as an accomplished poet. Daniel Ladinsky, after his excursions into Hafiz, also worked on translations of Rabia.

Ironic, but one of the most intimate acts/ of our body is death./ So beautiful appeared my death – knowing who I would then kiss,/ I died a thousand times before I died.

Sufism urges us to seek death always, but without dying. We have to allow the ego to be slaughtered within our everyday lives, to lose ourselves. And suddenly my own perennial death wish took on a new meaning. What if it was more than simply a mark of emotional and psychological wounds? What if it was, underneath, a longing for union with the divine: a desire to fall into the arms of perfect love and become one with the One? As Hafiz puts it, *our separation from God has ripened./Now fall like a golden fruit/Into my hand.* Ever since the night I first saw the film of Meher Baba in Norwich, and had a taste of that union, I'd tried to find it again, to recapture it in human relationship. But perhaps I'd been looking in the wrong place.

In one of my healing sessions with one of the Sufi teachers in the States, she delved back to try to find the root cause of my pain.

'Did you have a sister?' she asked. I told her about my mother's still-born baby. 'That baby was you,' she said. 'You didn't want to come into life because you knew how hard it would be. So you left, then came back again a few years later, as the 'you' you are now.'

Although I knew how utterly bizarre and risible this would sound to materialist thinkers, it also felt uncannily right, and fit perfectly with the sense I'd always had of being haunted by part of myself.

'But this second time,' the teacher went on, 'you didn't come in completely. Part of you was left behind in the realm of the dead. That's why you've always felt incomplete, never fully alive.' Was it this, I wondered, which accounted for my attraction to the Gothic? Was this why I'd been so drawn to the story of Mary Shelley, with her baby that died and then, in her dream, came back to life? Was this why I identified with Persephone, that daughter lost in hell? I had no proof whether this idea of division and loss, like the other past life work I'd done, was fact or fiction, but I didn't let that worry me. It was enough that I found it healing. As Blake said in the *Marriage of Heaven and Hell*, *Everything possible to be believed is an image of truth.* The teacher did some further work involved in soul retrieval, and slowly I began to feel more human, more whole.

By 'coincidence' too, this healing school in the States was exactly the same lineage of Sufis who had set up the community in Norfolk, where I'd been to Nefissa's wedding and my spiritual awakening had begun thirty years before. I met people at the school who'd helped establish that very community. The path had come full circle. 'Allah is calling you,' the women at the wedding had told me. '*La ilaha ill-allah,*' ran the lines I'd found after the wedding farce with Tony: *There is no god but God*. I recalled my dream of Jung, the embodiment of wisdom, smiling patiently on his chair on the edge of the woods, able to wait forever. In such matters, time is irrelevant. Love will always find you.

For years now my work had been the hidden, inner work on the self, but now, on my return to the UK, worldly employment also found me. Very part-time and ill-paid, but deeply fulfilling. I became involved in the Arts and Health sector, taking creative writing and art into mental health care. A perfect fit at last. I could draw on the best of my experience from teaching, writing and therapy, and harvest some of the bittersweet fruits of my own difficult inner journey. I ran workshops in Dorset with Marc Yeats, a brilliant self-taught artist and composer, and we watched people change under our eyes from week to week, adults who'd gone through different traumas and diagnoses – anxiety, bipolar, depression, life-threatening illness, redundancy, bereavement, divorce.

This expansion of psychological therapies, a rare collaboration between the Arts Council and NHS, received unconditional positive feedback and the overall project in the South West won a national Public Health award. It was therapy without the label of therapy, creativity the third party that filtered everything and made communication easier. Unsurprisingly, some of the most 'damaged' people, with self-inflicted scars visible on their bare arms in summer, were the most creative, and the most bereft when the trial stopped.

Funding for the project, alas, wasn't sustained – too simple and cheap a solution to mental health issues, too non-medical to be 'proven' – but participants went away with new self-esteem, as did I. My passion for the creative arts as a therapeutic tool was confirmed. I might be Chiron, another wounded healer who couldn't cure herself, but I could perhaps help others. I started to tutor writing groups, ran various projects in Arts and Health, worked with cancer patients and wrote the Charter for the National Arts and Health Alliance. Abandoning fiction writing, I embarked instead on memoir and poetry.

I'd always written poems in secret, but now, thanks to the encouragement of Frome's Poetry Café, I dared to read my work in public, and sent it to journals and anthologies. One sonnet found its way onto a GCSE syllabus, another poem was made into a copper sculpture by Andrew

Whittle for the grounds of a new mental health unit in Dorchester. I discovered that, during my time in the underworld, the landscape of poetry had changed. Back at Bristol in the 1980s, it had been a battle to get women poets onto the undergraduate syllabus. Now many brilliant female voices had risen to the surface and I devoured them greedily: Jane Hirshfield, Eavan Boland, Sharon Olds, Alice Oswald, Penelope Shuttle, Carol Ann Duffy, Mary Oliver, Naomi Shihab Nye, many more.

Bloodaxe published the magical anthologies *Staying Alive*, *Being Alive*, *Being Human*, along with rich volumes which revealed the possibility of new kinds of writing. Poetry, I discovered anew, breaks though isolation, mirrors something of ourselves when we feel outcast or invisible. It holds a kind of kinship, what Jo Bell calls 'Kith', defying separation. Life seen through this new lens started to feel different, full of unexpected beauty, all our lives full of cracks, all able to be filled with gold. I discovered South West England to be full of generous, talented poets. I joined the Knucklebones and Subversifs poetry groups in Bath; attended workshops led by Roselle Angwin, William Bedford, Jo Bell, Sue Boyle, Carrie Etter, Philip Gross, Mimi Khalvati, Jenny Lewis, Tim Liardet, Pascale Petit, Hilda Sheehan. I had at last found my kith: a community of writers who embraced and fostered my own work.

In 2014 Poetry Salzburg published my first pamphlet, *What the Ground Holds*. Penny Florence made a welcome reappearance in my life and came to the launch, giving me a book written by the mother of a friend of hers: a close study of the relationship between the ideas of Meher Baba and Carl Jung. In 2015 and 2016 I had a flurry of wins and placements in poetry competitions: Bath, Wells, Swindon's Battered Moons, Bridport, Berkshire, Cheltenham, Torbay. Spring 2016 saw my first full collection of poetry *The Light Box* published by Cultured Llama, with packed houses at launches at Topping's Bookshop, Bath and Frome's Poetry Café. Jo Bell gave an exuberant endorsement: 'Stonking good poems'; Roselle Angwin talked of their 'deft sleights-of-hand, shifting personae, lightly-handled depths of wit, heart-intelligence, compassion, perceptiveness,' the way they merged 'the numinous with the power of the sensory world.' 'Jackson,' claimed one reviewer, 'writes about pain with some exactitude and wit.'

For the front cover, I used Stanley Spencer's *Resurrection*: a reparatory vision of loved ones returned from the underworld and reunited after death in an earthy paradise. I'd long known that the classic story of

Demeter and Persephone was central to my personal mythology: the brutal severance of mother and child; the angry and despairing mother; the lost daughter who has to make her necessary descent into darkness; their longed-for reunion; the partial return to the light. Now I realised that the writing of this memoir had unconsciously fallen into the same mythic structure – opening at the point where I leave my mother's world and step into the realm of higher education – one could say the world of patriarchy – and ending after I've left that world behind, having re-surfaced into my 'light box' of poetry, love and humanity.

In July 2015, while I was working on poems for *The Light Box*, jazz pianist John Taylor – husband of my dear friend Di, who had passed away from cancer in 2004 – died from a sudden heart attack while playing at the Saveurs jazz festival in France. Two weeks later, I received news – casually, passed on by a third party on email – that John Harlow, my ex-husband, had also died suddenly: struck out of the blue by a pulmonary embolism as he sat working – forever working – in his studio. He was sixty-nine; he'd always said he'd never 'make old bones'. By now he'd retired from Bath university, sold our married home at The Old Bakehouse and bought a substantial small-holding in north Devon, where he kept sheep and horses. He and Mary were still in a relationship, though they'd never married or even lived together; in one of our last conversations, years before, John had told me he knew now he was 'too selfish' to be married, and wanted a life of solitude.

When I heard the news of his passing, I couldn't help unearthing the beautiful hand-written letters of enduring love John had once sent me, and recalled the poignant time of his own father's funeral, soon after we'd met. Having witnessed his mother's grief as she said goodbye, John turned to me with a rare display of feeling, and murmured, 'One day, one of us will have to do this for the other.'

But now, my sad farewells were done in private. Following his autopsy and cremation, with no funeral, wake or shared ceremony for any of his friends, John's ashes were scattered on Dartmoor by his two sons and a woman I'd never met. And I found myself looking back with nostalgia to that blissful summer's day in the orchard when John and Diana Taylor had visited John and me at the Bakehouse; how strange it felt, now all three of them were gone, to be the only one left alive holding the memory.

26

After So Many Deaths
I Live and Write

Flesh ripe with joy now they are touching again,
lovers, mothers, children, fathers, plumped-up wives,
in this light that is never switched off,
these bodies that cannot have enough of each other,
this love that is always being made.

Rosie Jackson, 'Resurrection'

O N ONE OF MY return trips to India, I again met Tom Hopkinson's daughter, Lyndall Passerini. She invited me to stay with her in Italy and a few months later I arrived in Cortona. The 17th century palazzone her husband inherited is set on a hillside outside the town, its tall stone tower visible for miles around. The main part of the building Count Passerini bequeathed to Pisa's Scuola Normale Superiore when he died, leaving Lyndall to live in a wing beneath the imposing tower.

We sat on the terrace in the evening sun, drinking white wine and talking about Meher Baba and Italy; we were planning to make a trip together to Assisi, where Baba had visited in 1932. I was trying to fathom why the name Cortona rang such a bell. *Under the Tuscan Sun* was set there, I knew; indeed Francis Maye's house was barely a mile away from the palazzone and Lyndall admitted she figured in the book under an alias. But I was sure the name went back further. Then I remembered Gay Clifford.

'I had a friend who used to come somewhere near here in her summer holidays,' I said. 'I don't suppose you know where Germaine Greer had her house?'

Lyndall didn't seem at all surprised. 'Are you thinking of Gay?'

'Yes. Gay Clifford. You knew her? She taught me at Warwick. She was one of the greatest influences in my life.'

'*Pianelli*,' Lyndall said. 'That's the name of the house where they stayed.'

'*Pianelli*. I remember now. Gay thought it paradise.'

'We used to own it,' Lyndall explained. 'We sold it to Germaine. I think Gay was rather upset. She'd have liked to buy it for herself.'

The connection felt uncanny, as if the mixture of heat and wine was making my mind play tricks. Here was Lyndall, whom I'd met thousands of miles away in India, at Meherabad, saying she owned *Pianelli*, the very house Gay Clifford had described to me in such loving detail four decades before. I remembered the excitement of reading her letters in the flat in Leamington Spa, while one-year old Adam played with his building blocks on the floor. How bizarre, that these two chapters of my life should dovetail so completely. I told Lyndall how beautiful I'd found Gay, what an inspiration.

'Without her,' I said, 'I don't think I'd have gone back to finish my degree. I wouldn't be who I am at all.'

We agreed what a tragedy Gay's stroke and early death had been.

'She stayed here too,' Lyndall said. 'She rented the house next door. Though she was a little wild by then. Knocking on doors in the early hours, after she'd drunk too much. We often had to get her to bed.'

I was sure I saw Gay, or the ghost of her, that week, as I walked in the olive groves behind the palazzone. For so long I'd followed in her footsteps, and here she was again, in the white silk shirt and Italian suit she'd worn when I first caught sight of her in the corridors at Warwick. I followed her past the derelict shepherd's hut, up the winding road to the top of the hill, where the view towards mountains showed sunflower fields, and cypresses punctuated the hills like dark exclamation marks. I breathed in the sweet fragrance of sage and pine.

Perhaps it was on this walk that Gay had thought of Donne's poem, which she used in her book on allegory. *On a huge hill,/Cragged, and steep, Truth stands, and hee that will/Reach her, about must, and about must goe;/ And what the hills suddennes resists, winne so.* From this summit of the old fortress above Cortona, she too would have looked down from the medieval stone walls towards the valleys and brambled woods where nestled *Le Celle*, the simple hermitage cells of St Francis. Here, perhaps, Gay wrote notes for her own poems: *I take out of my pockets /the past.*

The strings of loving, /the pressed flowers which bridged time... in search of the oil of grace.

Writing this book has helped put my narrative to rest; it was just my story, and can now give way to something else. The poet and visionary Kathleen Raine, after I met her at a conference a few years before her death, sent me a moving letter where she talks about our human lives no longer being the centre: how they are 'peripheral to something much bigger.' 'My own story,' she wrote, 'has no more importance or reality for me than any other life, and all lives are surely different paths by which we travel... Love, one way or another, is the only teacher, the only path.'

I have not entirely relinquished my dream of finding an enduring human union – after all the travesties in my life, it would be wonderful to have a happy ending of sustained, reciprocal human love, a kind of *Eat, Pray, Love* finale – but my sporadic attempts at relationship suggest I still choose badly. Despite many very good friends in my life, both men and women, I currently live on my own. Perhaps this is the cost of that other love, the pearl of great price. As Kathleen Raine also wrote in her letter: 'all traditions demand total, not partial, sacrifice as the price of enlightenment, and we all try to offer the gods what *we* think appropriate, but they want always the very thing we are not prepared to give.'

When I finally found a home I loved and was just able to afford, a 17th century cottage in a village outside Frome, Adam came to help me decorate. He was affectionate and loving, ready to talk more freely about things.

'I'm writing a memoir,' I told him. 'Is that OK with you?'

'I see it all differently now,' Adam replied, 'everything that happened. I don't blame you for anything.' He wrote in my visitors' book that he hoped I'd be happy and settled in my new house. '*It's about time!*'

But I knew our story remained bittersweet, these moments of seeming reconciliation all too liable to lapse again, the closeness interspersed by long periods of silence. When he'd married his childhood sweetheart, the same girl who'd visited Bristol when I lived there, I wasn't invited to the wedding. Perhaps they didn't trust that David and I could be civil to each other. They had no children and later, when they divorced, Adam returned to the partner with whom he had his daughter, and resumed the responsibilities of parenting. Maybe the broken template can be repaired.

The task for me, as a mother, and now as a grandmother too, seems to be to love at a distance, to go on loving, even if that love isn't visibly received, wanted or returned. Like the ending of 'Spice Island,' the short story I wrote about Adam's visits to me in York when he was little, I have to trust that, on some level, the love will go in. 'It is like the sudden shaft of light that touched you that morning when you were sleeping in my bed: the radiance that was yours without your knowing it.'

I too, of course, have been a glass mother in my way. But now, maybe, I can give that image a different meaning, invoke the positive associations of glass – transparent, open, hiding nothing; a conduit for the light.

And suddenly, as I write these words, I find myself phoning Adam. It's lunchtime, he's at work; I interrupt him painting a skirting board. To my surprise, I feel compelled to say something I've never said; something my mother never said.

'Adam, this may surprise you, but I need you to hear this. I *failed you as a mother*. There were reasons for it, of course, which you might understand more if you read my book. But nevertheless, the fact remains that I failed you. I see it more clearly now. I would like to make that up to you from now on, in whatever way I can.'

Adam's response is quick and warm. 'It must have taken you a lot to say that.'

But it didn't. I no longer feel driven by guilt or shame, apology or self-justification. Just honesty. Taking responsibility. Setting the record straight.

I believe, too, that my own mother's love, though locked away and gone underground, unable to show itself in words or gestures of affection that could reach me, was there underneath like a subterranean water-source, persisting in the few ways she could manage: sewing clothes, saying prayers. She was the one who taught me to read, after all; she gave me the gift of words. What seemed her uncaring behaviour towards me was not, I am now sure, driven by malice, nor even selfishness, but by unawareness, ignorance, and the limitations imposed by her undiagnosed Asperger's. The result – an absence of natural parent-child love and affection – was tragic for us both, and this inevitably impacted on my mothering of Adam. But the worse pain, I am now convinced, was hers: going through life with no emotional *affect*; never being able to be joyful or angry, passionate or sad; not knowing how to respond to her baby's needs, nor to any emotional intimacy. It's true that I had to step through decades of pain to counter all this, but at least I know how to feel. *I feel, therefore I am.*

And I was grateful that, shortly before she died, my mother not only managed to admit her love in a way she hadn't in sixty years, which felt a kind of completion, but she also filled a gap in her own family narrative, one which threw new light onto her story.

Until then, I'd thought she'd had only two siblings: her much loved brother who died in World War II, and her much younger sister, Margaret. Now, Mum shared with me the major trauma of her childhood. When she was only young herself, she had walked into her mother's bedroom one morning and found on the bed her little sister's corpse. No one had told her that the sister, three years old, had died in the night. Mum admitted that this scene haunted her all her life; added to the loss of her own stillborn daughter, it helps explain why her emotions were so blocked, that she might not feel this underlying grief and terror. Maybe the age three is also significant: Adam's age when I 'lost' him, and his daughter's age when he and his partner first split up. I knew better than to share with Mum the theory, from the Sufi teacher in the States, that I might have *been* that lost stillborn first daughter. It was too strange and personal a notion to have it scoffed at.

Whether conditions such as my mother's Asperger's are partly fostered by our upside-down culture, with its left-brain dominance, is a debate outside the scope of this book, but Ian McGilchrist makes persuasive arguments in that direction in his brilliant study *The Master and his Emissary: The Divided Brain and the Making of the Western World*. He suggests it is no accident that Asperger's, autism and many forms of mental illness have become far more prevalent over the last century, with its technological arrogance and mechanistic way of seeing. What is missing, McGilchrist reminds us, is a more embracing, coherent view of the world: one that honours mystery and unknowing, that takes us away from self-interest and control into a place of service and surrender. One might say, what is missing in our whole earth-destroying culture is the heart, the soul, the lost 'feminine'.

My brittle mother wasn't the only one whose behaviour I had to forgive, understand, love and accept. I knew now that to stop my constant running away from myself, I had to live consciously and willingly with everything that had happened to me. I had to acknowledge that all I'd done, whatever the cause, had consequences. I must abandon envy and rejoice in the success of my peers. I must accept without bitterness what I saw as John's and other men's betrayals. It was time to cease seeing the world through the filter of my glass mother, to remove the brittle shards that influenced how I saw other people, all too often imagining sharpness or hostility where there was none.

Most importantly of all, I had to see the story about Adam from his and his father's point of view as well as my own. This was the saga, after all, which had put me back on the human map. If I hadn't gone through the experiences with him – the pregnancy, loss, heartache, pain – my heart would not have been wedged open with suffering, would have been less able to relate to other people with compassion and empathy. This was my version of the 'happy fall', the *felix culpa*, about which I'd written with such prescient conviction at Warwick, in my exam on *Paradise Lost*, so many years before. Something in me had invited all this to happen to undermine the *hubris* of my 'successful' but neurotic academic life, to remind me what really mattered. What have I lost after all, in leaving that world, but the baubles of academic acclaim and a fat bank balance, a few more titles and letters after my name?

As I finish writing this in the quiet attic of my old cottage, I'm looking at a photo of me taken in India. I'm in my early thirties, my face a little plump, standing next to Meher Baba's right-hand man, Eruch Jessawalla, in his white T-shirt. Eruch, along with all of Baba's close disciples, is dead now, the men buried beyond the railway track at lower Meherabad, the women at the top of the hill alongside the *Samadhi*. 'Proof,' one American woman laughed, 'that Baba was a feminist!'

One of the last times I saw Eruch was when I was at my most distraught over the break-up with John. We were in *Mandali* Hall, where Eruch always sat on the floor, with no cushion, and I was next to him on a small pouffe, like one we had when I was a child. Above our heads, a net curtain at the window was yellow in the sun, shielding us from the fierce Indian heat. I was lamenting how hard I found the spiritual path, no let-up, and Eruch, who never uttered a word of complaint about his advanced *myasthenia gravis*, looked at me with compassion.

'You must remember, Rosie, what Baba said. *Suffering is the sharpest spear I use to bring my lovers to me.*'

'Sometimes,' I persisted, 'I'd rather be dead than alive.'

'There are two kinds of suicide,' Eruch continued. 'The suicide of the coward, and the suicide of the brave. If you want to die because you just can't do it, this is the suicide of the coward. But if you carry on and die to yourself, no matter how impossible it is, this is the suicide of the brave. This is what the Sufis mean, when they say *Die before you die*. This is what Meher Baba wants. To die to ourselves. This is the right kind of suicide.'

So, day by day, and moment by moment, I try to die before I die. Sometimes, it feels remarkably like living. Sometimes, it even feels like joy.

Lying awake one night, wondering who to approach for an endorsement for this memoir – always a tricky thing – I turned on the radio: a woman talking about Virginia Woolf. I was sure I recognised the voice. Gillian Beer, now Dame Gillian, the Cambridge professor who examined my D.Phil. thesis all those years before. She generously read *The Glass Mother*, following her words of endorsement with a postscript which brings another circle of my story to completion.

Gillian told me that she and Allon White were close friends; he'd asked her to read at his funeral. 'At his request, I read George Herbert's "The Flower".' When she sent me the poem, which I didn't know, I was struck by its aptness and beauty; it felt to be a kind of blessing from Allon. 'It seems so appropriate,' Gillian reflected, 'to the life that you have lived.' A perfect epilogue, indeed.

> *Who would have thought my shrivel'd heart*
> *Could have recover'd greennesse? It was gone*
> *Quite under ground;*
> . . .
> *And now in age I bud again,*
> *After so many deaths I live and write;*
> *I once more smell the dew and rain,*
> *And relish versing: O my onley light,*
> *It cannot be*
> *That I am he*
> *On whom thy tempests fell all night.*

Acknowledgements

I am greatly indebted to novelist Lindsay Clarke, who understood what I was trying to convey and who kept my feet to the fire with astute feedback and unflagging friendship. Thanks to my invaluable writing friends in Frome: Crysse Morrison, Frances Liardet and Alison Clink, who read work in progress; Rosie March-Smith, for encouragement of an early draft; Claire Dyer for help in editing the final one. I'm grateful to Dame Gillian Beer, Jane Rusbridge, and Daniel Ladinsky for their endorsements.

Thank you to Kate Lynch for the generous use of her painting for the front cover: 'Five Minutes Before the World Begins' is held in the Royal West of England Academy Talboys Collection; Lyn Davies for his book design; my agent, Annette Green, and Robin Jones at Unthank Books, for their enthusiasm.

I'm deeply grateful to the Royal Literary Fund for essential support in times of need; my therapist N, for patiently enabling my recovery; my fellow spiritual travellers in India and round the world; many friends who have sustained me over the years; and my wonderful memoir students in Frome. Finally, thank you to my son, Adam, for allowing me to write this honestly.

Acknowledgements are due to all the following copyright holders for their kind permission to reprint the quotations used as epigraphs.

Jane Hirshfield, 'The Weighing' and 'The World Loved by Moonlight', from *Each Happiness Ringed by Lions* (Bloodaxe Books, 2005).

Etty Hillesum, *An Interrupted Life: The Diaries and Letters of Etty Hillesum 1941-43* (Persephone Books, London 1999).

Maggie Mountford, 'When I Speak', first published in Rosie Jackson, *Mothers Who Leave* (Harper Collins, London, 1994).

Lesley Saunders, 'Particulare Care', from her pamphlet *Ordinary Treasure*, 2012.

Coleman Barks, 'Low in the Roots', 'The Great Wagon', 'Sell your cleverness', from *Rumi: The Big Red Book* (Harper Collins, 2010).

John Wheway, 'Success', first published in Alex Pirani, *The Absent Father: Crisis and Creativity* (Penguin Arkana, 1989).

Daniel Ladinsky, *I Heard God Laughing: Renderings of Hafiz* (Penguin 1996 & 2006) and *Love Songs from God* (Penguin, 2002).

Rosie Jackson, 'Love Letters', and 'Resurrection: After Stanley Spencer's *The Resurrection: Reunion 1945*', from *The Light Box* (Cultured Llama, 2016).

Stanley Kunitz, 'The Layers', from *The Collected Poems of Stanley Kunitz* (W. W. Norton & Company, 2002).